Genomics and Society

Legal, Ethical and Social Dimensions

Edited by
George Gaskell and Martin W. Bauer

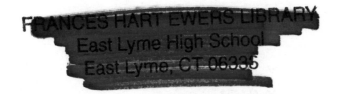

EARTHSCAN

London • Sterling, VA

First published by Earthscan in the UK and USA in 2006

ISBN-13: 978-1-84407-113-5 hardback
ISBN-10: 1-84407-113-8   hardback

Typesetting by Keystroke, Jacaranda Lodge, Wolverhampton
Printed and bound in the UK by TJ International Ltd, Padstow, Cornwall
Cover design by Susanne Harris

For a full list of publications please contact:

Earthscan
8–12 Camden High Street
London NW1 0JH, UK
Tel: +44 (0)20 7387 8558
Fax: +44 (0)20 7387 8998
Email: earthinfo@earthscan.co.uk
Web: www.earthscan.co.uk

22883 Quicksilver Drive, Sterling, VA 20166-2012, USA

Earthscan is an imprint of James and James (Science Publishers) Ltd and publishes in
association with the International Institute for Environment and Development

A catalogue record for this book is available from the British Library

Library of Congress Cataloging-in-Publication Data
Genomics and society : legal, ethical and social dimensions / edited by George Gaskell
  and Martin Bauer.
    p. ; cm.
  Includes bibliographical references.
  ISBN-13: 978-1-84407-113-5 (hardback)
  ISBN-10: 1-84407-113-8 (hardback)
  1. Medical genetics. 2. Genomics. 3. Medical genetics–Social aspects. 4. Medical
genetics–Moral and ethical aspects. 5. Genomics–Social aspects. 6. Genomics–Moral
and ethical aspects.
    [DNLM: 1. Genetic Engineering–ethics. 2. Genomics–ethics. 3. Bioethical Issues.
4. Organisms, Genetically Modified. 5. Public Policy. WB 60 G335 2006] I. Gaskell,
George. II. Bauer, Martin W.

  QH438.7.G46 2006
  174′.957–dc22
                        2006000302

The paper used for the text pages of this book is FSC certified.
FSC (The Forest Stewardship Council) is an international network
to promote responsible management of the world's forests.

Printed on totally chlorine-free paper

FSC

Mixed Sources
Product group from well-managed
forests and other controlled sources

Cert no. SGS-COC-2482
www.fsc.org
© 1996 Forest Stewardship Council

Contents

List of Figures, Tables and Boxes

Figures

Tables

Boxes

List of Contributors

Editors

George Gaskell
Professor of Social Psychology, Director of the Methodology Institute and Associate Director of BIOS, the Centre for Bioscience, Biomedicine, Biotechnology and Society, London School of Economics and Political Science, UK

Martin W. Bauer
Reader in Social Psychology and Research Methodology at the London School of Economics and Political Science, UK

Authors

Agnes Allansdottir
Lecturer in Social Psychology and Communications at the Faculty of Letters and Philosophy, University of Siena, Italy

Siv Froydis Berg
Researcher at the Centre for Technology, Innovation and Culture (TIK Centre), University of Oslo, Norway

Daniel Boy
Director of research at the Centre d'Études de la Vie Politique Française (Cevipof), Paris, France

Aglaia Chatjouli
PhD student, Department of Social Anthropology and History, Aegean University, Greece

Suzanne de Cheveigné
Sociologist at Centre National de la Recherche Scientifique (CNRS), Shadyc, Marseille, France

Susana Costa
Researcher at the Centre for Social Studies and PhD Student at the School of Economics, University of Coimbra, and Fellow at the FCT University of Coimbra, Portugal

Urs Dahinden
Senior researcher and lecturer at the IPMZ – Institute of Mass Communication and Media Research, University of Zurich, Switzerland

Carmen Diego
Researcher in the Sociology of Communication, Culture and Education, University of Lisbon, Portugal

Robert Downey
PhD student in the Faculty of Communications and Culture at the University of Calgary, Canada

Edna Einsiedel
Professor of Communication Studies at the Faculty of Communication and Culture, University of Calgary, Canada

Toby Ten Eyck
Associate Professor in the Department of Sociology and the National Food Safety and Toxicology Center at Michigan State University, USA

Björn Fjæstad
Adjunct Professor of Science Communication at the Department of Social Science, Mid Sweden University, Östersund, and Docent of Economic Psychology at the Stockholm School of Economics. He is also editor and publisher of the Swedish popular science journal *Forskning & Framsteg.*

Petra Grabner
Research Assistant at the Department of History and Political Science, University of Salzburg, Austria

Jan Gutteling
Associate Professor of Risk and Crisis Communication at the University of Twente, the Netherlands

Jürgen Hampel
Senior lecturer in the Sociology of Technology at the University of Stuttgart, Germany

Aiko Hibino
Researcher at the Graduate School of Biostudies, Kyoto University, Japan

Jonathan Jackson
Lecturer in Social Research Methodology at the London School of Economics, London, UK

Erling Jelsøe
Associate Professor, Department of Environment, Technology and Social Studies, Roskilde University, Denmark

Mercy Wambui Kamara
Research Associate at CESAGEN, University of Lancaster and Teaching Assistant at Roskilde University, Denmark

Matthias Kohring
Assistant Professor of Communication and Media Science at the Department of Media Science, University of Jena, Germany

Nicole Kronberger
Lecturer at the Department of Social and Economic Psychology, Johannes Kepler University, Linz, Austria

Nicola Lindsey
EVO Research and Consulting, London, UK

Marisa Matias
Research assistant at the Centre for Social Studies and graduate student in sociology at the School of Economics of the University of Coimbra, Portugal

Jörg Matthes
PhD student at the Institute of Mass Communication and Media Research, University of Zürich, Switzerland

Anneloes Meijnders
Assistant Professor of Human–Technology Interaction at Eindhoven University of Technology, the Netherlands

Cees Midden
Professor of Psychology at the Department of Technology Management, Eindhoven University of Technology, the Netherlands

Arne Thing Mortensen
Professor of Philosophy at the Department of Communications, Roskilde University, Denmark

Motohiko Nagata
Associate Professor of Social Psychology at the Faculty of Humanities and Social Sciences, Mie University, Japan

Torben Hviid Nielsen
Professor, Department of Sociology, University of Oslo, Norway

João Arriscado Nunes
Associate Professor of Sociology at the School of Economics, researcher at the Centre for Social Studies, University of Coimbra, Portugal

Susanna Öhman
Senior Lecturer in Sociology and Head of Department, at the Mid Sweden University, Östersund, Sweden

Anna Olofsson
Senior Lecturer in Sociology at the Mid Sweden University, Östersund, Sweden

Susanna Hornig Priest
Associate Professor and Director of Research, College of Mass Communications and Information Studies, University of South Carolina USA

Maria Rusanen
Researcher in Risk Analysis and Communication at the National Public Health Institute of risk communication and management at National Public Health Institute, Kuopio, Finland

Timo Rusanen
Senior Research Fellow, Head of Joensuu Centre for Ethnic Studies, ETNICA, University of Joensuu, Finland

Georgios Sakellaris
Research Director, Institute of Biological Research and Biotechnology, the National Hellenic Research Foundation

Toshio Sugiman
Professor, Graduate School of Human and Environmental Studies, Kyoto University, Japan

Helge Torgersen
Researcher at the Institute of Technology Assessment, Austrian Academy of Sciences, Vienna, Austria

Tomasz Twardowski
Professor and department head in the Institute of Bioorganic Chemistry, Polish Academy of Sciences, Poznań, and Professor in the Faculty of Biotechnology, Technical University of Łódź, Poland

Wolfgang Wagner
Department of Social and Economic Psychology, Johannes Kepler Universität, Linz, Austria

Acknowledgements

This is the fourth volume from the 'International Research Group on Biotechnology and the Public'. The European Commission Directorate General for Research provided the core funding for the project 'Life Sciences in European Society' (QLG7-CT-1999-00286). We acknowledge with thanks the contribution of DG Research and in particular the support of Alessio Vassarotti, Maurice Lex and Mark Cantley.

Special thanks to Morag Brocklehurst, our project manager, and to Sue Howard, who helped with the production of this book. And finally, a word of thanks to all our colleagues in Europe, North America and Japan who made 'Life Sciences in International Society' a stimulating, productive and enjoyable experience.

George Gaskell
Martin W. Bauer
London: February 2006

List of Acronyms and Abbreviations

AEBC   Agriculture and Environment Biotechnology Commission
BSE   bovine spongiform encephalopathy
CBAC   Canadian Biotechnology Advisory Committee
CCNE   Comité Consultatif National d'Éthique (National Ethics Committee in France)
CIHR   Canadian Institute of Health Research
CNECV   Portuguese National Committee for Ethics in the Life Sciences
DCE   Danish Council of Ethics
DEFRA   Department for Environment, Food and Rural Affairs (UK)
EC   European Commission
EFSA   European Food Safety Authority
ELM   elaboration likelihood model
ES   embryonic stem
ETENE   (Finland's Health Care Ethical Committee)
EU   European Union
FARSUL   Federação de Agricultura do Rio Grande do Sul
GAIC   Genetics and Insurance Committee
GE   genetically engineered
GM   genetically modified
GMO   genetically modified organism
HFEA   Human Fertilisation and Embryology Authority
HGAC   Human Genetics Advisory Commission
HGC   Human Genetics Commission
HP   heuristic processing
HSM   heuristic systematic model
IAP   Inter-Academy Panel
IARC   International Agency for Research of Cancer
IDEC   Consumer Protection Institute, Brazil
INSERM   Institut National de la Santé et de la Recherche Médicale (French Health and Medical Research Institute)
IVF   in vitro fertilization
MST   Movimento dos Trabalhadores Rurais Sem Terra (Rural Landless Workers Movement)
NBAB   Norwegian Biotechnology Advisory Board

NBAC	National Bioethics Advisory Commission
NGO	non-governmental organization
NOAH	Friends of the Earth Denmark
NOU	Norwegian Offentlige Utredninger (Norwegian Governmental Task Force Report)
NZZ	*Neue Zürcher Zeitung*
PT	Partida dos Trabalhadores
R&D	research and development
SCOT	Social Construction of Technology
SMART	Self-Monitoring Analysis and Reporting Technology
SP	systematic processing
UN	United Nations
UNESCO	United Nations Educational Scientific and Cultural Organization
WHO	World Health Organization
WTO	World Trade Organization

1

The Genomic Society and its Public: Introduction

George Gaskell and Martin W. Bauer

In an editorial in *Science*, coinciding with the American Association for the Advancement of Science's annual conference in 2005, Alan Leshner addressed the growing tensions between science and society (Leshner, 2005). As research tackles value-laden issues, for example in areas such as therapeutic or research cloning and stem cell research, so, he argues, is the public increasingly claiming a voice in the regulation of science and in the shaping of research agendas. Science, he suggests, is moving beyond the period when it was evaluated on the criteria of potential benefits and risk, to a future in which value-related dimensions will need to be taken on board. Rather than rejecting such changes, Leshner calls for scientists to adopt an inclusive approach and through open and rational discourse to find common ground with other communities on the ethical, legal and social implications of science and technology. This challenge to the traditional independence of science was paralleled by a call in *Nature* for 'upstream engagement' – the involvement of non-specialists to bring a broader range of views into decision making on research agendas (*Nature*, 2004).

These ideas have been circulating among academic 'observers' of science for some years. More recently we have seen major research funding bodies in the US, Canada, the European Union (EU) and a number of the EU member states requiring research grant applications to elaborate on the social, legal and ethical dimensions in their proposed research and to demonstrate a commitment to public engagement.

The fact that following these developments we now see two of the leading journals of the scientific establishment calling for a radical shift in science policy is suggestive of a sea change in thinking about the governance of science and its relations with wider society. For here is a challenge from the 'insiders' of science to recognize that the idea of science as a self-regulating profession, independent of wider society, is no longer tenable. What has driven this change? Among the many candidate explanations is the eventful history of modern biotechnology from 1973, about which some of the many contributing authors of this book, and other researchers, have written extensively. Here, we would like to highlight one issue – the lost opportunity in the early days of biotechnology to recognize that the public was interested, and had a legitimate interest, in the development of the science.

The discovery of the technique of recombinant deoxyribonucleic acid (DNA) by Cohen and Boyer in 1973 revolutionized biology and laid the foundations of modern biotechnology. Scientists soon became aware of and concerned about the implications of recombinant DNA. Charles Weiner provides a fascinating account of the motives behind and the outcomes of the series of Asilomar conferences in the 1970s (Weiner, 2001). The famous 'Berg' letter to *Science* and *Nature* in 1974 on the potential biohazards of recombinant DNA molecules sets the scene (Berg et al, 1974). The letter, signed by a number of leading researchers, invited scientists around the world to 'join with members of this committee in voluntarily deferring the following types of experiments' until 'the potential hazards of such recombinant DNA molecules have been better evaluated or adequate methods are developed for preventing their spread'. This led to a self-imposed moratorium on research that was intended to protect society against hazards and to protect science from over-enthusiastic regulation. But, crucially, the discussions at the Asilomar conference in 1975 focused on hazards associated with the means (technical scientific issues) and not with the ends (the consequences of the technology for society).

One of the organizers of the conference put it this way:

> *There are two issues which are peripheral to this meeting and which could confuse it in a number of ways. One of these is the utilization of this technology in what's been called gene therapy or genetic engineering. Which leads one into complicated questions of what's right and what's wrong, of complicated questions of political motivations, and which I do not think this is the time to discuss. And secondly, an issue which is very serious and which many of us care about and have cared about for a long time, which is the possibility to utilize such technology in biological warfare. And, again, although I think it's obvious that this technology is possibly the most potent potential technology in biological warfare, this meeting is not designed to deal with that question. The issue that does bring us here is that a new technique of molecular biology appears to have allowed us to outdo the standard events of evolution by making combinations of genes which could be immediate natural history. These pose special potential hazards while they offer enormous benefits. We are here in a sense to balance the benefits and hazards right now and to design a strategy which will maximize the benefits and minimize the hazards for the future. (see Weiner, 1979, 2001)*

Thus, the social, ethical and legal aspects of recombinant DNA research were categorized as peripheral and a source of potential confusion. One wonders what the history of biotechnology would have looked like if these issues had been regarded as confusing but potentially central. In the event, the moratorium was short lived. Scientists satisfied themselves on the safety issues and beyond that, to quote Rumsfeld, 'stuff happens'. In this case, the 'stuff' was economics and the biotechnological equivalent of the arms race as the technology became, in a number of countries, a national priority. By the early 1980s, Weiner reports that all of the 11 signatories of the Berg letter were involved with the biotechnology industry. This was a time for exuberant visions of the improvements in the quality of life, for patents and profits; not an auspicious period to muddy the waters with concerns about social, ethical and legal issues.

Of course there were voices sounding the alarm. For example, in 1979 Weiner wrote the following prophetic statement:

> *Nothing will be solved by facing the future with a 'scientists versus the public' attitude. Instead of belittling and ridiculing public concerns it would be far more constructive to attempt to understand the basis of public perceptions and the need for public participation in decisions. In addition, confidence in the credibility of technical experts could be enhanced rather than diminished if they are open and explicit about their professional and financial interests in the outcome of the issues being discussed; and if they admit when they do not have the answers, or when the available data are ambiguous, or when uncertainty prevails, or when there is disagreement among experts. (Weiner, 1979)*

So, looking at the articles with which we started this introduction we see that the clock has turned full circle. It may be that this is just a case of good ideas taking some time to mature, or it may be that the eventful history of biotechnology suggests that there is no alternative but to change.

That said, there are many unresolved issues about the practicalities of an inclusive science policy and of upstream engagement in scientific decision making. Let us consider two of the many tricky issues. First, with whom should science be inclusive? This raises questions about who defines the relevant constituencies of society; what is the public interest and how does this relate to public opinion? Here perhaps we should look towards political science for some suggestions. The second issue concerns what is meant by, or what would be, effective engagement? Is it a matter of actual engagement with the public (however defined), in which case the larger the number of people or groups the better, or should engagement be with ideas and concerns circulating in the public domain? It is likely to be a long and experimental road before procedures achieve both the desired outcomes and general support.

These reflections put the present series of chapters into context. This collection of chapters is one of a number of outputs of a research project 'Life Sciences in European Society'. This brought together a multinational and multidisciplinary group of European researchers, who were joined by colleagues from Japan, the US and Canada. The chapters are divided into three parts: Emerging Issues and Debates, The Efficacy of Public Opinion and Global Perspectives.

Recombinant DNA research and genetic engineering have raised many issues over the years, and those of health and safety, environmental impacts and ethical qualms have been with us since the 1970s. The 1990s saw a widening and differentiation of this range of concerns. In Part 1, 'Emerging Issues and Debates', we define and explore some of the new and pressing issues. Chapter 2 features genetic information, which brings a new facet to the ongoing debates over the information society and social control. What is it that 'genes' tell us about ourselves and others, what can and should we do and not do with such information? Is this a particular kind of information that needs special attention (genetic exceptionalism), or is it just a form of knowledge among many others? Organ transplantation has been within the scope of surgical interventions since the famous heart transplants of the 1960s. Chapter 3 on 'spare parts' explores the discussions in several countries arising from the developments and prospects of genetically engineering animals as organ providers for humans; for example, pigs to provide hearts for so-called xenotransplantations. Genetic diagnostics, spare parts engineering and stem cell research have put bioethics centre stage in many of these public discussions, and have even created a new field of expertise – bioethics. Chapter 4 shows that bioethics does not offer fixed benchmarks against which to judge and evaluate the issues, but is moving along with the development of technological prowess. The fact that a new technology puts everything up for grabs, even the ethical foundations of the discussion, might be a cause for concern for some, but reassuring for others. The discussion over genetically modified (GM) food has foregrounded a crucial ingredient of social life: trust. Paranoia is not a sustainable frame of mind. The rediscovery of the centrality of trust in everyday life makes the foundations of trust a quest for many researchers. What determines this key lever of 'public acceptance'? Chapter 5 demonstrates what might and might not be achieved through an experimental analysis of the phenomenon of trust.

Part 2 explores the efficacy of public opinion, the second hurdle for a new technology (regulation being the first one) which has proven to be a force to reckon with. Chapter 6 shows that public opinion is a multifaceted creature that variously impacts the new developments. In Chapter 7, experiences from a number of countries that have experimented with or even institutionalized new forms of public participation around the issues of genetic technology are discussed. Such forums of public involvement offer an opportunity for public opinion to affect technological trajectories, for example through policy making.

Public opinion is mobilized by various groups in civil society, and awareness of emerging issues is raised, catalysed and circulated by mass media coverage. This is the focus of Chapter 8. For long periods of their life cycle, new technologies are little more than figments of technical imagination and expectations to guide research and enthuse private and public sector investment. As such, they are beyond the direct experience of most people in any population. The mass media play a crucial role in mediating this secluded reality, in raising awareness, creating public perceptions and framing the expectations for things to come. And for genetic engineering this has a rich history of more than 30 years at least. The idea that bioethics might be a way of calming the debate and keeping out politics is shown to be an illusion in Chapter 9. The stem cell debate shows that this is as much a technical debate as a competition between different bioethical principles or styles. As shown in Chapter 10, the public perception of genetic technology is not only rooted in scientific information, but also influenced by cultural resources from our mythological past. Ancient myths stay with us, alive and kicking, despite repeated obituaries from the enlightened and positivist notions of scientific progress. Ideas of 'monsters' frame and fuel some of the anxieties surrounding GM food and other forms of genetic modification.

Finally, the third part of the book shows that these issues have become globalized over the course of the 1990s and into the 2000s. A first marker of globalization is the penetration of things genetic into 'pop culture', the focus of Chapter 11. The gene not only is a point of reference in scientific news and business information, but crops up in sports news, in literature, music and film and thus becomes an integral part of the everyday imagination. And because US pop culture is a global culture, the analysis of American pop is likely to show us the future trend around the world. But while there may be a convergence in popular culture, we also see tensions over genetic technologies within and between countries. Chapter 12 looks at North America and shows contrasts between Canada and the US in the framing of biotechnological issues. And, across the Atlantic, Chapter 13 reviews the tussles between the EU and the US over GM food with implications for international trade negotiations. In Chapter 14, we find that Japan is developing experiences of genetic engineering along the lines of its own traditions. Chapter 15 contrasts North and South America with a focus on Brazil, which did not follow the path laid out by the US. It supported de facto a European policy and reaped the benefits by resisting the second Green Revolution.

Our introduction concludes with a few words on what this book is not about. Any book covering the past and present of biotechnologies will be of necessity selective, and to enumerate all the omissions would be long and pointless. Nevertheless, two lacunae are worth noting. First, our focus was, and is, the efficacy of public opinion in framing the agenda in various public spheres. We set out to document the fact that public opinion is not an epiphenomenon of technological determinism. We wanted to highlight the spaces for civic action. But even here we are geographically limited. Our book is rather short on Asia, represented solely by Japan; India and China are not covered, nor is the continent of Africa. This has many reasons, not least practical ones of coordinating an international research project with focus on Europe over many years.

Second, of the key issues that emerge from genetic and genomic technology, we do not cover the issue of 'a changing human nature' itself. For many anthropologically minded observers this technology puts 'human nature' itself at science's disposal, with all the ramifications this has for our ethical and legal self-understandings. We are rather short on Foucauldian analysis of 'discourse of self', pertinent as this may be. The changing content of arguments of natural law or human rights in the light of projects of human design does not belong in a book focusing on public opinion. The threats to 'human nature' emerge in the horizons of public concern and unease discussed in Chapter 10, but beyond this our readers are invited to look in numerous other publications.

References

Berg, P. et al (1974) Letter: 'Potential biohazards for recombinant DNA molecules', *Science*, vol 185, p303; *Nature*, vol 250, p175

Leshner, A. I. (2005) 'Where science meets society', *Science*, vol 307, p815

Nature (2004) 'Going public', *Nature*, vol 431, p883

Weiner, C. (1979) 'Historical perspectives on the recombinant DNA controversy', in Morgan, J. and Whelan, W. (eds) *Recombinant DNA and Genetic Experimentation*, Pergamon, New York, pp81–87

Weiner, C. (2001) 'Drawing the line in genetic engineering: Self regulation and public participation', *Perspectives in Biology and Medicine*, vol 44, no 2, pp208–220

Part 1

Emerging Issues and Debates

2

Dilemmas of Genetic Information

*Urs Dahinden, Nicola Lindsey, Aglaia Chatjouli,
Carmen Diego, Björn Fjæstad, Marisa Matias,
João Arriscado Nunes and Timo Rusanen*

The past decade has seen an increase in public concern about genetics and the
life sciences in Europe and the US. Some applications of the technology have
barely infiltrated the public arena before they have been rejected, as was the case
with genetically modified (GM) foods in much of Europe. Others have been
infiltrating slowly, held up by the limits of the technology and our knowledge about
genes. Genetic testing is one such area. Despite the great promises of the Human
Genome Project to identify the roles of genes and gene sequences in simple and
complex diseases and physical traits, the number of clinically relevant genes that
can be directly tested for is small. Nevertheless, there is an underlying assumption
that comprehensive information about an individual's genetic constitution will be
readily available.

We report on public debates surrounding genetic testing and the use of this
information. The aim is to investigate some of the properties of genetic information, how it is interpreted in different contexts, and why it may warrant special
attention. The text is interspersed with country case studies on particular issues.

What is genetic information?

First we need to define what is meant by *information*, and then *genetic* information.
Information is simply a representation of reality by means of symbols (i.e. words,
numbers, technical codes and so on). *Genetic* information, then, can be sym-
bolically coded at different levels of abstraction: tests for the presence or absence
of a particular allele, tests for deoxyribonucleic acid (DNA) sequences near the
gene or genes (genetic markers) and tests for gene products or proteins. Genetic

information can derive from observing a person's physical characteristics, such as their eye and hair colour, or from observing their family members.

Information, therefore, represents genetic reality but is not the gene in and of itself. Information selects and highlights specific features of that reality. This selectivity results from the economic constraints that surround the collection of information. It is a cumbersome process and must be justified by a specific need or purpose. For example, in the clinical context, genetic information is used to diagnose or predict disease.

Information is immaterial, that is, it is not dependent on the continuing existence of the reality it represents. Although information does require some kind of physical storage and management (in the form of texts on paper or electronic data on hard disks), the resources involved are small. Due to its immateriality, information is difficult to destroy. It can be stored at very little cost over a long period, and after the original rationale for collecting it has changed or expired. As a result, information can easily transcend time, space and the social context to which it refers. The immateriality of information also means that it can be efficiently managed – analysing and manipulating symbols requires less effort than managing the physical and social realities themselves.

Information is produced for specific purposes. The process of 'informatization' involves different forms of re-contextualization. Information is gathered and encoded according to the context of collection, it is then stored and transmitted across time, space and social contexts and is finally decoded and re-contextualized by a receiver. As a result, information is multifunctional and can be used for unintended purposes. For example, credit card statements do not just reveal evidence of expenditure but also trace the user in space and time. The possible uses of information are, therefore, multiple and often unexpected.

Modern western societies have often been described as 'information societies' (Bell, 1976, republished in 1999). The debate over the definition of 'information society' and the assessment of its implication remains contested (Castells, 1996; Webster, 2003a, b). Information societies trade tacit and explicit knowledge, and see the development of science and technology as the most important activity. Scientific knowledge and technological products have been seen as the main source of societal and economic change, reshaping societal structures and redefining social values. Freed from the constraints of traditional structures, information societies accelerate fragmentation and individualization. Members of (post-)modern societies do not so much inherit identity by birth and socialization, but rather must construct an identity from a patchwork of social roles and markers.

The emergence of the information society is intimately linked to the globalization of commerce. Genetic information is a new field for business opportunities. This is true for forensic applications as well as medical and pharmaceutical research. The ownership and the access to genetic information is a highly commercial import. Genetic information thus presents a conflict between public and private ownership. The Human Genome Project demonstrates that information that was once hidden and private is being reified and thus made public and a potential commodity. Indeed, the rhetoric of the Human Genome Project

Box 2.1 Case study 1: Patents on nature?
The 'Gene Protection Initiative' in Switzerland 2001

Urs Dahinden

The role of patents for the development of biotechnology is controversial. This controversy is by and large an expert debate between a few representatives from industry, public authorities and non-governmental organizations (NGOs). Switzerland is one of the few countries in which a public debate followed by a democratic vote has taken place over this controversy.

What are the main positions in the patenting conflict? On the one hand, the biotechnology industry claims that patents are an important requirement for the commercialization of a new technology. Patents are intellectual property rights that define ownership of scientific and technical information. Patents are the legal instrument by which information can be transformed into a commodity with a private owner and a price. On the other hand, NGOs criticize the current legal practice of patenting biotechnology.

The main source of controversy in patenting is the distinction between discovery and invention. Both invention and discoveries provide new information, but in most legal systems, only inventions can be patented. This distinction is justified as follows: a discovery provides new information about natural laws which are public goods that cannot be privatized and commercialized. By contrast, an invention may be based on natural laws, but adds to those an element of creativity and human culture. At first glance, this differentiation between discovery and invention seems simple and straightforward, but its application in the realm of biotechnology is complex and contested. According to this logic, the discovery of a new gene responsible for a specific disease should not be patentable because it does not include a new invention in the sense of a technology. However, current legal practice allows the patenting of this discovery in the sense that the patent covers those innovations (e.g. therapeutic treatments) that are going to be developed in the future based on current information from the discovery.

The question of what can be patented is decided by national and international patenting offices through a combination of theoretical reasoning and pragmatism. They are in charge of drawing a line between discovery and invention, between public and private information, between open access and commercial restriction. However, patenting offices work in an area of conflicting interest and conflicting parties with unbalanced lobbying power. The industry has a strong interest in gene patenting, whilst NGOs oppose this trend.

The Swiss public debate on patenting followed in most respects the general patterns and argumentation discussed above. The debate was triggered by a popular initiative: 'Gene Protection Initiative' (German 'Genschutz-Initiative') (Bonfadelli et al, 2001). This initiative was launched by environmental NGOs and called for the prohibition of the following three things:

1   the production and sale of GM animals;
2   the release of GM plants and animals;
3   the patenting of GM plants and animals.

The motive of the initiative committee was clearly anti-biotechnology (points 1 and 2) and also against patents for genes (point 3).

In the media debate on the initiative, the issue of patenting was not the main topic. The opponents of biotechnology were making their case of ethics, environmental protection and animal protection, while the supporters of biotechnology emphasized biomedical and economic prospects. In the referendum of 7 June 1998, the Swiss electorate rejected this constitutional amendment with a majority of 66 per cent. A follow-up survey of the voting motives (Hardmeier and Scheiwiller, 1998) showed that the issue of patenting was not the determining factor for either side of the conflict: The ban on patenting was only mentioned by those citizens who were supporting biotechnology; only 2 per cent of them mentioned this as an argument to vote against the initiative (Hardmeier and Scheiwiller, 1998, p11). This is an indication that even in Swiss direct democracy, the issue of patenting remains an expert topic.

emphasizes the interests of the 'public good' that the project will serve, while the 'gold rush' for gene patents puts it back into private hands. The controversy over patenting became a national referendum issue in Switzerland, described in case study 1 (Box 2.1).

Uses of genetic information in the European context

Medical uses

The potential uses of genetic information have been publicly debated across Europe over the past decade, triggered by the rhetoric of progress emanating from the Human Genome Project since 1990. Currently, the most common setting for the production and use of genetic information is the clinic. Genetic testing of consenting adults for disease-related genes, for both diagnostic and predictive purposes, is well supported and fairly widespread across Europe. In most countries, the testing service is offered in nationally approved clinics where adequate counselling can be provided, and not over the counter or through the internet. There has been greater concern about the genetic testing of children, and about prenatal diagnosis and pre-implantation genetic diagnosis. Regulation varies, and some countries have debated more or less pragmatically what traits it should be permissible to test for. These are usually disease related, and exclude diagnosing the sex of an embryo.

Clinical practice is closely related to research. Many mutations are very rare. Patients coming forward for testing for rare mutations may be asked to take part in research studies. However, in order to identify the significance of these mutations in the population, and to develop drug and gene therapies more efficiently, large numbers of participants are needed. Many countries have put forward proposals for large-scale population databases where cohorts of up to a million people can have their lives followed and their diseases monitored and

Box 2.2 Case study 2: Uman Genomics: Biobanking between public and private ownership (Sweden)

Björn Fjæstad

The medical biobank of Västerbotten County Council and Umeå University was founded in 1987. Västerbotten County in northern Sweden has a population of just over 250,000. The county council provides public medical services. At health examinations, patients are asked to donate blood and fill out a questionnaire about health and habits. The biobank consists of some 130,000 samples from 90,000 donors.

In 1999, the stock company Uman Genomics was founded and was granted a monopoly for commercial activities based on the samples (Michael Lövtrup, science journalist, has kindly provided information about the history of Uman Genomics). The product sold was to be knowledge, not blood samples. Up to half of the volume of each sample may be used by Uman Genomics. The privacy protocols and the fact that Uman Genomics had a majority public ownership meant that the design of the operations was seen as ethically exemplary (Abbott, 1999).

The company was not a commercial success. In April 2002, the county council approved a revised contract. Uman Genomics is no longer required to report the results of the analyses to the biobank but can wait until a patent is sought. The requirement for a majority public ownership was revoked.

The legality of this new contract was challenged in court by some biobank employees concerned about who has the right of disposal of the samples and the right to decide over the biobank – the county council or the biobank scientists? The biobank scientists have continuously been encouraged by the county council to seek external funding, which could suggest the biobank is the physical result of a research project and is governed by its main investigators, rather than an integral unit of the county council's normal medical operations. In October 2002, the county administrative court ruled in favour of the county council. This verdict is being appealed against. A higher court will decide whether undue favours were granted to a single business enterprise. Meanwhile the uncertainty in the matter has led to a situation whereby the company is having difficulty finding investors, and in 2003 all employees were given notice.

Another point of conflict involves the conditions of commercialization. The new Swedish biobank law states: 'Tissue samples or parts of tissue samples kept in a biobank must not be transferred or given out for profit purposes'. Some are convinced that the revised contract, fixing a yearly sum, is in agreement with the new law. The critics are just as certain that the opposite is true. In addition, the monopoly granted to Uman Genomics, valid for 20 years, may violate fair competition laws. Some external science funding agencies and the cancer agency of the World Health Organization (IARC) have questioned the formation of Uman Genomics and its use of up to half of the samples in commercial activities.

When Uman Genomics was formed, a new donation document was introduced stating, among other things, that the stock majority is owned by the county council and Umeå University and that transparency is guaranteed. However, the leaders of the county council and the Umeå University have now stated that donors are to be given the opportunity to decide how their blood is to be used.

> One of the main founders of the medical biobank has formed a new board for the biobank since they do not accept the new organization created by the county council and Umeå University. The future of Uman Genomics is thus wide open.

compared with their genetic profiles. The best example of this is Iceland, where in 1998 the parliament allowed the whole population's individual health records to be passed on to a large database without patients' explicit prior consent. Individuals are given the opportunity to opt out should they *not* wish to be a part of the study. Access is in the hands of a private company, DeCode. They use this information in conjunction with widely available records of Icelandic family histories and donated genetic material to identify genes involved in simple and complex diseases. Similar databases have been created elsewhere (Maschke, 2005). Governments promote these databases as a valuable economic and national resource.

Sweden and the UK have had such proposals widely debated. Unlike the Icelandic model, these are publicly run and participation is voluntary. Biobank UK, formerly known as the UK Population Biomedical Collection, a database of 500,000 people funded by the Medical Research Council and the Wellcome Trust, has been given government approval. Case study 2 (Box 2.2) reports on the controversy over the commercialization of genetic information in Sweden.

Non-medical uses

Genetic information is also used in non-medical contexts. Genetic fingerprinting, used as person identification, has become an important tool for solving crime in Europe: see case study 3 (Box 2.3). In many countries, massive public and media support have backed high-profile criminal investigations using this technology. This information is also stored in forensic databases, sometimes even if the suspect is not charged or is acquitted, as is the case in the UK. DNA analysis is now used as a routine procedure in paternity testing and has been used in some high-profile paternity suits involving well-known public figures from rock stars to sportsmen. Paternity testing, together with forensic testing, is probably the area where the greatest volume of genetic information has been generated. Despite its relative acceptability, there are still questions about whether the information could be used for other purposes in the future, for example in crime prevention.

Of more serious public concern has been the use of genetic test information by insurance companies and employers. This issue has been debated across Europe, although perhaps not to the same extent as in the US. Currently, legislation prevents insurers using genetic information in Austria, Denmark and Norway, while the Netherlands, France, Sweden and the UK have moratoria in place. The European Council Convention on Human Rights and Biomedicine places a ban on all forms of gene-based discrimination that restricts the use of genetic tests for medical purposes.

Finally, genetic information and the identification of specific genes have raised concern over intellectual property rights. In July 1998, the European directive on

---

Box 2.3 Case study 3: The forensic use of genetic information in Portugal

João Arriscado Nunes and Marisa Matias

In Portugal, the use of standardized genetic techniques and practices of DNA profiling is now routine in the investigation of criminal cases and paternity claims, and in the identification of victims of disasters.

Scientific and technical standardization, however, is at odds with the specificities of the Portuguese legal system, particularly the admissibility and weight of forensic evidence, and the role of both expert witnesses and judge (Costa and Nunes, 2001). The former are usually forensic scientists working either for the National Institute for Forensic Medicine, for the Laboratory of Scientific Police or for research units licensed for this kind of work. They appear in court as experts of the court, not as experts for the prosecution or the defence. Counter-expertise is rare, although its possibility is inscribed in the law. Judges retain considerable discretionary power in weighing forensic evidence, even if they are compelled to justify its dismissal on scientifically admissible grounds.

The issue of the integrity and quality of the material is critical in so far as this kind of evidence has to withstand scrutiny both as scientific-technical evidence and as legal evidence. The integrity and quality of the biological materials collected in crime scenes is often poor (due to the lack of training in crime scene techniques by police agents). The concept of a chain of custody, as a warrant of the integrity of the evidence, is known in Portuguese legal discourse, but its implementation is contingent on the action of the police, as has been shown by ethnographic research (Costa and Nunes, 2001; Costa et al, 2002; Costa, 2003). Biological material for investigations of paternity claims is collected by medical personnel and its integrity and quality are preserved.

In paternity claims, the use and scrutiny of genetic profiles often takes place as one form of evidence – albeit a crucial one – in a context of conservative conceptions, held by the judge and public prosecutors, of appropriate sexual and procreative behaviour by women and of their moral standing (Machado, 2002). Based on the constitutional right that every citizen has to know the identity of her/his father, Portuguese civil law requires that the public prosecutor's office launch an investigation if the father of a child is unknown. DNA profiling has become the successor technique to blood tests in these investigations.

The creation of genetic databases for forensic purposes has been under discussion over the past two years, but the debate on this issue has been confined mostly to forensic scientists and legal scholars and practitioners.

---

the legal protection of biotechnological inventions came into force. Essentially, this directive allows genes to be patented provided they have been characterized in isolation of the genome. This has caused debate in Italy, France, Norway, the Netherlands and Germany. Nevertheless, it will be adopted by most European countries. The British debate and the regulation of gene testing for insurance purposes are presented in case study 4 (Box 2.4).

Box 2.4 Case study 4: Genetic testing and insurance in the UK

Nicola Lindsey

The UK has seen three fundamental changes in policy in the past few years on the issue of genetic testing and insurance. In 1997, the insurance industry entered into a voluntary agreement with the government whereby, under the auspices of self-regulation, it would not ask applicants to undergo genetic testing. Moreover, it would only use genetic test information above a certain financial limit. In 1999, the Government decided that if the industry were to be using genetic test information, it ought to be approved officially, and it therefore set up an independent advisory body, the Genetics and Insurance Committee (GAIC), to assess and monitor the industry's use of tests on a case-by-case basis. In September 1999, the committee approved the first test – that for Huntington's disease – to be used in relation to applications for life insurance. The approval triggered a fairly widespread media and public debate and prompted another government advisory body – the Human Genetics Commission (HGC) – to launch a public consultation on the issue. Finding a high degree of public and political concern about the issue, the HGC called for a moratorium on the use of genetic test results just six months later. Finally, in October 2001, faced with growing public pressure the Government conceded to a five-year moratorium, extending the boundaries of the industry's own moratorium in terms of time, financial limits and the range of insurance products covered. It kept the GAIC in place to regulate tests above this limit and monitor the industry's observance of the moratorium.

The two committees were therefore working independently within government and in fact advising the Government on the same issue in opposite ways. The Genetics and Insurance Committee was a technical committee set up to consider the scientific, clinical and actuarial relevance of genetic tests. For this committee, insurance was viewed as a private contract between individual and insurer which is based on the principle of equity – that is, that neither side should be in possession of more relevant information than the other. The evidence that the committee used to assess the relevance of genetic tests was fundamentally quantitative, whereby the insurance company applying for approval must demonstrate that a positive result for the test in question will increase an individual's mortality rate by at least 50 per cent or their morbidity rate by at least 25 per cent. The assumption underlying the existence of the committee is that genetic testing will become more prevalent in the future and therefore it represents an effort to get the regulatory mechanisms in place now.

In contrast, the Human Genetics Commission is a strategic committee set up to consider the social, ethical and legal implications of developments in human genetics. For this committee, life insurance was seen as a social good, that is, something that all individuals should have access to in order to function normally as part of society. In their report on insurance the committee expressed fears that discrimination on genetic grounds by insurance, companies might lead to the exclusion of new social categories and this might therefore discourage individuals from undergoing genetic testing. This was seen as a serious public health issue. In addition, the committee viewed genetic information not simply as the results of genetic tests, but as including family history information. Finally, it argued that genetic tests are not accurate but are always open to interpretation.

Therefore, the two committees may be seen to be operating on different sides of the paradoxes inherent in genetic information and research. The result for policy making in this area in the UK is that the overall regulatory picture is inconsistent and difficult to define.

Regulatory issues

These uses of genetic information raise difficult issues for regulators and policy makers. Genetic information raises questions of consent. For example, is the collection voluntary or coerced? Is informed consent, once given, valid for repeated sampling? How is consent dealt with in cases where the individual is incapable of giving it? Under what circumstances (if any) should individuals be coerced into giving tissue or fluid samples for genetic information? What about forensic settings? Should the sampling of genetic material be compulsory for criminals, suspects or victims of crimes? If the answer is 'yes', what crimes should be included? Should sampling be coercive in cases of paternity claims, and for whom (mother, child, putative father)? Who should be entitled, in each circumstance, to collect the genetic information: medical personnel, research scientists, law enforcement officers? Where should responsibility for authorizing genetic testing lie: with courts of law, medical authorities, research institutions? What are the criteria for inclusion in and exclusion from databases?

Second, questions arise about how genetic information is managed. Who is entitled to manage the information and in what format? Who is in charge of the custody of samples, profiles and of codes for matching individuals with samples and profiles? Should these be kept in separate institutions? What institutional arrangements provide adequate safeguards of privacy? How can intervening institutions and agents be made accountable? What are the mechanisms for controlling violations?

Third, what are the legitimate uses of genetic information and genetic data-bases? Who is entitled to access the databases, for what purposes, under what circumstances, and how? What are the specific conditions of access for research, medical intervention and forensic uses? Are uses for insurance purposes legitimate? When is it legitimate for employers to use genetic testing for hiring staff and for workplace safety purposes? What safeguards against abusive access are available? Are the threats of misuse or abuse of genetic information different from those that apply to other, more common forms of use of medical or personal information?

Fourth, who owns the genetic information? Is it the person who provided the materials or their family, if the information is relevant for its members or is likely to be sensitive, damaging or a possible source of discrimination for family members (in cases of detection of genetic traits 'running in families', for instance)? Is it the research institute that turned it into manageable and usable data? Can materials or processes based on genetic materials be patented? Who owns the materials stored in forensic databases? Who is entitled to decide which information to include or exclude from databases?

Discriminatory practices

Finally, how can discriminatory practices based on genetic information be prevented? Are there legitimate forms of discrimination? If so, in which areas and for what purpose? Can individuals be removed from a job on the basis of genetic testing, by invoking the need to safeguard their health and safety? Is it legitimate for an insurance company or an employer to discriminate against non-symptomatic carriers of a genetic trait or a genetic polymorphism ('healthy ill'), invoking increased risk of a disabling disease? How do questions of discrimination relate to current definitions of proportionality and equity in criminal law? Does the inclusion of genetic profiles in databases of convicted criminals violate the rights of those who have been convicted but then released? These and many other questions relating to the safeguarding of citizens against discrimination on the basis of genotypical characteristics need to be examined from regulatory, legal and constitutional points of view. How do such safeguards appear in international and European conventions and how are they then transposed into domestic law?

The above questions reflect the range of complex issues surrounding genetic information with which policy makers in many countries have been grappling. However, in many ways questions relating to genetic information are questions of information in general. The aim of the following sections is to identify the properties of genetic information that render it a particular challenge.

Particularities of genetic information

Genetic information is pervasive and has relevance on many different levels. It has the unique ability to define both individuality and membership of a social group. Individuals construct their identities with reference to membership and non-membership of social groupings or 'microcultures', hence building a dichotomous concept of togetherness and belonging and of otherness. Such typical reference systems include those of kinship, age, gender, ethnicity, economic status and profession. Genetic information may act to reinforce these social groupings, which are also conceptual categories within which the self is constructed, either by adding value to the existing connecting threads that bond the group, or by devaluing them, resulting in the impoverishment of the sense of belonging. In other cases, genetic information could also be constructing new connecting threads, leading to the formation of novel collective structures in formal or informal forms, whether institutionalized or not. Hence, genetic information has the potential power to change the boundaries between the self and the other.

According to Martin (1987), the interpretation process of genetic information by non-experts is not random; it varies according to social status and often reveals other aspects of people's lives. In addition, genetic information and the interpretation of it may lead to the construction of new social communities based on

---

Box 2.5 Case study 5: The role of genetic information in reproduction among same-sex couples in Finland

Timo Rusanen

In Finland, same-sex unions have been legal since 2002 as marriage-like registered partnerships giving many of the legal rights typical for married heterosexual couples. Whether or not same-sex couples should have the right to adopt children is still being debated. More pertinent to this debate is that the existence of fertility treatments using artificial insemination opens up the possibility of biological parenthood for one of the partners in a same-sex couple.

The role of genetic information is highly relevant for biological parenthood, where the homosexual couple have to make a decision about whose eggs or sperm of the two partners will be used for the treatment. In addition, a decision has to be made about the origin of the eggs or sperm to be used as a complement from the donation bank. No matter what selection criteria the couple may apply, these decisions rely heavily on genetic information about the potential parents and about the egg or sperm donors. In sum, the artificial insemination technique offers to homosexual, and incidentally to heterosexual, couples the possibility of a biological parenthood that can be designed, based on genetic information.

Finland's Health Care Ethical Committee (ETENE) allows fertility treatment only to heterosexual couples. Treatment for single women, but not for homosexual couples, is allowed. One reason for this is that the current bill on the registration rights of same-sex couples does not allow adoption (HS 2001). The Ethical Committee allows fertility treatments to heterosexuals only on the basis that the position of the child is paramount. However, there is also a view that prohibiting same-sex couples from acquiring joint children would be a form of discrimination against sexual minorities. Furthermore, if homosexual couples had access to fertility treatment, this would be inconsistent with the situation where same-sex couples have no right to adopt each other's children. Under the present Finnish legislation, if one partner in the homosexual couple has a biological child, the other partner cannot adopt it. In this respect, allowing infertility treatment without the possibility of adoption would be illogical in the context of the existing legislation (www.etene.org).

---

shared genetic traits. Genetic information has the potential to redefine the social in biological terms. Rapid advances in the production of genetic knowledge bring the 'biological' into sharp focus. This process has become known as 'geneticization'. Geneticization is a reductionist process that places the organic, the mechanistic and the biological as the basis of human existence while devaluing social experiences and feelings (Lippman, 1992; Nelkin and Lindee, 1995). According to this geneticization trend, the self, the personality and the potential of the individual are genetically determined. The relationship between the 'social' and the 'biological' has historically been a source of controversy and hence the evident power of genetic information to reorganize this relationship explains, in part at least, its controversial nature.

Genes and personal identity

This redefinition of the social order creates new dilemmas that may threaten an individual's sense of autonomy. This can be witnessed, for example, by the emergence of people born through sperm and egg donation who now want to trace their biological fathers and mothers. In addition, new reproduction technologies open the possibility of biological parenthood to same sex couples. Case study 5 (Box 2.5) sketches some of the questions and conflicts regarding the role of genetic information in reproduction among same-sex couples in Finland.

Reproduction technologies are changing our understanding of what it means to be a parent. Individuals who undergo genetic testing are simultaneously implicating members of their own family in both present and future generations. Some family members may not want to know they are at risk. Those who have tests have to decide whether and how to act on the information – should someone who knows that they carry the Huntington's gene go ahead and have children of their own, knowing they have a 50 per cent chance of passing it on? Should they actively screen out embryos that carry that gene?

Discourses and social representations of genetic information highlight the multiplicity of meanings that can be given to this information in different socio-cultural contexts, beyond, or apart from, its scientific-biological meaning. Genetic information brings novel meanings and at the same time strengthens old meanings, symbols and myths all of which make up the material used in the process of constructing one's identity and the boundaries that separate the 'self' from the 'other', 'us' from 'them'.

Redefinition of kinship, disease and ethnicity

The three most obvious areas where genetic information can be seen to redefine social groupings are the family, the disease group and the ethnic group.

Family members are biologically related, that is, they share inherited biological substance. In addition they are connected by emotional feelings and economic relationships. The strength of these connections may differ in different cultures. In the west, for instance, biological relatedness has been the prevalent determinant. In Euro-American kinship, blood ties and the sharing of bio-genetic substance make up central organizing symbols in lay concepts about kinship. The idiom of nature is central in the American kinship system. 'The family is formed according to the laws of nature and exists according to laws that are experienced by the people as natural' (Schneider, 1980, p34).

However, in many cultures the extended family form has been devalued. For example, second cousins are often not felt to be relatives. In such contexts, the appearance of genetic information may emphasize the biological connections (geneticization). Once a family member is informed of an inherited genetic condition, he/she will be challenged to inform the other family members and to trace the specific genotype in the family tree. In this example, the family as a group is then defined via its biological/genetic characteristics.

People who have a specific genetic disease in common may form social groupings. In this case, genetic information might be the cause of the formation of the grouping, which enables the members to adopt common ways of dealing with the problem they share. They might evolve a collective discourse that will represent them in society and will have an economic, political and emotional impact. We are witnessing the emergence and empowerment of such groups that elaborate political and ideological discourses regarding their 'special' conditions and use the genetic information in multiple ways. For example, some groups via their collective actions argue that their unique genetic profiles should not be stigmatized and, drawing on their human rights, they may embrace their genetic difference rather than trying to change it with future gene therapies (the case of congenitally deaf people is often quoted in this context). Other groups try via their collective actions to demand attention from the various stakeholders, and ask for special treatment, in the workplace or in economic support. In many cases, they ask the scientists to give priority to their problem, and to drive research towards a direction best suited to their specific problem.

The progress of genetics has revealed information regarding the differences and similarities of the genetic profiles between and within ethnic groups. This genetic information has mainly been produced by the Human Genome Diversity Programme and has begun to play an important role in the process of the construction of ethnic identities. Ethnic groups may use the information in multiple ways, and may allocate different meanings to it. For instance, such information may reconstruct the foundations of an ethnic group, in terms of the determinants that make members of an ethnic group different from the rest. Alternatively, ethnic groups may use this information on a political level, in order to claim their difference, or even to claim separate land, extra rights and so on. For example, there is evidence to suggest that native Australian Aborigines are adopting genetic testing technologies in deciding their new political representatives.

The multifunctionality of genetic information

Human genetic information is comprehensive and therefore multifunctional. Our current scientific understanding of human genetics is limited. Even though it is known that many human properties are determined to a greater or lesser extent by genetic predispositions, the determining influence of other factors such as environment or individual choice is not known. While there is scientific and political controversy about this topic, it is illuminating that in this discussion on heredity virtually every human property is addressed, ranging from physical (e.g. body size) to social (e.g. criminality), psychological (e.g. mental health, homosexuality) and intellectual characteristics (e.g. intelligence). It is this comprehensiveness that enables genetic information to be used for very different purposes: for identifying a person or for determining his or her predisposition for specific illnesses. This multifunctionality of genetic information presents a key challenge for data protection and privacy. Genetic information that has been gathered for diagnostic purposes might potentially also be of interest for insurers, employers and public health administrations. However, the norm of privacy states that individuals should be in control of their personal information.

We are witnessing in western countries via the symbolic use of the 'genetic' a 'new cartography of the body redefining health, disease and fault in a realistic, biologically deterministic way' (Strathern, 1992). This phenomenon is part of a wider turn according to which inheritance and nature are being reproduced as techniques (Rabinow, 1996) and blood kinship is being geneticized, medicalized and instrumentalized.

Power and hierarchy: The lay–expert divide

The genetic testing procedure is unlike most other medical testing procedures in that the patient not only receives medical or technical advice but also undergoes intensive counselling from a trained genetic counsellor. This need for counselling is driven by the complexity and sensitivity of the information rather than the physical pain associated with the procedure itself, which is minimal. A hierarchical divide and possibly a power differential are thus created between those who possess the information and those who are authorized to access and interpret it. As the importance of genetic testing grows, this divide will inevitably grow wider.

Sociological researchers have shown how the development of genetic testing and the focus on the genetic basis of disease have led to a reclassification or 'geneticization' of disease diagnoses in the clinic. So, those who have non-familial breast cancer are treated differently from those who have inherited forms, despite having virtually the same clinical symptoms. But more seriously, as genes involved in more complex traits are identified, a process of medicalization is taking place where the boundaries of what is normal are constantly being shifted with the identification of each new gene and mutated allele. The label 'medicalization' summarizes the trend, that more and more societal problems are defined in terms of medical categories. Examples can be found in other policy fields, for example in relation to drugs, crime and the labour market. The results of pre-symptomatic tests challenge the current social definition of health and illness: having a positive test result without symptoms of a disease does not fit into either category. Behavioural traits, such as aggression, sexuality and alcoholism, are in the process of being redefined in medical terms. With the power of access to our genes lying in scientists' hands, will the result be that normality becomes a medical condition? Will we be turning to scientists to define who we are? Or worse, will large social institutions like insurance companies be able to find out things about us before we even know them ourselves?

The twin processes of medicalization and geneticization challenge a traditional understanding of how we view disease and the inheritance of particular traits. Although the genetic definition of a disease may be new, beliefs about inheritance are not. They have long been part of social and family cultures, for example through the identification of family resemblances. They may also be associated with social and cultural practices concerning the inheritance of wealth and personal possessions. These beliefs are likely to affect how people of different cultures react to genetic information in the clinic. For example, clinicians have reported how patients with inherited forms of breast cancer fail to consider that the gene may have been inherited through the paternal line because they assume it can only be passed on by women. These beliefs cannot be ignored, because they influence how information is processed and understood by patients. Similarly, the experts' understanding of inheritance and the context in which they work will influence the conception of the genetic testing procedures and the destiny of the results. Factors concerning the management and ownership of the testing will also influence the relationship between patient and medical expert. Therefore, given the complexity of the genetic testing and the sensitivity of the information, these procedures require not only medical, but also psychological and sociological expertise, usually provided in the form of genetic counselling both before and after testing.

While accepting that the way in which scientific and technological knowledge circulates is influenced by the expert perspective (insiders) on sharing knowledge with lay people (outsiders) (Bauer and Gaskell, 1999), it should also be recognized that lay–expert hierarchies are not simple power relations defined over who does know (experts) and who does not know (lay) about genetic testing. The complexity of the issue and the constraints of our knowledge affect all the people involved, with the result that experts in some fields are at the same time lay people in others. Therefore, the separation between lay and expert knowledge is not a simple one (Moscovici, 1981) and we must consider several types of expertise and lay knowledge (Wynne, 1995, 1996; Irwin and Wynne, 1996). As an alternative to the so-called deficit model of the public understanding of science, Wynne (1995, 1996) and Irwin and Wynne (1996) suggest a process of 'creative construction' in which expert knowledge is transformed into lay knowledge, where the representations of science are seen as a common-sense answer to the challenges made by science and scientists in present-day societies.

Thus, the relations between lay people and experts are deeply related to the contexts, norms and rules of testing procedures as well as to the understandings of cultural inheritance on the part of both groups.

Limitations of genetic prediction and intergenerational responsibility

Cultural understandings of inheritance, family and social relationships add a further layer of interpretive complexity to genetic information. At the same time, genetic information is inherently probabilistic information. On its own, genetic information cannot predict when a disease will develop, what the symptoms will be or how severe it will become. Genetic tests can never be 100 per cent predictive because the same disorder can be caused by many different gene mutations and can arise spontaneously in the population. Lifestyle choices or prophylactic treatments may help to combat some genetic diseases, but it is uncertain what the effect of these and other environmental influences will be on any given individual.

Therefore, genetic information – the quantitative estimate of disease – is virtually useless on its own; it must always be accompanied by an interpretation or a qualitative element. But difficult decisions often rest on these interpretations, such as whether to go ahead with a pregnancy or whether to inform existing children and siblings of their risk. The meaning of genetic risk is therefore more global than just an index or statistical statement can provide. Not only are the risk estimates intrinsically difficult to understand in real terms, but they are also affected by the seriousness of decisions that must be based on them. These decisions will be laden with fundamental social and personal values as well as psychological factors and, as a result, negative and positive outcomes may be attributed with greater significance than is predicted by their statistical risk alone. At the same time, clinically, the information is often of little value at all if tests become available before any preventive treatment or therapy is developed. It is not surprising then that a large proportion of people at risk of Huntington's disease – a highly penetrant neurological disorder of later life – choose not to undergo genetic testing.

A further implication of this is that the new production of genetic information is intimately linked with developments in information technology. On the one hand, the success of modern human genetics would not have been possible without large computers and robots doing much of the analysis in an automatic, reliable and fast way. There is indeed a new academic discipline emerging from this successful cooperation, called bio-informatics. On the other hand, modern computer technology is also making some of the problems related to the abuse of genetic information worse, due to the size of genetic databases and the speed at which they can be accessed, not to mention the restrictions over who is able to access it.

Finally, genetic information is also fundamentally temporal information. It is diagnostic and predictive. Genetic information has implications not only for the individual concerned but also, crucially, for future generations. Through the use of family history, it draws past, present and future generations into a single experience. However, it is the history of past uses of genetic information that causes people to fear the future. One need only look at the eugenic policies of the 1930s and 1940s to know how risky the use of genetic information for some people might be. There is a fear among many people that the use of genetic information to select desired traits or characteristics and to penalize those without is a 'slippery slope'; once going down that route, there is no breaking the trend. There is a sense that genetic information is irreversible – once we know, there is no way of ignoring it. We have to carry the burden of that knowledge with us throughout our lives. It is no surprise that people who are found to carry a disease-linked gene perceive the positive test result as the first discernible symptoms of that disease – even if the gene is recessive and they are not actually at risk of developing symptoms. The enlightenment imperative of 'dare to know' might appear in a new light: knowledge as an unwanted curse or burden.

Some paradoxes by way of conclusion

In this chapter, we map out some of the features of genetic information that define its 'special' status. In doing so, a number of paradoxes have been uncovered. Genetic information can be both *concrete* and *abstract*. We cannot experience a gene, only its effects. Yet to identify a 'gene' is to reify a physical property present in every cell of the body. Genetic information is both *simple* and *complex*. It is simple to obtain and can be reduced to a single yes/no presence or absence of an allele, but at the same time it can only have relevance within a system – the environment of other genes, the cell, the body, nature and so on. Genetic information is often presented statistically, while its social *meaning is not quantifiable*. While we do not have the technology to treat genetic diseases, is it worth knowing that we have a higher chance of developing a problem? At the same time, genes interact in a system with each other and with the environment. Is it worth knowing about one gene if it can be mitigated by another about which we do not know? Genetic information has the power to define both *individuals* and *groups*. It is inherently structural information. It can redefine social relationships and the social order. Genetic information can show *unity* or *diversity*, depending on the focus of public discourse. On the one hand, genes are something that belong to all of us – the human genome – and are therefore a public good of humanity as a whole. On the other hand, an individual's genome is also personal and should therefore be in the control of that private person. So, genetic information has the power to make the public private and the private public. It is something that might be traded as a private good while used for the public good. Genetic information is *multifunctional*. It can describe medical and non-medical traits and be used for medical and non-medical purposes. Genetic information is often thought of as new because it requires the application of new and better technology. But we have long been aware of our physical differences, of how these are passed on in families and how they may be associated with different social groups. Genetic information is therefore not new, but a redefinition of old information in new terms. This process of valuing genetic information is often referred to as 'geneticization'. Some genetic information is not particularly sensitive, such as blood groups, gender, fingerprinting for crime. In other contexts, it is extremely sensitive, such as carrier status of a genetic disorder.

These paradoxes highlight the ambivalent nature of genetic information. Similar to the development of other technologies, one would expect that this ambivalence means a temporary openness that will close in the social shaping of technology. What will be the societal impact of genetic information? Will the current trend of geneticization in medicine and childbearing prevail? It is premature to provide definite answers, because conflicting tendencies coexist. On the one hand, genetic information is a complex issue debated only within a small expert community. On the other hand, our case studies showed public sensitivity towards this topic in many European countries, not least because the very definition of personal identity is at stake. The future of genetic information is wide open.

It is the enduring belief in the potential of genes that causes the debate around the use of genetic research to persist. Therefore, any usage of genetic information in individual and political decisions should proceed cautiously. The certainties of today might prove to be the errors of tomorrow. On the other hand, scientific progress is a strong legitimization for current efforts in the collection and analysis of genetic information. As the Iceland example shows, a popular pastime of family interests in genealogy has become a valuable resource for modern medical research. The question arises: if at all, then to what extent does anticipated future progress justify the partial suspension of fundamental rights (e.g. protection of privacy and personal data) at the present time.

References

Abbott, A. (1999) 'Sweden sets ethical standards for use of genetic "biobanks"', *Nature*, vol 400, no 6739, p3

Bauer, M. and Gaskell, G. (1999) 'Towards a paradigm for research on social representations', *Journal for the Theory of Social Behaviour*, vol 29, pp163–185

Bell, D. (1976, republished in 1999) *The Coming of Post-Industrial Society: A Venture in Social Forecasting*, Basic Books, New York

Bonfadelli, H., Dahinden, U., Leonarz, M., Schanne, M., Schneider, C. and Knickenberg, S. (2001) 'Biotechnology in Switzerland: From street demonstrations to regulations, in Gaskell, G. and Bauer, M. W. (eds) *Biotechnology 1996–2000: The Years of Controversy*, Science Museum, London, pp282–291

Castells, M. (1996) *The Information Age: Economy, Society and Culture*, Blackwell Publishers, Malden, MA

Costa, S. (2003) *A justiça em laboratório: A identificação por perfis genéticos de ADN entre a harmonização transnacional e a apropriação local*, Almedina, Coimbra

Costa, S., Machado, H. and Nunes, J. A. (2002) 'O ADN e a justiça: A biologia forense e o direito como mediadores entre a ciência e os cidadãos', in Gonçalves, M. E. (ed) *Os Portugueses e a ciência*, Publicações Dom Quixote/Observatório das Ciências e das Tecnologias, Lisbon, pp199–233

Costa, S. and Nunes, J. A. (2001) 'As atribulações da ciência 'impura': A harmonização da biologia forense e a diversidade dos sistemas jurídicos', in Nunes, J. A. and Gonçalves, M. E. (eds) *Enteados de Galileu? Semiperiferia e Intermediação no Sistema Mundial da Ciência*, Afrontamento, Oporto, pp107–141

ETENE (2004) Homepage of the Finnish National Advisory Board on Health Care Ethics (ETENE), www.etene.org

Hardmeier, S. and Scheiwiller, D. (1998) 'Analyse der eidgenössischen Abstimmungen vom 7 Juni 1998: Volksinitiative "Zum Schutz von Leben und Umwelt vor Genmanipulation" (Genschutz-Initiative)', *Vox-Analysen eidgenössischer Urnengänge*, vol 63, GfS-Forschungsinstitut, Bern, Institut für Politikwissenschaft der Universität Zürich, Zürich

HS (2001) 'Ethical committee would allow fertility treatments only to heterosexuals', *Helsingin Sanomat*, 1 February

Irwin, A. and Wynne, W. (1996) *Misunderstanding Science? The Public Reconstruction of Science and Technology*, Cambridge University Press, Cambridge

Lippman, A. (1992) 'Led (astray) by genetic maps: The cartography of the Human Genome Project and health care', *Social Science and Medicine*, vol 35, no 12

Machado, H. (2002) 'Tribunais, género, ciência e cidadania uma abordagem sociológica da investigação judicial de paternidade', Doctoral dissertation in Sociology, Universidade do Minho, Braga

Martin, E. (1987) *The Women in the Body: A Cultural Analysis of Reproduction*, Beacon Press, Boston

Maschke, K. J. (2005) 'Navigating an ethical patchwork – Human gene banks', *Nature Biotechnology*, vol 23, no 5, pp539–545

Moscovici, S. (1981) 'On social representations', in Forgas, J. P. (ed) *Social Cognition: Perspectives on Everyday Understanding*, Academic Press, London, pp181–209

Nelkin, D. and Lindee, S. (1995) *The DNA Mystique: The Gene as a Cultural Icon*, W. H. Freeman, New York

Rabinow, P. (1996) *Essays on the Anthropology of Reason*, Princeton University Press, Princeton, NJ

Schneider, D. M. (1980) *American Kinship: A Cultural Account*, 2nd edn, University of Chicago Press, Chicago

Strathern, M. (1992) *After Nature: English Kinship in the Late Twentieth Century*, Cambridge University Press, Cambridge

Webster, F. (2003a) *Theories of the Information Society* (International Library of Sociology), Routledge, London and New York

Webster, F. (ed) (2003b) *The Information Society Reader*, Routledge, London and New York

Wynne, B. (1995) 'Public understanding of science', in Jasanoff, S., Markle, G., Pinch, T. and Petersen, J. (eds) *Handbook of Science and Technology Studies*, Sage, London

Wynne, B. (1996) 'May the sheep safely graze? A reflexive view of the expert–lay knowledge divide', in Lash, S., Szerszynski, B. and Wynne, B. (eds) *Risk, Environment and Modernity: Towards a New Ecology*, Sage, London, pp44–83

3

Spare Parts for Human Bodies?

Suzanne de Cheveigné,[1] *Edna Einsiedel and*
Jürgen Hampel
with Jacqueline Chervin and Robin Downey

Until recently, modern biotechnology aroused debate mainly in the field of food applications, around a number of genetically modified plants such as maize or soya. Various surveys indicated that medical applications of biotechnology were receiving far more support from the general public than applications in the field of agriculture and food production (Durant et al, 1998; Gaskell and Bauer, 2001). However, some specific medical applications are not without controversy, especially the new regenerative medical techniques such as xenotransplants, cloning and stem cell research. This chapter will examine the recent evolution of public debate around these techniques, based on an analysis of the situation in three countries, Canada, France and Germany, in order to reach a better understanding of the role societal processes play in the development and implementation of new technologies.

Our analysis will be situated in the general perspective of the theoretical approach known as the Social Construction of Technology (SCOT). While older analyses of technological development saw it as a process following its own technological rationality (Ellul, 1954, 1964), or a process of diffusion (Rogers, 1983), more recent innovation research has demonstrated that the shaping of new inventions is a social process in which different actors and different social phenomena are involved (Flichy, 1995; Bijker, 1995; Callon et al, 2001). From this perspective, looking at the technological aspects of inventions is not sufficient for the analysis of innovation processes where actors play a crucial role, actors in science, industry and the state as well as non-governmental organizations (NGOs) and the public. It is necessary to analyse the role that a broad range of social groups play in determining the trajectory of technologies from the stages of innovation to an eventual stabilization around a dominant form. It means focusing both on the technologies and on the actors that shape and amplify their meanings, widening the analytical perspective and including decision processes in the 'developing system'.

Public debate is an essential element of this process. The discussions presently surrounding stem cells, cloning and xenotransplants, in the media and elsewhere, signify that these technologies are still in a state of transformation and have not yet reached closure. The way that they are framed in the public sphere and the way they move from one arena to another (Hilgartner and Bosk, 1988; Renn, 1992; Callon et al, 2001) play an essential role in the collective elaboration of their future. The importance of such processes has been demonstrated in the case of agricultural biotechnology in Europe, where public rejection has prevented many implementations of this technology (see Hampel et al in this volume).

With these elements in mind, we wish to compare the state of public debate around three controversial medical techniques in three countries with quite different histories: Canada, France and Germany. The three techniques, xeno-transplantation, human reproductive cloning and stem cell research, can all be described as potential techniques for the replacement of human organs and tissues. Functionally equivalent, they can be described as providing 'spare parts' for the human body. While even the more realistic of these techniques is still at the research level, their medical, ethical and social dimensions as well as their potential risks and benefits have provoked widespread debates and controversies which we wish to examine here, as an element of the social construction of these technologies.

We shall begin our analysis in 1997, the year of the announcement of the birth of Dolly the cloned sheep. The event aroused considerable awareness and emotion worldwide, and the possibility of applying the same technique to human cloning was immediately taken up by the media (Einsiedel et al, 2002). From that point on, the intensity of public debate concerning all sectors of biotechnology increased and medical applications of biotechnology became a frequent topic of controversy – especially human reproductive cloning. The issue was apparently not only a virtual one, even though human cloning is considered to be very far from serious implementation by most scientists. Immediately after the birth of Dolly, a series of projects for the cloning of humans was announced, first by Dr Richard Seed from Chicago, then by Dr Severino Antinori, a fertility specialist from Rome. Recently, the Raelian sect – founded in Canada – even claimed that the first human had effectively been cloned on Christmas Day 2002. More than a year later, the claim had still not been substantiated. Reproductive human cloning, teetering on the boundary between science fiction and reality, remains, potentially, a technique that could provide a reservoir of compatible organs or even permit the regeneration of entire human beings.

Xenotransplantation and stem cell research can also be described as potential techniques for the replacement of human organs and tissues, providing 'spare parts' for the human body. While human cloning has triggered science fiction-like debates, the problem of research with human embryo stem cells, possibly obtained by therapeutic cloning, has become a major regulatory issue in many countries (Knowles, 2004). Xenotransplantation, on the other hand, has not raised public

controversy in the same manner. These differences are what we wish to understand, in three countries with quite different traditions: Canada, France and
Germany. But first, let us point out some elements of their common context.

A common horizon

Although public debates tend to remain on the national level, the trajectories
of public debate around cloning, stem cells and xenotransplants share a common
background, made up of scientific discoveries and international regulations.
Although events and norms may be diversely adopted and interpreted in different
countries, a brief history of the development of the techniques we are discussing
here and of some of the regulatory acts that have had a global echo is needed.

Xenotransplantation, that is, the replacement of deficient humans organs and
tissues with organs coming from animals, was the first of these 'spare parts'
techniques to be implemented – before 1920 (Réal, 2001; Schicktanz, 2000) with
organs from baboons and chimpanzees. Today, pigs have been identified as
the likeliest candidates, genetically modified (i.e. 'humanized') to eliminate the
production of the proteins responsible for their rejection. Although human
identity, crossing the boundaries between humans and animals, and animal
protection are an issue, scientists are at present most concerned about the possible
transmission of disease. Indeed, on 29 January 1999, the Council of Europe called
for a moratorium on all tests because of the risk of infection by porcine retroviruses
that could lead to a modification of human genetic heritage.

Stem cells, which are unspecialized cells that can evolve to become specialized
ones – of the heart muscle or the pancreas, for instance – will also be examined
here. There are two kinds: embryonic stem cells and adult stem cells, which are
found in some tissues of adult organisms. The best known of the latter are bone
marrow cells, which can become blood cells, but adult stem cells have also been
found in skin and muscles. They serve to regenerate cells that are lost through
normal wear, injury or disease, but they appear to have less possibility of evolution
than embryonic ones. At present, scientists are working on the premise that stem
cells, either embryonic or adult, may become the basis for treating degenerative
diseases such as Parkinson's disease, diabetes and heart disease, by replacing
failing cells. In spite of such bright prospects, the use of embryos raises delicate
ethical questions about respect for this early element of life – embryo research is,
for instance, totally condemned by the Vatican and has raised much debate in the
United States. The use of adult stem cells would avoid the ethical dilemma, but
their possibilities seem, for the time being, to be more limited.

The problem has become decidedly more complicated since the idea of
obtaining stem cells from embryos by *therapeutic cloning* appeared. This brings
us back to human cloning, a technique that seemed, until the birth of Dolly, to
have more potential as a science fiction story – as in Aldous Huxley's *Brave New
World* – than as a real prospect. This process involves transferring the nucleus of
an adult cell from the organism to be cloned – containing all its genetic information
– into an unfertilized, enucleated ovula, then, by various techniques, activating

the development of the egg. One possibility is then to reimplant the egg in a 'mother', as was done for Dolly and as would be done in the case of human reproductive cloning. For humans, this perspective is nearly unanimously rejected – with the few exceptions we mentioned in the introduction. UNESCO adopted the Universal Declaration on the Human Genome and Human Rights on 11 November 1997, which says that states must not allow 'practices which are contrary to human dignity, such as reproductive cloning of human beings'. Paradoxically, however, an international regulation against reproductive cloning has not yet been set up, because of the opposition of countries (the United States, Spain, the Vatican) that want therapeutic cloning and not only reproductive cloning to be forbidden.

The other possibility is not to implant the egg into a uterus but instead to allow it to develop in vitro to the stage where it produces embryonic stem cells. The resulting stem cells would be genetically identical to the cloned cell – which would come from the person in need of treatment. Transplantation of organs between individuals requires close tissue compatibility. One solution, widely rejected as we said, could be to use human cloning to produce individuals solely for organ donation. Stem cells obtained by therapeutic cloning, on the other hand, as the US National Bioethics Advisory Commission Report (1999) pointed out, would avoid producing such instrumentalized individuals: 'a morally more acceptable and potentially feasible approach is to direct differentiation along a specific path to produce specific tissues (e.g. muscle or nerve) for therapeutic transplantation rather than to produce an entire individual'.

The idea of using this nuclear somatic transfer technique, also known as therapeutic cloning, to produce embryonic stem cells genetically compatible with the patient emerged in 1999 and has multiplied the ethical problems around stem cells. They now combine at least three sensitive points: destroying embryos; opening the way to cloning – although proponents of the technique insist on the fact that the embryo clone will never be allowed to develop into a human adult; and possible trafficking of ova. Therapeutic cloning is a strong point of divergence among countries. It was authorized in Great Britain at the end of 2000 and, in Europe, is now allowed in Sweden, Norway, Finland and Belgium. In the United States, the government decided that public funds should not support this type of research. The first report of the production of stem cells by therapeutic cloning was announced in South Korea in February 2004 (Hwang et al, 2004). While apparently human cloning more imminent, the fact that the use of somatic cell nuclear transfer attempted on 242 eggs yielded 30 embryos and only one viable stem cell line was again a reminder of the major technical challenges still entailed in these procedures. However, this research was subsequently retracted.

To conclude this brief description of the scientific and regulatory horizon common to our three countries, we can note that the regulatory debates on medical biotechnology are following a different pattern from those on agricultural biotechnologies. To date, because of lack of consensus on the question, there is no common European regulation of medical biotechnology equivalent to the Directives passed in 1990 in the agricultural domain (Torgersen et al, 2002), and the same holds in the case of Canada. Medical applications of biotechnology are regulated in some countries, such as Germany and France (see below), but at the level of the European Union they are clearly not a field in which common guidelines can be set up. Strong positions were taken in 2000 against therapeutic cloning by the European Parliament and by the European Ethical Group but the United Kingdom legalized the technique at the end of the same year. Only in November 2003 did the European Parliament vote to allow the Commission to fund stem cell research.

Different stories in different countries

Xenotransplantation

Among the techniques discussed here, xenotransplantation has attracted the least public attention in the three countries. Survey data show differences in perceptions between countries, Germany being, for example, more favourable to the technique than France: of the people interviewed who had heard of the technique, 50 per cent thought its development should be encouraged (as opposed to only 36 per cent in France) (Eurobarometer, 2002).[2] In Canada, six out of ten agreed that this application should be encouraged. Between countries, there are differences not only in public perception, but in the way the media take up the issue and in the way it is regulated.

In Canada's opinion-leading newspaper *The Globe and Mail*, only 11 stories mentioning the word xenotransplantation were published from 2000 to 2001. Reports of specific scientific studies are the only new stories that present xeno-transplantation as their primary topic and they typically quote university scientists. Groups such as the Islet Foundation, an international NGO that advocates science and research in the interests of finding a cure for diabetes, weigh into the debate, promoting the technology, while a few medical ethicists provide perspectives that challenge the ethics of rashly embracing this technology.

The Canadian 'debate' has been occurring primarily under the jurisdiction of the health ministry, which oversees the conduct of clinical trials as well as pre- and post-market surveillance of drugs and medical procedures. Existing legislation covered in the Food and Drugs Act and regulations pertaining to medical devices cover the use of xenotransplants, which would require a formal application for a clinical trial. Nevertheless, because of the challenges posed with regard to risk and ethics, the ministry embarked on a lengthy process of preparing a specific regulatory framework. In 1997, it held a 'National Forum on Xenotransplantation – Clinical, Ethical and Regulatory Issues'. The forum – which included health professionals, special interest groups, industry and university researchers – identified that Canada needed both a regulatory framework to set safety standards and wide public consultation to engage and inform the public. An expert group was created to propose a regulatory framework and has produced several drafts. A public consultation effort was also initiated to inform the regulatory process and to stimulate public interest and debate, in the form of citizen juries and two national surveys funded by the health ministry. Lay publics consulted on this issue recommended that the government hold off on approving clinical trials, a position based on concerns about risks posed by the potential transfer of animal viruses to humans. Other concerns such as animal welfare, the viability of other alternatives to animal tissues and organs, the adequacy of a regulatory framework, were additional considerations, while the issue of cross-species transplants had minimal significance. As of the beginning of 2004, Canada had no formal regulations pertaining specifically to the use of xenografts in humans. The level of controversy on the issue remains relatively low, and xenograft research on non-human cross-species transplants is ongoing in several universities.

In France, xenotransplants have received very little media attention (there were only seven articles on the subject in *Le Monde* in 2000 and 2001) and the general consensus is that they have little future. The risk of infection by porcine viruses has become the main argument against them, replacing rejection problems. Contrary to the Canadian example, however, they have been regulated without any public consultation, a clear case of technical regulation. The law of 1 July 1998 on the safety of products destined for human use governs xenotransplants. It stipulates that research on the therapeutic use of animal organs or cells must receive specific authorization from the Ministry of Health and that rules of good practice (concerning breeding and tracing animals, etc.) are to be set up by a newly created agency in charge of the safety of all medical products.

In 1999, the National Ethics Committee declared that the technique was 'premature' due to the risk of infection by porcine viruses but it did not call for a moratorium on research. It also recommended 'psycho-social studies' because 'xenotransplants violate the border between man and animal, with all the signification attached. Those who refuse or are unable to make a difference between their humanity and their material being will not accept xenotransplants. They will feel that the grafted organ puts them on the level of a man–animal chimera in which their humanity is dangerously dissolved' (CCNE, 1999).

In France, at present the common opinion on xenotransplants is that their prospects are poor. For instance, the Council of State, in its report of 29 November 1999 on the renewal of the bioethics laws, considered that 'their future seems compromised' due to technical difficulties and to the risk of infection. Public opinion, as we have said, is not favourable to the technique. However, in interviews or focus groups the dynamics of reactions were interesting. The immediate reaction was generally negative, but in the course of the discussion, the usefulness of a transplant often overcame the initial rejection. Their perceived utility outweighed other considerations, which in this case were less a question of material risk (although that aspect was present) than of ontological questions of human identity and of the human/animal boundary (de Cheveigné et al, 2002).

In Germany, xenotransplantation is also a topic of little public controversy. In the *FAZ*, the most important daily elite newspaper, 13 articles were published dealing with the topic, most of them in the science section, over 2000 and 2001. This coverage is also quite low in spite of the fact that Germany comes third, after the US and the UK, in research activity on the application. In 1998, scientists and industry representatives working on xenotransplantation founded a study group on xenotransplantation (Deutsche Arbeitsgemeinschaft Xenotransplantation) to deal with questions and problems of basic research as well as to advise national and international authorities. The group is composed of surgeons, immunologists, microbiologists, physiologists and virologists as well as ethicists, representatives from public life and representatives from approving regulatory institutions. Scientists agree that, at the moment, the risks associated are too high and that further research is needed: any application of this technology is considered pure science fiction and not a realistic option (Denner, 2000).

Public opinion, as we have said above, is nevertheless more favourable than in France, but the topic is almost invisible to the German public, so the application remains a subject which is discussed only within the scientific arena. The lack of regulation of xenotransplantation was pointed out by a study of the German parliamentary Office for Technology Assessment, which called for international, but also national, regulation. The report recommended the establishment of a provisional regulation agency as in the UK and called for a discussion about a temporary moratorium and a general societal debate (Petermann and Sauter, 1999). These recommendations were not implemented and no special legal regulation of xenotransplantation exists.

The only regulatory institution is the Federal Chamber of Physicians, which was planning to formulate a directive for dealing with xenotransplantations in 2002 – it is not yet in force in 2004. Its scientific advisory board sees opportunities especially in the replacement of the pancreas and the heart, but is very sceptical about kidneys and livers. The risks are more strongly emphasized than the benefits, and ethical problems (concerning animal protection and human identity) are raised. Because the scientific community did not view xenotransplantation as viable in the near term, it is not surprising that the question was not included in the task list of recently established institutions like the National Ethics Council and the Parliamentary Commission on 'Law and Ethics of Modern Medicine'. Political parties do not deal with the question either. In this respect, Germany is similar to France: the subject is reserved for specialists and, contrary to the Canadian case, no public participation has taken place. Neither the scientific community nor political actors made efforts to trigger a public debate about xenotransplantation.

Reproductive cloning

Unlike xenotransplantion, reproductive cloning is a highly publicized topic in all three countries. The 1997 announcement that scientists had cloned Dolly the sheep brought both visions of scientific progress and nightmares of human cloning together, as was evident in the coverage of the announcement in the media (Einsiedel et al, 2002). Canada's national newspaper the *Globe and Mail* carried 3 articles on cloning in 1996 but the figure shot up to 36 in 1997, the year Dolly was cloned. This decreased by about one-third in the next three years but increased significantly again to 47 stories in 2001. Until 2000, the dominant news story was about cloning animals such as mice, pigs, goats and cows. In 2001, however, stories about therapeutic and reproductive cloning overwhelmingly outnumbered animal cloning stories. Interestingly, the media's coverage of these two types of human cloning was and continues to be very different.

In Canada today, the concept of reproductive cloning is, as it was when Dolly was cloned, still very much shrouded in a cloud of rejection. Evidence of this occurred in December 2002 when Clonaid, a company associated with the Raelians, made the announcement that it had cloned the first human child. Clonaid's declaration provoked headlines of scepticism and horror from papers across Canada, with the Raelians generally considered a fringe group lacking in credibility. By March 2004, the Senate, following the lower House of Parliament's lead, finally passed a wide-ranging bill regulating assisted human reproduction but additionally barring human cloning.

In France too, human reproductive cloning has been condemned by all actors since the announcement of the birth of Dolly, usually calling upon Kantian ethics: a human being must never be considered only as a means – a position often presented in opposition to Anglo-Saxon utilitarian ethics.[3] The National Ethics Committee condemned human cloning two months after the announcement of the birth of Dolly. It first underlined the fact that genetic identity doesn't imply personal identity, then declared that 'the uniqueness of each human being which supports the autonomy and dignity of the person' depends on the uniqueness of appearance and that 'the idea of descent itself would lose all meaning'. A final argument concerned the instrumentalization of the person: clones would not be 'free ends unto themselves but pure means in the service of prior aims that would be, whatever the appearances, fundamentally exterior to them' (CCNE, 1997). When the possibility of human cloning is reported in the media, for instance when Dr Antinori drew public attention in early 2001, the arguments against it are practical (the high failure rate in animals) but also legal (it is pointed out that the plans come from two countries lacking laws against cloning, Italy and the United States). The nature/nurture debate often underlies the discussions.

Public opinion in France, as in the other two countries, is clearly against human cloning. When the idea of 'cloning a human adult to allow a sterile couple to have children' was submitted to focus groups in 1999, it evoked responses such as 'science fiction, loss of identity, loss of control, monotony, horror' (de Cheveigné et al, 2002). Human cloning is likely to be explicitly outlawed under the new bioethical law that is presently going through Parliament as a 'crime against the human species'.

In Germany, public awareness of human cloning is higher than of xenotransplantation and the theme is more present in the media (Hampel et al., 2001). After the birth of Dolly the sheep, human – and not animal – cloning dominated the headlines of journals and newspapers. No supporters of the technique were visible; the reaction from media, politics and scientific institutions to announcements of Dr Seed, Dr Antinori and the Raelians was, without any exception, negative. There is a general consensus, even among those who wish to liberalize regulations of biotechnology, that human reproductive cloning should be forbidden in all cases and, in consequence, it evokes no public or regulatory debate. However, while the intense public and political debates persisted in several European countries and in the US to cope with the regulatory needs imposed by the new technology (Einsiedel et al, 2002), the reactions of the public as well as the reactions from political actors were rather modest in Germany. The cloning of humans had appeared on the agenda, but not as a real political problem. Two months later, in April 1997, a commission of the Ministry for Research and Technology, directed by the head of the German Research Association and including representatives from science, law, the humanities and theology, came together to evaluate the existing regulation in Germany and decided that the Embryo Protection Law was sufficient since it forbids artificially creating a human embryo with the same genetic information as another embryo.

Rejected practically without exception in our three countries, human reproductive cloning is, or will soon be, explicitly forbidden. This is a case where relatively intense public discussion – contrary to the xenotransplantation case – has taken place practically without controversy. Spectacular but unfounded announcements only seem to act as a foil, allowing an exceptionally wide consensus to be reaffirmed – a consensus to which even those who wish to liberalize biotechnology regulations also subscribe. At the international level, however, efforts to pass a convention in the UN prohibiting human reproductive cloning, led by France and Germany, have been unsuccessful because of disagreements on scope, with a few countries (the United States, Spain, the Vatican) trying unsuccessfully to include therapeutic cloning in this treaty (Knowles, 2004).

Stem cells and therapeutic cloning

Stem cell research, in so far as it can imply carrying out research on embryos and/or their creation by therapeutic cloning, is by far the most controversial of the biomedical technologies discussed here. For this reason, the possibility of extracting stem cells from adult – rather than embryo – tissues has often been picked up enthusiastically as a way of avoiding an ethical dilemma.

In Canada, it was chiefly the attention paid to stem cells that revitalized regulation on reproductive technology, which had languished in legislative limbo for close to a dozen years. On the whole, however, the debate on stem cells remained mainly at the expert and stakeholder levels. Patient advocacy groups, for instance, have articulated the need for continued research in this area (Downey and Einsiedel, 2003). One arena where these expert deliberations took place was within the research granting council for health and medical research. The Canadian Institute of Health Research (CIHR) released guidelines that would specifically address stem cell research in the face of quite vocal opposition. This effort was part of the scientific community's attempts to lobby Parliament and to pre-empt legislation that was seen to stifle research. These scientists were particularly mindful of what was happening in the US regarding restrictions on embryo research. They wanted to ensure that a line was drawn between therapeutic cloning ('good' cloning) and reproductive cloning ('bad' cloning), and the fear within these circles was that policy makers examining legislative options would lump these two together and, worse, ban them altogether. The guidelines allow for human stem cell lines from pre-existing embryos, foetal tissue, amniotic fluid, the umbilical cord, placenta and other body tissues. There was a lot of support for the guidelines from some experts. Health and legal experts applauded the CIHR guidelines as 'a wonderful example of the potential for a tempered Canadian approach – a balance between the apparently restrictive US policy and the more flexible UK approach' (Caulfield et al, 2002).

On the other side of the debate, ethicists, conservative religious communities, pro-life pressure groups and politicians have all raised doubts about stem cell research. The pro-life lobby targeted both regulatory circles and patient groups that supported the CIHR guidelines. Patient groups responded to the controversy by creating strategies to lobby for the passage of Bill C-13. These groups are especially aware of the advantages of making embryos legally accessible for research purposes. An organized group of children with diabetes marched on Parliament Hill, websites promoted ways of contacting and pressuring MPs, and patient groups gave presentations to the Standing Committee on Health that was deliberating over the bill. There was some support from a number of parliamentary members on both the government and the opposition party sides for the pro-life position (Downey and Einsiedel, 2003).

In terms of public opinion, stem cell research, where stem cells were derived from fertility clinics' leftover embryos less than 14 days old, was judged to be 'very acceptable' by 29 per cent and 'somewhat acceptable' by 39 per cent of the Canadian public (Pollara/Earnscliffe, 2003). Closure was finally reached on the issue when the legislation on assisted human reproduction was passed by the Lower House in 2003 and the Senate in 2004. This same act, which will bar human cloning, will also pave the way for limited use of human embryos in medical research. This regulation would allow a government-appointed agency to oversee the use of embryos left over from fertility clinics for stem cell research.

In France, the present state of regulation allows the import of stem cell lineages for research purposes. The new bioethical laws under discussion in Parliament will probably allow research on leftover embryos but forbid therapeutic cloning, even though most scientists push strongly for it (with one or two prominent exceptions). Public opinion is moderately favourable since 58 per cent of those who had heard of 'cloning human cells or tissues' thought it should be encouraged, compared to 50 per cent in Germany and a European average of 55 per cent (Eurobarometer, 2002).

The Catholic Church has one of the least ambiguous positions in this debate: the embryo is sacred from its conception on. In his Encyclical Letter on life (Evangelium vitae) of March 1995, Pope John Paul II declared that 'the use of human embryos or fetuses as an object of experimentation constitutes a crime against their dignity as human beings who have a right to the same respect owed to a child once born, just as to every person'. The Protestant, Muslim and Jewish points of view are less categorical, either because they adopt a more relational definition of the beginning of life or because they set it at a later moment (40 days after conception). The position of the Catholic Church, to which many of the members of the right-wing majority in Parliament adhere, is an element of the French debate.

In other sectors, there is a wide consensus on the acceptability of research on existing but unwanted embryos that would otherwise be destroyed. For instance, the National Commission for Human Rights (July 2000) and the Council of State (December 1999) both agreed to this type of research, and the Academy of Medicine even considered that there is an 'obligation' to carry out research on embryos. On the other hand, the creation of embryos and, even more so, their production by therapeutic cloning are perceived as much more problematic. Therapeutic cloning is advocated essentially in scientific circles, with, for example, favourable reports from the Academies of Medicine and of Science in June 2002 and January 2003. The National Ethics Committee was divided on the question in its report of January 2000, with a majority in favour. The arguments it gave against therapeutic cloning are that it would mean creating embryos, that it would open the way to reproductive cloning, that it would put pressure on women to sell or give up ova and that adult stem cells might make it unnecessary. The arguments in favour were the competitiveness of French research and industry and the therapeutic prospects. Outside scientific circles, adult stem cells are widely advocated as a way to avoid the ethical problems that embryo research entails.

In November 2000, Prime Minister Jospin presented a project for the revision of the bioethics laws that would have allowed therapeutic cloning. President Chirac opposed it, in one of the first battles of a presidential election campaign that he would finally win, and the government withdrew the clause. In December 2003, the bioethics laws returned to Parliament, after several previous debates. The National Assembly adopted a very contrived text: research on embryos is in principle forbidden but is exceptionally authorized for five years if it 'may allow major therapeutic progress'. Therapeutic cloning, on the other hand, is absolutely forbidden. The debate followed traditional political positions, the (now small) left-wing opposition taking a pro-research stance. The text still has to go back again to the Senate to be adopted, so the situation may yet change again, more than four years after the date the law was due to be revised.

In Germany, the debate about stem cells developed against the backdrop of the widespread discussions provoked by a lecture by the German philosopher Peter Sloterdijk in July 1999 dealing with Martin Heidegger and his letter on humanism (in which Heidegger claimed that humanism had not reached its goal to civilize man). In his lecture, entitled 'Rules for the human park', Sloterdijk talked about 'anthropotechnologies' and asked whether humankind will move towards optional birth and prenatal selection. Critics accused him of supporting eugenic applications of biotechnology. A series of articles appeared in the weekly *ZEIT* and in other elite newspapers, and television channels changed their programmes and broadcast discussions on modern biotechnology and its applications to humans.

The debate on the use of human embryo stem cells for research purposes began in this context and became one of the major debates in Germany at the turn of the century. Initially, the scientific community recommended research with adult stem cells, which were seen as offering scientific opportunities without raising ethical problems and, until 2000, research with human embryo stem cells was not supported by academic institutions. This position weakened when research with animal embryo stem cells proved to be promising. In August 2000, a neurologist, O. Brüstle, requested a research grant to start a project with cells to be imported from Israel. After some hesitation, the German Research Foundation officially called for a modification of the law to allow research with imported human embryo stem cells, with an evaluation after five years.

The debate was framed as a debate concerning the importing of human embryo stem cells. Because the German law for the protection of embryos forbids not only any use of human embryos but also the production of human embryos for other purposes than for human reproduction, no superfluous embryo stem cells are produced. The situation is therefore quite different from that of France or Canada, where large stocks of unused frozen embryos exist. The position of the German government was not clear. In January 1999, the Ministry for Justice argued in favour of a modification of the Embryo Protection Law in order to make it more restrictive, while the Ministry for Research argued in favour of a more liberal regulation and for the use of human stem cells obtained abroad from aborted embryos. Both were members of the Social Democratic Party.

Advisory bodies established by different constitutional institutions came to divergent interpretations. While the Parliamentary Commission established to discuss the 'legal and ethical problems of modern medicine' advised Parliament in November 2001 not to modify the law and not to allow the import of human embryo stem cells, the majority of the National Ethics Council supported a limited importation, even though a minority group voted against. On 30 January 2002, Parliament decided to allow the import and use of these cells if they came from lines created before 1 January 2002. After this decision, it seems that the debate almost totally disappeared from the public agenda.

Two elements were important in the German debate. First, there was a common consensus based on Kantian ethics. Even utilitarian arguments had been embedded in a Kantian argumentation structure: human beings are ends, not means. This position was not challenged by the supporters of research with human embryo stem cells, who instead disputed the exact definition of when human life starts. Nevertheless, researchers added arguments about international competition, stressing the importance of scientific and economic developments. Scientists argued that there was a conflict between the constitutional right of freedom of research and the right of human embryo stem cells to become a human being. On the other hand, both dominant churches, the Protestant and the Catholic,[4] rejected human stem cell research with the argument that human embryo stem cells are not cells but humans, with all their rights and dignity. The second characteristic of the German debate was the coexistence of a broad intellectual debate about human dignity and the conditions of human existence, and a very restricted regulatory debate which was focused on stem cell research. Up until now, there has been no societal debate about therapeutic cloning because of a lack of supporters, the scientific community succeeding in restricting the debates on medical biotechnology to those applications where immediate regulatory modifications are needed to enable further research in a field seen as being promising by scientists.

Controversy and debate

We have examined the trajectories of three different regenerative medical techniques in three different countries: human reproductive cloning, which is universally rejected for ethical reasons; xenotransplants, which raise some practical doubts about current abilities to manage the risks; and finally, stem cells and therapeutic cloning, which are moving ahead in spite of the ethical worries they raise. On these topics, both debates and regulation remain mainly on the national level: medical biotechnologies are following a different trajectory compared to agricultural biotechnology. Due to lack of consensus, there has been no common European regulation comparable to the Directives of the early 1990s on genetically modified organisms (GMOs).

Reproductive cloning has remained relatively uncontroversial in all three countries, provoking a common rejection and a move to stricter regulation when deemed necessary. Scientists, political groups, politicians and the general public have a high degree of consensus that this was terrain very few wanted to tread, with the exception of the occasional flurry of media attention given to various groups interested in carrying out reproductive cloning to address infertility. In France, it is nevertheless frequently evoked as the consequence to which therapeutic cloning could lead.

We have pointed out greater national differences around xenotransplantation, which is still the topic of some scientific controversy about the possibility that applications may be reached in the near future, the French appearing globally less optimistic about the perspectives than the Germans. The issue has generated low levels of public debate even when the Canadian government organized a public consultation in the form of citizens' juries, because of risks and ethical concerns. No advocacy group in these countries has staked out this issue for major attention and it remains relatively dormant in the public arena.

Of the different technologies discussed here, stem cells and the related questions of embryo research and therapeutic cloning are the most controversial. Indeed, in all three countries, a number of actors hope that adult stem cells will provide a way of avoiding ethical issues raised by embryo research, but scientists strongly advocate pursuing work on embryo stem cells. Embryo stem cell research has powerful proponents and opponents: the scientific community agrees that such research should be developed and argues in favour of more liberal regulations. On the other side, there are other institutional groups – churches, patient organizations and others – for whom human embryo research is not acceptable. On this topic, historical and cultural differences clearly appear between our countries. Germany, sensitive to the memory of the eugenic experiments under the Third Reich, has developed a very restrictive legislation on the embryo, which rules out the production of spare embryos as well as prohibiting therapeutic cloning. Public debate developed on an exceptionally wide and philosophical basis but has subsided since the import of stem cells has been permitted. In France, rapid evolution in positions on research on embryonic stem cells has taken place, paradoxically causing much delay in the updating of the bioethics laws of 1994, which originally forbade any research on embryos. Allowing therapeutic cloning was even envisaged, then rejected. The final issue seems to be (the legislative process is not yet finished) that only research on supernumerary embryos will be allowed, on a temporary basis. This is a position similar to the one Canada has adopted on the question, but it was reached in a context that is less open and with little debate. A common position shared by our three countries should be noted: the abortion question has never been linked to the discussion on embryo research to the degree that it has in other countries such as Norway or the US.

Each in their own way, the medical applications discussed here raise the most difficult questions: What does it mean to be human? When does life begin? What constitutes identity? Where is the limit between animality and humanity? The tapping of these deep-seated values suggests that these debates will continue to play out and any regulatory or legislative initiative either will be stalled or will be a series of compromises. The question then may be as much to do with the sorts of 'political opportunity structures' that can facilitate these debates and discussions as with the technologies themselves.

A number of authors have reported a movement in western societies towards more public participation in science and technology questions. Generally speaking, social groups are increasingly inserting themselves earlier on in a technology's trajectory, as the science is still developing – all the technologies discussed here are still far from being put into application. We have seen little sign of organized debate, except in the case of Canada on the issue of xenotransplantation. It would no doubt be a mistake to restrict the notion of public participation to organized processes. The discussions triggered in Germany by Sloterdijk's lecture are an example of a more informal debate which nevertheless played an important role in defining positions on medical biotechnologies. France, on the other hand, traditionally a technocratic country, has offered very little room for public debate.

Most of the debate on medical biotechnology is more or less restricted to scientific experts, a major difference from the issue of agricultural biotechnologies, particularly GM foods, where deliberative public engagement exercises in the form of consensus conferences have become more common (Einsiedel, 2001). With public participation and debate increasing, scientists can no longer remain above the fray. They have increasingly articulated their interests beyond the laboratory, in the public sphere, be it via official reports from scientific bodies (academies, professional associations, etc.), individually or through strongly science-based ethics committees (Galloux et al, 2002). The evolution in legislation on embryo research shows that they find some degree of success.

Notes

1   The authors wish to thank Agnes Allansdottir and Siv Berg for very stimulating discussions in the early conceptualizing stages of the preparation of this chapter. The Canadian sections of this study were made possible by a grant from Genome Canada for a genomics, ethics, environmental, economic, legal and social studies project with E. Einsiedel as Principal Investigator (PI).
2   Percentages quoted aggregate those who tend to agree and who definitely agree with the proposition.

3   For an example of this confrontation see the debates on the subject in *Nature* (May and July 1997) and in *The Lancet* (17 January 1998).
4   Discussing stem cell research, the Protestant Church in Germany has a similar position to that of the Catholic Church, a remarkable difference to the French situation.

References

Bijker, W. E. (1995) *Of Bicycles, Bakelites, and Bulbs: Toward a Theory of Sociotechnical Change*, MIT Press, Cambridge, MA

Callon, M., Lascoumes, P. and Barthes, Y. (2001) *Agir dans un monde incertain. Essai sur la démocratie technique*, Seuil, Paris, 2001

Caulfield, T., Daar, A. S., Knoppers, B. M. and Singer, P. A. (2002) 'Stem cell research', *Globe and Mail*, 2 May, A2

CCNE (Comité consultatif national d'éthique) (1997) Avis 54, www.ccne-ethique.fr

CCNE (Comité consultatif national d'éthique) (1999) Avis 61, www.ccne-ethique.fr

Cheveigné, S. de, Boy, D. and Galloux, J. Ch. (2002) *Les Biotechnologies en débat*, Balland, Paris

Denner, J. (2000) 'Mikrobiologische Risiken der Xenotransplantation', in Engels, E. M., Badura-Lotter, G. and Schicktanz, S. (eds) *Neue Perspektiven der Transplantationsmedizin im interdisziplinären Dialog*, Nomos, Baden-Baden, pp142–169

Downey, R. and Einsiedel, E. (2003) 'Life and death politics: social movements and stem cell research', paper presented to the Society for the Social Studies of Science conference, Atlanta, Georgia, 4–6 October 2003

Durant, J., Bauer, M. W. and Gaskell, G. (eds) (1998) *Biotechnology in the Public Sphere: A European Sourcebook*, Science Museum Publications, London

Einsiedel, E. F. (2001) 'Citizen voices: Public participation on biotechnology', *Politeia*, vol 17, no 63, pp94–104

Einsiedel, E. et al (2002) 'Brave new sheep – The clone named Dolly', in Bauer, M. and Gaskell, G. (eds) *Biotechnology: The Making of a Global Controversy*, Cambridge University Press, Cambridge, pp313–347

Ellul, J. (1954) *La Technique ou l'enjeu du siècle*, Colin, Paris (English version 1964, *The Technological Society*, Alfred A. Knopf, New York)

Eurobarometer 58.0 (2002) europa.eu.int/comm/public_opinion/archives/eb/ebs_177_en.pdf

Flichy, P. (1995) *L'Innovation technique*, La Découverte, Paris

Galloux, J.-C., Thing Mortensen, A., Cheveigné, S. de, Allansdottir, A., Chatjouli, A. and Sakallaris, G. (2002) 'The Institutions of Bioethics', in Bauer, M. W. and Gaskell, G. (eds), *Biotechnology: The Making of a Global Controversy*, Cambridge University Press, Cambridge, pp129–148

Gaskell, G. and Bauer, M. W. (eds) (2001) *Biotechnology 1996–2000: The Years of Controversy*, Science Museum, London

Hampel, J., Pfennig, U., Kohring, M., Görke, A. and Ruhrmann, G. (2001) 'Biotechnology boom and market failure: Two sides of the German coin', in Gaskell, G. and Bauer, M. W. (eds) *Biotechnology 1996–2000: The Years of Controversy*, Science Museum, London, pp191–203

Hilgartner, S. and Bosk, C. L. (1988) 'The rise and fall of social problems: A public arenas model', *American Journal of Sociology*, vol 94, no 1, pp53–78

Hwang, W. S. et al (2004) 'Evidence of a pluripotent human embryonic stem cell line derived from a cloned blastocyst', *Sciencexpress*, doi:10.1126/science.1094515

Knowles, L. (2004) 'A regulatory patchwork – Human ES cell research oversight', *Nature Biotechnology*, no 22, vol 2, February, pp157–163

National Bioethics Advisory Commission (1999) Report, http://www.bioethics.gov/

Petermann, Th. and Sauter, A. (1999) *Xenotransplantation. Sachstandsbericht*, Arbeitsbericht No. 64, Büro für Technikfolgenabschätzung beim Deutschen Bundestag, Berlin

Pollara/Earnscliffe(2003) 'Public Opinion Research into Biotechnology Issues in the US and Canada', Eighth Wave Report to the Biotechnology Coordinating Committee, Government of Canada, March

Réal, J. (2001), *Voronoff*, Stock, Paris

Renn, O. (1992) 'The Social Arena Concept of Risk Debates', in Krimsky, S. and Golding, D. (eds) *Social Theories of Risk*, Praeger, Westport CT and London pp179–196

Rogers, E. (1983) *Diffusion of Innovations*, Free Press, New York

Schicktanz, S. (2000) 'Aus der Geschichte lernen? Die Entwicklung der Idee der Xenotransplantation', in Engels, E.-M., Badura-Lotter, G. and Schicktanz, S. (eds) *Neue Perspektiven der Transplantationsmedizin im interdisziplinären Dialog*, Nomos, Baden-Baden, pp239–256

Torgersen, H. et al (2002) 'Promise, problems and proxies: Twenty-five years of debate and regulation in Europe', in Bauer, M. and Gaskell, G. (eds) *Biotechnology: The Making of a Global Controversy*, Cambridge University Press, Cambridge, pp21–94

4

Moving the Goalposts in Bioethics

Erling Jelsøe, Arne Thing Mortensen, Mercy Wambui Kamara, Maria Rusanen, Susana Costa, Torben Hviid Nielsen and Nicola Lindsey

Since the announcement of the birth of Dolly, the cloned sheep, in late February 1997, debate and controversy over cloning have been ongoing in countries around the world and on the international scene. From the moment of the announcement, it was clear that the same technique that was used to create Dolly could, in principle, be used for cloning humans. Thus, the immediate reaction was a series of statements and policy initiatives aimed at the prohibition of human cloning. Such an initial 'veto' against the cloning of human beings was characteristic of both international institutions like UNESCO (1997) and the Council of Europe (1998) and national bodies such as the National Bioethics Advisory Commission (NBAC, 1997) established by President Clinton, or the UK Government, stating that 'We regard the deliberate cloning of human individuals as ethically unacceptable' (House of Commons Official Report, 1997).

Almost simultaneously, interest in the scientific and medical prospects of cloning was expressed. Pressures for drawing limits between, on the one hand, what should be permitted in order to take advantage of the perceived benefits and, on the other hand, the ethical and safety issues that gave rise to the widespread concern were articulated by both the medical community and politicians, and encapsulated in the quotation 'the challenge to public policy is to support the myriad of beneficial applications of this new technology, while simultaneously guarding against its more questionable uses' (NBAC, 1997, p107).

However, a distinction of greater immediate political importance was proposed in the British report *Cloning Issues in Reproduction, Science and Medicine* (HGAC and HFEA, 1998). This report distinguished between reproductive and therapeutic cloning. While cloning of an entire human individual was called human reproductive cloning, the term 'therapeutic cloning' was introduced to characterize other applications of the same technique, such as nuclear replacement technology, which led to the birth of Dolly. An example of therapeutic cloning was the creation of stem cell lines for developing therapeutic applications. This distinction soon gained importance when, later in 1998, US scientists succeeded in isolating and culturing human embryonic stem cells.

The distinction between reproductive and therapeutic cloning became important because it provided concepts for drawing the line between something considered absolutely unacceptable, namely human reproductive cloning, and something that might be acceptable in light of the scientific and therapeutic promises it offered. Thus, while the rejection of human reproductive cloning formed for the first time what was almost a global moral standard on a bioethical issue (Grabner et al, 2001; Lindsey et al, 2001) and the few proponents of human reproductive cloning, like Dr Seed or Clonaid, were regarded as outrageous, the important social and political conflicts have been over whether and to what extent human therapeutic cloning should be permitted.

The social and political conflicts have centred round the setting of boundaries that will limit research and development into cloning while enabling these activities to take place legitimately within certain legal frames. This *boundary work* has involved debates about ethical principles resulting in a continuous process of institutionalization of ethics. This in turn has led to a codification of ethical principles or rules in the form of legal frameworks or the institutionalization of norms.

In this chapter, we show how this institutionalization of bioethics has taken place over several decades. Our main focus is on European countries, but we also review the broader international development. The emergence of ethics in the field of biotechnology applied to humans as a global policy issue and controversy appears to be one of the most remarkable features of the development since Dolly. Paradoxically, despite the enormous global outcry that followed the announcement of the birth of Dolly, neither research in cloning nor its regulation was anything new. Dolly's emergence was the result of several decades of research that, unlike her appearance, raised little media interest. (Kolata, 1997; Shickle, 2000; Daar and Mattei, 2002). Similarly, in many countries human cloning was already prohibited and several international institutions, such as the European Parliament, the Council of Europe and the World Health Organization (WHO), had made statements against human cloning dating back to the middle of the 1980s. We focus mainly on cloning and human reproductive technologies but the processes of institutionalization have, in many cases, been more broadly related to medicine or medical biotechnologies.

Institutionalization of bioethics in Europe

The institutionalization of bioethics is divided into three phases. Each phase differs on three criteria: the character of the institutional framework, its specific focus and the degree of public attention it receives (Lindsey et al, 2001; Bauer, 2001; Galloux et al, 2002). The first phase reflected historical experiences dating back to World War II and the general development in medical sciences in the post-war period. The second phase was closely connected with the development of new medical biotechnologies and associated controversies, whereas the third phase denotes a period in which ethics seems to become omnipresent and which was heavily influenced by the debates about cloning and stem cell research. Despite common features across countries in the developed world, such as the establishment of research ethical committees and ethical advisory bodies, there are still considerable variations between countries. Along with the internationalization of the debates and increasing commercial interests, these differences with respect to policy initiatives and regulation seem to be an issue in themselves and we indicate some of the most important features of the 'regulatory patchwork' (Knowles, 2004).

Self-regulation of scientific and medical research

Until the 1970s, bioethics was not an issue of scientific or political concern, and in some European countries, such as Austria and Germany, it was even a taboo subject due to the eugenic policies before and between the wars. The first initiative in the institutionalization of ethics did not come from policy makers, but from the medical community itself. The World Medical Association's Declaration of Helsinki, released in 1964, was the first international report to set out ethical guidelines for medical research involving human subjects. An important contributory reason for the code was the Nuremberg Process and the documentation of the severe violations of human rights that medical doctors had taken part in during World War II, in particular the use of humans as subjects in fatal experiments. However, the declaration had only a limited impact until 1975, when it was extensively revised and re-released as the Helsinki Declaration II. The Declaration recommended that the design and performance of all experimental procedures involving human subjects should be clearly formulated in an experimental protocol, which should be submitted for consideration and approval to a specially appointed independent ethical review committee. Another important principle was that of informed consent of the patient as a prerequisite for approval of any medical trial that involved human subjects. Thus, the Declaration may be said to be the first step in the institutionalization of ethics, since it specifies the incorporation of ethics into the research process itself.

In the years immediately after the first Helsinki Declaration, research ethics committees appeared in the US, and early initiatives were also taken by Sweden and the UK in the 1960s. By the time of the first amendment of the Declaration in 1975, and in the following years, the phenomenon had spread across Europe. Ethics committees were established in hospitals, in research departments of universities and/or as regional bodies. However, countries differed in the speed and efficiency with which they complied with the Declaration. For example, in Austria the first ethics committee was established by the Medical Faculty of the University of Vienna in 1979, but the full implementation of ethics committees in all hospitals did not occur until 1994, when it became a requirement for full EU membership. Similarly, in Portugal there were no local ethics committees until 1995, when, again, full EU membership required their establishment. Thus, for some of the latecomers, the impetus for the establishment of ethics committees in fact came from the EU.

In almost all cases, ethics committees were established and controlled by the scientific and medical communities. Their decisions were not legally binding ethical codes but recommendations on the conduct of experimental research. In most countries, the composition of local ethics committees was dominated by professionals in medicine, law, religion, philosophy and science. Few countries had committees with any lay members or other representatives of the public, with the exception of Denmark, where there was an equal representation of biomedical researchers and lay members. The fact that it was the scientific and medical communities, rather than policy makers, who established these committees is significant, for it reflects not just a recognition of bioethical issues by scientists, but a desire to keep them within their power and to shield research from political debates and, ultimately, state legislation. Indeed, not many countries had any central or coordinating committee at this time, with the exceptions of France (where the main state medical research institution, the Institut National de la Santé et de la Recherche Médicale (INSERM), established the Bioethics Committee in 1974) and Denmark (which established a nationwide system of one central and seven regional science ethical committees in 1979–1982). However, in both these cases the function of these central committees was simply to coordinate or act as a body of appeal; they had no advisory or political role. In general, policy makers left concerns that arose in the course of research to be dealt with by the scientific community. As a result, the field was largely self-regulated.

Ethics and the new biotechnologies applied to humans: A role for public policy

Thus, until the late 1970s, biotechnology did not appear to raise any moral or ethical concerns that extended beyond medical research in general, and the system of localized research ethics committees seemed adequate. However, with the development of in vitro fertilization techniques and the birth in the UK of the world's first test tube baby in 1978, new public concerns about biomedical technologies arose, attracting the attention of Europe's policy communities. As the technology spread across Europe, emerging debates became interlocked with older debates about abortion, the status of the embryo and the eugenic consequences of intervening with the natural processes of conception and birth. As the 1980s progressed, biotechnological techniques began to be applied in even wider contexts, and as a result the debate surrounding their implications diversified to encompass issues that were broader than simply the technical risks associated with the techniques themselves. For example, the emerging techniques of gene therapy and embryo diagnostics raised the possibility of irreversible manipulations of human genes, while for many even in vitro fertilization (IVF) denoted the first step towards manipulation of human gametes. The combination of these issues pointed to the great potential of the technology and served to mobilize ambivalence and mistrust among the public about how these techniques would be developed and used in the future.

Consequently, in order to address emerging public concerns about the technology, the policy communities of Europe were now forced to take on ethical issues not simply as a function of the medical research process, but as a consideration in strategic public policy making as well. This resulted in three overlapping trends: first, the formalization of local research ethics committees, leading eventually to centralization (often through a single overarching body) and state control. Second, the establishment of national ethics bodies to consider the ethical implications of broad trends in biomedical research. And third, the implementation of regulation encompassing specifically moral and ethical principles and, in some cases, the legitimization of ethical institutions dealing with biotechnology, through enactment in law. The process of institutionalization has, therefore, been both a continuation of earlier trends initiated by the scientific community and an intervention by the policy communities as an additional means of legitimizing the development of the technology.

The first, and in political terms most significant, expression of the new situation, in the early 1980s, was the almost simultaneous appointment of commissions dealing with the ethical aspects of biotechnology on humans. The Warnock Commission in the UK, the so-called 'Gen-etikkomité' in Sweden, the Benda Commission in Germany and the Danish Ministry of the Interior's Commission on Ethical Problems in Egg Transplantation, Artificial Fertilization and Embryo Diagnostics are all examples of government-appointed bodies. Similarly, the National Ethics Committee in France (CCNE, see below) made recommendations about the treatment of embryos and the development of techniques for genetic diagnostics after it was formed in 1984.

Cloning technologies were also considered by these bodies, but despite the fact that research in this field was ongoing, the issue was generally not extensively reviewed. The Warnock Commission, for instance, mentioned embryo division, which at that time had been used on farm animals, but then briefly noted that this type of cloning had not 'to the best of our knowledge' been used on human embryos. It also mentioned that 'another technique, which has sometimes been referred to as cloning, but which may be more accurately described as nucleus substitution, would raise more fundamental discussions' (Warnock, 1985, pp72–73). However, this reference to nucleus substitution, the technique that was later used for the creation of Dolly, was very brief and held in hypothetical terms, even though some potential applications were mentioned. The Danish commission simply stated that cloning of a human individual could be ruled out as a possibility because differentiated cells in the process of division have lost their totipotency (i.e. their capability to develop). Nevertheless, it also stated its absolute rejection of cloning and creation of hybrids of human and animals (Ministry of the Interior's Commission on Ethical Problems in Egg Transplantation, Artificial Fertilization and Embryo Diagnostics, 1984, pp10, 60). The scepticism and apparent disbelief in the possibility of cloning that was expressed in these and other reports at that time reflected not only a scientific assessment but also the scientists' discomfort and fear of compromising the ongoing biomedical research activities.

All these commissions proposed rules related to the new technologies; some also proposed that permanent national bodies with consultative and/or administrative functions should be formed. There followed lengthy debates and negotiations on the issues within the national parliaments. Thus, six years passed from the publication of the Warnock Report in the UK in 1984 until finally in 1990 the Human Fertilisation and Embryology Act was passed (Bauer et al, 1998; Mulkay, 1997). Similarly, in Germany it took five years after the report of the Benda Commission until the German Bundestag passed the Law on Protection of Embryos (Hampel et al, 1998). Norway is an even more exceptional case. In 1987, an act, said to be the world's first on in vitro fertilization, was passed by the Norwegian parliament. But it was not until 1994, after several additional parliamentary debates and new reports from various commissions, that the Act relating to the Application of Biotechnology in Medicine was passed. The Norwegian Biotechnology Advisory Board (NBAB) had already been established before the act was passed. It was an advisory and consultative body with a remit to promote debate about the social and ethical consequences of modern biotechnology. A characteristic part of the Norwegian policy processes was a careful reviewing and discussion of various ethical positions as a basis for making recommendations (Hviid Nielsen et al, 2001; NOU, 1991).

Despite different political cultures and ethical positions in the various countries (the UK with a tradition for a pragmatic and utility-oriented approach to ethics and Germany with an orientation towards Kantian duty ethics are often mentioned as two opposites) (Jasanoff, 1995; Coff 1998), the theme was basically the same and had to do with embryo research. The moral status of the embryo, 'the right to life' and the question of when life begins were arguments that were used repeatedly. The controversies in the UK probably attracted most attention internationally because of the relatively liberal attitude to embryo research expressed in the recommendations of the Warnock Report. It was also the Warnock Commission that proposed a limit of 14 days after fertilization for research on embryos, a proposal that has since been adopted as a standard in many countries. The ensuing and very polarized debates eventually led to the passing of the British act, which was a victory for the advocates of the new reproductive technologies (Bauer et al, 1998; Mulkay, 1997). The strong focus on the arguments related to the status of the embryo was also reflected in the Danish Council of Ethics Act, which stated that 'the Council must base its work on the prerequisite that human life begins at the time of conception' (Act on the Establishment of an Ethical Council, 1987).

Following the Human Fertilisation and Embryology Act in the UK, the Human Fertilisation and Embryology Authority (HFEA) was established in 1991. The HFEA undertakes various tasks, including licensing and monitoring of centres undertaking embryo research. It is both a consultative and a regulatory body. More generally, the establishment of national ethical bodies in Europe began some years earlier. The first country to establish a centralized body with a consultative function was France, where the CCNE (the Comité Consultatif National d'Éthique pour la santé et les sciences de la vie) was created by a presidential decree enacted in 1983. The main impetus for the establishment of a national body came from the scientific community, which wanted clear guidelines for the conduct of its research, and from the president, who acted politically to secure moral legitimacy in future legislative initiatives to regulate the field. In contrast, Denmark established its Council of Ethics (DCE) by law in 1987 as a separate body to work in parallel with the system of local science ethics committees and the overarching central committee. The French and the Danish approaches to the creation of national bodies for bioethical issues may be considered as opposite poles in the range of different models. The French model is elite not only in its origin and orientation, but also in its composition, while the Danish model is more participatory in its orientation, with the emphasis on promotion of public debate, and in its composition, with more than half of the members being lay persons.

During the 1990s, the trend for the establishment of national bioethics committees spread across Europe. The Italian National Committee on Bioethics was established in 1990, the Greek Bioethics Committee in 1997 (established in law in 1992) and the Portuguese National Committee for Ethics in the Life Sciences (CNECV) in 1989. The composition of these committees varies between countries, although it is only in Denmark that the committee has a majority of lay members. The elite-oriented model with a predominance of scientists and other professional experts is the most frequent. More recently, non-governmental organization (NGO) representatives and representatives from the public are also being appointed, in particular to the national consultative committees.

In general, such bodies have been established as a result of political initiatives but, as in France, some were prompted by calls from the scientific community, who were concerned about the rising opposition to the technology from non-scientific quarters (and in particular the emergence of critical NGOs) and the involvement of big business in the development of the technology. In the more religious countries, particularly Italy, the debate was raised by the Church and religious authorities. Indeed, the first initiatives in the institutionalization of bioethics in Italy were taken by the Catholic Church and its associated institutions. Thus, in 1985 the Università Cattolica del Sacra Cuore in Rome set up a centre of Bioethics in the Medical Faculty, and established the Institute of Bioethics in 1992. When the National Committee on Bioethics was formed in 1990, it was to be composed of religious and secular experts, but the first president was a Catholic senator and most of the first 40 members were Catholics. This tension between religious and secular factions has dominated the institutionalization of ethics in Italy. Similarly, the Portuguese National Committee for Ethics in the Life Sciences has been strongly influenced by the Catholic Church. Portugal is particularly interesting because the first policy initiatives came relatively early in 1986 and the CNECV was established in 1989. Nevertheless, only a few initiatives were taken by the committee during the 1990s and it did not promote public debate as it was supposed to. Furthermore, the activity of the committee had little effect on the drafting and implementation of specific legislation. All in all, the work of the committee reflected its composition, largely dominated by scientists and doctors of a strict Catholic persuasion (Jesuino et al, 2001).

By the 1990s, it became clear that the old style of self-regulation was no longer adequate to cope with the demands of biotechnology. The establishment of centralized ethics committees was one feature of policy makers' attempts to bring it under state control. Thus, bioethics became further institutionalized through the introduction of administrative or legal acts. The establishment of local and national committees was a predominant mode of regulation in the institution-alization of ethics in relation to biotechnology. This mirrors the conception of ethics as a politically intricate field most easily dealt with through expert advice. For most countries, however, the most controversial techniques, including genetic engineering on human gametes and embryos as well as cloning, seem to be explicitly prohibited.

Ethics take centre stage: The cloning and stem cell debates

From the early 1990s, public, policy and media interest in biotechnology began to grow exponentially as the different applications of biotechnology became increasingly common features of everyday life. Not only embryo research but also potential applications related to pre-implantation diagnostics, gene therapy, xenotransplantation and gene testing as well as in the Human Genome Project increasingly attracted attention. By the late 1990s, ethical discourse on biotech-nology had taken centre stage in public, policy and media debates. This was catalysed most significantly by the announcement, in February 1997, of the birth of Dolly. This was the 'first real global and simultaneous news story on bio-technology' (Einsiedel et al, 2002).

The cloning debate

From 1997 onwards, there was a proliferation in the number and type of bodies dealing with ethical issues, from national ethics bodies to centres of ethics and public consultations on ethical concerns. The issue of cloning forced further legislation, even though, as mentioned above, in a number of countries cloning was already prohibited in various ways. The ban was not always explicit: for example, in Denmark the ban on trials aimed at creating genetically identical human individuals continues to be interpreted as a general ban against cloning. Dolly had a significant impact in Italy, where there was no formal regulation of reproductive technology. On 5 March 1997, only about a week after the announcement of the birth of Dolly, the Italian Minister of Health banned all forms of experiments related to human or animal cloning. There has been some relaxation since then but all forms of human cloning are still prohibited. Portugal and Finland had no existing legislation on cloning and made no immediate attempts to establish any regulation. It was not until a Medical Research Act was passed in 1999 that cloning in Finland was covered by legislation. By this act, cloning of human individuals is prohibited, whereas research on embryos left over from IVF treatment is permitted under certain conditions. This reflects the positive views of the Finnish people on new biotechnologies as well as a 'wait and see' attitude on controversial issues (Rusanen et al, 2001). In Portugal, discussion about cloning was mainly an issue for scientists and members of ethical committees. The CNECV made an advisory statement at the request of the parliament, but no regulatory initiatives were taken. The Portuguese situation reflected the tensions and conflicts between the strict Catholic members of the CNECV and the attitude of the majority of the scientific community. Both

Finland and Portugal have signed the Convention of the Council of Europe on Human Rights and Biomedicine (Council of Europe, 1997) as well as the Additional Protocol on Prohibition of Cloning Human Beings (Council of Europe, 1998), and Portugal has ratified both.

Trends in the institutionalization of ethics have been mirrored at the European Union (EU) level. European Union institutions became interested in bioethics in the mid-1980s, stimulated by the organization of several international bioethics conferences. In 1989, the European Parliament passed a Resolution on the Ethical and Legal Problems of Genetic Engineering, and in line with trends emerging within its member states, the European Commission established its own bioethics committee, the Group of Advisers on the Ethical Implications of Biotechnology in 1991 (replaced in 1998 by the European Group on Ethics in Science and New Technologies). Similarly, the Council of Europe established the Ad Hoc Committee of Experts on Bioethics in 1989 (later renamed the Steering Committee on Bioethics). More recently, UNESCO released its Universal Declaration on the Human Genome and Human Rights in 1997, which was accepted by the UN Assembly in 1998.

In terms of European policy making, ethical issues were most significant in the ten-year debates in the European Parliament over patenting and intellectual property rights and in the preparations in the Council for a convention on bioethics. These debates culminated respectively in the European Directive on the Legal Protection of Biotechnological Inventions in July 1998, and with the European Council Convention on Human Rights and Biomedicine in April 1997. Both initiatives concern broad ethical debates surrounding the development of biotechnology. The Directive on the Legal Protection of Biotechnological Inventions effectively brings animal, human and plant biotechnology together and has implications for the progress and economic prospects of the technology. The Convention of the Council of Europe on Human Rights and Biomedicine, on the other hand, is a legal text designed to establish a common standard for bioethics across Europe, and internationally, to protect people against the misuse of biological and medical advances through a series of principles and prohibitions. For example, it prohibits the creation of human embryos for research purposes, bans germ-line gene therapy and in vitro fertilization where it is used for sex selection (except where it would avoid a serious hereditary condition), and it also prohibits genetic discrimination. In addition, the regulations extend to cover issues of consent, organ donation, the implementation of medical research and public consultation. Those who have signed the convention must align their laws accordingly. Indeed, for many countries – especially those in Eastern Europe – its assimilation will represent the first instance in which issues of bioethics have been addressed in legislation on medical biotechnology. Following the cloning debate, an Additional Protocol to the convention emerged in 1998 that prohibited cloning of human beings.

For a number of countries, it has been the incorporation of European Directives into national laws that has been the main stimulus for the institutionalization of ethics, as in Austria and Portugal. In Finland, ethics did not become a political consideration until 1995, when the Gene Technology Act fulfilled the requirement for the establishment in every country of a competent authority to oversee developments in gene technology. In order to align Finnish laws with other EU requirements (including bioethics), the Gene Technology Board has consequently been concerned mostly with the technicalities of legislation and the consideration of EU directives. This has also been the case for the bioethics committees in Switzerland and Greece.

All in all, by the middle of the 1990s quite comprehensive structures for dealing with bioethical issues existed in European countries. The cloning debate did not lead to fundamental changes with respect to these processes of institutionalization. In several European countries, there was extensive media coverage and a public debate that lasted for a while and then fizzled out, whereas in others it provided the impetus for introducing legislation or setting up new ethical bodies. The most significant outcome of the cloning debate was probably that it greatly enhanced the development of a bioethical discourse and regulatory activities on an international level.

The stem cell debate

About a year after Dolly was born, the cloning debate, at least at the policy level, became a debate about the creation and use of human embryonic stem cells. This change occurred following the publication of the British report distinguishing between reproductive and therapeutic cloning and the subsequent announcement from US researchers in November 1998 that they had succeeded in isolating and culturing human embryonic stem cells. Two questions divided the participants in the debate in many countries – should it be permitted to:

1   create human embryos by means of therapeutic cloning as a source of human embryonic stem cells; and
2   isolate and culture human stem cells from early embryos as a basis for research in stem cells?

Once again events in the UK soon attracted international attention. Following recommendations from the Human Genetics Advisory Commission (HGAC) and the HFEA in December 1998 to allow embryo research using cloning techniques, the British government announced a moratorium on the use of cloning techniques and set up a new independent advisory group. In April 2000, the Nuffield Council on Bioethics published a report that supported the recommendations of the HGAC and HFEA, and in August of that year the new advisory group published its report with the same conclusions (Chief Medical Officer's Expert Advisory Group on Therapeutic Cloning, 2000). This involved changes in the Human Fertilisation and Embryology (HFE) Act allowing embryo research with the aim of developing stem cell therapies (provided that the research had been licensed by the HFEA). The Government accepted the recommendations, which were also supported by Parliament, and on 22 December 2000 the changes to the HFE Act were passed. This happened just three months after the European Parliament had passed a resolution in September 2000 calling for a ban on all forms of human cloning throughout Europe.

The decision in the UK to permit embryo research and therapeutic cloning signalled to many that now the boundary was moving in favour of cloning and it fuelled the debate around the world. However, the situation differed in various European countries. In Finland, as mentioned above, research using embryos left over from IVF treatment had already been permitted a year before and the events in the UK did not prompt further policy initiatives. In Denmark, by contrast, in January 2001 the DCE recommended that research aimed at developing stem cell therapies should be permitted using embryos left over from IVF treatment, whereas therapeutic cloning should still be prohibited. Eventually, in June 2003, the Danish parliament enacted these recommendations in a change to the Act on Artificial Fertilization. In Norway, where cloning was explicitly prohibited by the 1994 Act relating to the Application of Biotechnology in Medicine, there was a move by the NBAB to revise the act and to permit research using embryos left over from IVF treatment. However, the Norwegian government chose to maintain the existing prohibition of both embryo research and therapeutic cloning and was supported by a majority in Parliament, when the revised act was passed in November 2003. Germany also maintained its prohibition of both cloning and embryo research, despite considerable criticism from the scientific and medical community.

Overall, there is a patchwork of different approaches to regulation (Knowles, 2004) across Europe. An increasing number of countries seem to be opening the way for embryo research. During 2004, France adopted an act on bioethics permitting research on embryos left over from IVF treatment. A referendum in Switzerland in November 2004 resulted in majority support for an act that permitted embryo research under similar conditions, and in Spain the new socialist government passed an act permitting embryo research and at same time making conditions for the research less restrictive than under the former Conservative government. Thus, a general picture is emerging whereby research on embryos left over from IVF treatment is permitted but therapeutic cloning is not.

On the broader international scene, the picture is still more chequered, in particular since stem cell research in the US became part of the political battlefield under the presidential election campaigns during 2004. Ironically, at the same time as George W. Bush, who strongly resists stem cell research, was re-elected president, in California an ambitious programme for the promotion of stem cell research has been launched. Furthermore, the US Federal policy against stem cell research only concerns the use of Federal money, whereas there is no regulation regarding privately funded research. In any case, the Bush policy has had repercussions in the UN, where an attempt to agree on a ban on reproductive cloning since 2001 has been blocked because the US, together with Costa Rica and followed by a number of other countries, wanted a ban on all types of cloning. In November 2004, it became clear that no treaty on cloning could win sufficient support: neither one that prohibits all forms of cloning, nor one that only implies a ban on therapeutic cloning. However, following a proposal from Italy, the General Assembly adopted the U.N. Declaration on Human Cloning in March 2005, in which member states were called upon to adopt the necessary measures to prohibit human cloning 'inasmuch as they are incompatible with human dignity and the protection of human life'.

Also in 2004, two events related to the actual research efforts pointed to the fact that, parallel to the political turmoil related to the cloning issue, scientific progress in the field is proceeding. In February, a team of Korean researchers reported that they had succeeded in making human embryos by cell nuclear replacement and harvested stem cells from these embryos. In culture, the stem cells had formed the tissue types that normally appear in the first stages of embryonic development (Pilcher, 2004). This 'stem cell breakthrough' was welcomed by the HFEA, which later, in August, granted the first therapeutic cloning licence for research to the Newcastle Centre for Life in the UK (HFEA, 2004). Adding to the controversy, a Korean investigation revealed that the 'breakthrough' had been deliberately fabricated.

Future directions

The boundary work related to the regulation of cloning is still ongoing. In the broad international context, the boundary has only moved a little over the years that have passed since the birth of Dolly, and therapeutic cloning has been permitted in very few countries. Shortly after Dolly, the political controversy developed into a debate about stem cells. This was welcomed by proponents of therapeutic cloning since research into stem cells is associated with a number of positive connotations for medical progress and treatment of serious diseases. The focus on stem cells also made it possible to argue for using other sources of embryos than those that could be created by means of therapeutic cloning. Thus, in most countries that have permitted embryo research, the only acceptable source of embryos is that of those left over from IVF treatment. This is considered to be less controversial because in these cases the embryos are not created for research purposes alone.

Pressure for therapeutic cloning

Scientists in the field still want to have access to the use of therapeutic cloning, however, and there have been constant pressures and arguments on this issue from the scientific community. The most prominent argument is that embryos from IVF treatment will be too limited as a source of stem cells, but permission to use therapeutic cloning would also give researchers the opportunity to develop the nuclear replacement technology. Furthermore, many scientists fear that there will be an embryonic stem (ES) cell 'brain drain' and flow of research funds to countries and states where therapeutic cloning is allowed (see, for instance, Resnik, 2004). Interestingly, within the international scientific communities there are strong proponents for an international ban on human reproductive cloning, which they hope will make therapeutic cloning more acceptable. The Inter-academy Panel (IAP), an international network of science academies, made a statement in 2003 advocating a global ban on human reproductive cloning while at same time speaking in favour of therapeutic cloning (IAP, 2003). Some scientists in the cloning field, however, advocate the view that the problem of human reproductive cloning only has to do with risk, and when the technical problems associated with the nuclear replacement technology have eventually been solved, there will be no serious arguments against using reproductive cloning, for instance to help infertile couples to have a child.

The slippery slope: Fear of cloning

A position like the one expressed by the IAP is easy to understand within a discourse of 'medical progress'. Nevertheless, cloning is still a widely contested issue, just as it was in the 1980s, when a ban on cloning was introduced in a number of countries even though the possibility of cloning was regarded with much reservation among scientists at that time. The symbolic significance and the connotations of cloning, such as 'brave new world', Frankenstein and mad scientists, have given cloning a position of its own in the public debate about modern biotechnology. Despite all assurances that if therapeutic cloning is permitted there will be no risk of reproductive cloning, there will still be fears that once permitted, no matter what type, the development of cloning will not be possible to control. Here we have the effect of another strong metaphor, which has been frequently used in the cloning debate, that of the *slippery slope*. If the regulatory boundary is moving, such fears will be invoked.

An event is needed to trigger debate

The astonishment and uproar that surrounded the announcement of the birth of Dolly may still seem paradoxical. Despite years of research efforts and legal provisions against cloning in many countries, the debate and controversy did not come until the news about the successful cloning of a mammal became known. This has been a recurrent feature of the debates throughout the 30-year history of modern biotechnology. Debates are created not by reports about activities in research laboratories but as a result of the announcement of concrete new products or inventions. This was the case in relation to cloning and genetically modified crop plants in the late 1990s, just as it had been in 1980, when the debates about embryo research started in the wake of the birth of the first test tube baby.

Moral status of embryo carries more weight than therapeutic benefits

In addition, it is remarkable how much the arguments related to embryo research in the 1980s, following the introduction of in vitro fertilization at the end of the 1970s, resemble those that have been used by most of the actors in the stem cell debate in recent years. It is still the moral status of the embryo that is at the core of the debate. To some, like George W. Bush or the Pope, it is the sanctity of life itself which is important, while others are worried about the instrumental use of the embryo as a means of creating new tissues and organs. More societal perspectives such as the question of what should be the priorities for the future development of the health care sector, both in the developed world and more globally, have not carried the same weight (Koch, 2003).

Slow-moving boundaries, bureaucracy and the expert

Much of the societal regulation in relation to bioethics was already established in 1997 and there are not many countries that have made important changes, such as the introduction of new basic legislation or the establishment of new advisory or administrative bodies, in response to the cloning debate. Change in regulation in order to permit research in embryos and stem cells with the purpose of developing stem cell therapies or acquiring new knowledge about embryo development has often been a matter of minor, albeit important, changes to existing legislation. In many countries, however, advisory and consultative bodies have worked overtime to produce a large number of statements, reports and discussion papers on ethical aspects of cloning and stem cells and thereby cemented the work of ethical committees and councils as part of bioethical governance. Since in most countries the ethical committees and councils have a majority of professional bioethicists among their members, a new group of experts is being established as governmental advisors and consultants. There is an obvious analogy to the way the scientific risk discourse was established during the 1980s as the response to the debate about agricultural biotechnologies. However, since the bioethical issues are overtly normative in character and, furthermore, in the case of biotechnology on humans, are culturally sensitive, the expert-oriented approach to bioethical regulation may be even more likely to experience a crisis of legitimacy than the scientific risk discourse.

References

Bauer, M. W. (2001) 'Biotechnology: Ethical framing in the elite press', *Notizie di Politeia*, vol 17, no 63, pp51–66

Bauer, M. W., Durant, J., Gaskell, G., Liakopoulos, M. and Bridgman, E. (1998) 'United Kingdom', in Durant, J., Bauer, M. W. and Gaskell, G. (eds) *Biotechnology in the Public Sphere: A European Sourcebook*, Science Museum, London, pp162–176

Chief Medical Officer's Expert Advisory Group on Therapeutic Cloning (2000) *Stem Cell Research: Medical Progress with Responsibility*, Department of Health, London

Coff, C. (1998) *Bioteknologipolitik i England, USA, Tyskland og Norge* (Biotechnology Policy in the UK, USA, Germany and Norway), Danish Ministry of Business Affairs, Copenhagen (report in Danish)

Council of Europe (1997) *Convention for the Protection of Human Rights and Dignity of the Human Being with regard to the Application of Biology and Medicine: Convention on Human Rights and Biomedicine*, European Treaty Series – No 164, Council of Europe, Paris

Council of Europe (1998) *Additional Protocol to the Convention for the Protection of Human Rights and Dignity of the Human Being with regard to the Application of Biology and Medicine, on the Prohibition of Cloning Human Beings*, European Treaty Series – No. 168, Council of Europe, Paris

Daar, A. and Mattei, J.-F. (2002) *Medical Genetics and Biotechnology: Implications for Public Health*, World Health Organization, Document No WHO/EIP/GPE/00.1

Einsiedel, E. et al (2002) 'Brave new sheep – The clone named dolly', in Bauer, M. W. and Gaskell, G. (eds) *Biotechnology: The Making of a Global Controversy*, Cambridge University Press, Cambridge

Galloux, J.-C., Thing Mortensen, A., Cheveigné, S. de, Allansdottir, A., Chatjouli, A. and Sakallaris, G. (2002) 'The Institutions of Bioethics', in Bauer, M. W. and Gaskell, G. (eds) *Biotechnology: The Making of a Global Controversy*, Cambridge University Press, Cambridge

Grabner, P., Hampel, J., Lindsey, N. and Torgersen, H. (2001) 'Biopolitical diversity: The challenge of multilevel policy-making', in Gaskell, G. and Bauer, M. W. (eds) *Biotechnology 1996–2000: The Years of Controversy*, Science Museum, London, pp15–34

Hampel, J., Rurhmann, G., Kohring, M. and Goerke, A. (1998) 'Germany', in Durant, J., Bauer, M. W. and Gaskell, G. (eds) *Biotechnology in the Public Sphere: A European Sourcebook*, Science Museum, London, pp 63–76

HFEA (2004) 'HFEA grants the first therapeutic cloning licence for research', Press Release 11 August 2004, Human Fertilisation and Embryology Authority, London

HGAC and HFEA (1998) *Cloning Issues in Reproduction, Science and Medicine*: A report from the Human Genetics Advisory Commission and the Human Fertilisation and Embryology Authority, December 1998

House of Commons Official Report (1997) Parliamentary debates (Hansard) 26 June 1997, Column 615

Hviid Nielsen, T., Haug, T., Berg, S. V. and Monsen, A. (2001) 'Norway: Biotechnology and sustainability', in Gaskell, G. and Bauer, M. W. (eds) *Biotechnology 1996–2000: The Years of Controversy*, Science Museum, London, pp237–250

IAP (2003) *Statement on Human Cloning*, The Interacademy Panel, Trieste, 22 September

Jasanoff, S. (1995) 'Product, process or programme: Three cultures and the regulation of biotechnology', in Bauer, M. (ed) *Resistance to New Technology: Nuclear Power, Information Technology and Biotechnology*, Cambridge University Press, Cambridge

Jesuino, J. C., Nunes, J. A., Diego, C., Alcantara, P., Costa, S. and Matias, M. (2001) 'Representation of biotechnology in Portugal', in Gaskell, G. and Bauer, M. W. (eds) *Biotechnology 1996–2000: The Years of Controversy*, Science Museum, London, pp258–266

Knowles, L. P. (2004) 'A regulatory patchwork – Human ES cell research oversight', *Nature Biotechnology*, vol 22, no 2, pp157–163

Koch, L. (2003) 'Har vi brug for stamceller?' (Do we need stem cells?), *BioZoom*, no 2, pp14–15

Kolata, G. (1997) *Clone: The Road to Dolly and the Path Ahead*, Allen Lane, London

Lindsey, N., Kamara, M. W., Jelsoe, E. and Mortensen, A. T. (2001) 'Changing frames: The emergence of ethics in European policy on biotechnology', *Notizie di Politeia*, vol 17, no 63, pp80–94

Ministry of the Interior's Commission on Ethical Problems in Egg Transplantation, Artificial Fertilization and Embryo Diagnostics (1984) *Fremskridtets Pris* (The Price of Progress), Report of the Ministry of the Interior's Commission on Ethical Problems in Egg Transplantation, Artificial Fertilization and Embryo Diagnostics, Danish Ministry of the Interior, Copenhagen (in Danish)

Mulkay, M. (1997) *The Embryo Research Debate: Science and the Politics of Reproduction*, Cambridge University Press, Cambridge

NBAC (1997) *Cloning Human Beings*, Report and recommendations of the National Bioethics Advisory Commission, Rockville, Maryland

NOU (1991) *Mennesker og Bioteknologi* (Humans and Biotechnology), Norges Offentlige Utredninger 1991:6, Oslo (report in Norwegian)

Pilcher, H. (2004) 'Cloned human embryos yield stem cells', *Nature Science Update*, 12 February

Resnik, D. B. (2004) 'The need for international stem cell agreements', *Nature Biotechnology*, vol 22, no 10, p1207

Rusanen, T., von Wright, A. and Rusanen, M. (2001) 'Biotechnology in Finland: Transcending tradition', in Gaskell, G. and Bauer, M. W. (eds) *Biotechnology 1996–2000: The Years of Controversy*, Science Museum, London, pp172–180

Shickle, D. (2000) 'When are we Capable of Understanding an Early Warning?', in Danish Council of Ethics (ed) *3 papers: Humans and Genetic Engineering in the New Millennium – How are we Going to Get 'Gen-ethics' Just in Time?*, Danish Council of Ethics, www.etiskraad.dk (only available online)

UN Press Release (2004) 'Legal Committee text calls for further discussions on human cloning aimed at "Declaration"', Press Release GA/L/3270, United Nations

UNESCO (1997) *Universal Declaration on the Human Genome and Human Rights*, Twenty-ninth session of the general conference, United Nations Educational, Scientific and Cultural Organization, Paris

Warnock, M. (1985) *A Question of Life*, The Warnock Report on human fertilization and embryology, Basil Blackwell, Oxford

5

Whom to Trust with Genes on the Menu?

*Matthias Kohring, Anneloes Meijnders, Cees Midden,
Susanna Öhman, Anna Olofsson, Jörg Matthes,
Maria Rusanen, Jan Gutteling and Tomasz Twardowski*

Food is something very special in our lives. This is not only and exclusively eating, calories and market. In the case of food, we have also to take into account the cultural aspects such as religion and tradition. For example, people were and still are told by religious authorities to eat only fish on Friday or to avoid pork. More recently, in the European Union (EU) we have witnessed a novel tendency: slow food. This new trend re-evaluates eating as having a social value. However, the case of authority has changed: whereas the evaluation of food is still dependent on cultural aspects, people now have to consider what scientific authorities tell them about the health consequences of food. For example, fat has been identified as a serious cause of heart diseases, and there are many other warnings that people were never concerned about in former times. Throughout the past decade, we have observed a new development on the food market: genetically modified (GM) food. Since people cannot directly smell and taste the genetic modification, that is, they cannot distinguish between a genetically modified and a 'normal' tomato, they are even more dependent on experts. The question of how non-experts can acquire knowledge to inform their own decisions about GM food leads to the crucial problem of trust in information sources.

The aim of the study reported in this chapter is twofold: first, we outline a theoretical concept which combines a modern sociological view of trust in information sources with social psychological considerations of how people process information when developing attitudes. Second, we try to test some initial predictions drawn from our model by analysing the effects of trust in information sources on attitudes towards GM food. Since most people inform themselves via newspapers and television, we focus on journalism as a source of information. First, we deal with the public perception of GM food. Then we describe our concept of trust and especially what trust in journalism refers to. In the next section, we introduce the heuristic systematic model that describes how people form attitudinal judgements and react to new information. From there, we derive our hypothesis that the impact of source trustworthiness on attitudes towards GM food should be higher if people's confidence in their own judgement is low than when it is high. We conducted two experiments in Germany and Sweden with a total of 224 individuals. Our data show that our hypothesis could not be confirmed, but nevertheless reveal interesting insights. The consequences of these results for future research are discussed in the last section.

The public perception of GM food

Several studies of public perception of gene technology conducted during the 1990s show that the European public is quite sceptical towards food applications of gene technology (Bauer and Gaskell, 2002; Gaskell and Bauer, 2001; Durant et al, 1998). Studies also show that in the US people are less concerned about gene technology compared to people in Europe (Gaskell and Bauer, 2001). In the late 1990s, this starts to change and the US is closing in on Europe when it comes to scepticism towards the technology (Hornig Priest, 2000). The study by Hornig Priest indicates that the US public has quite stable and negative opinions about GM food, but compared to other kinds of food concerns (e.g. diseases from animals that can pass to humans) GM food is the least controversial food concern. However, in a student survey comparing the US, Japan, Norway and Taiwan, the US public is still the most positive towards consuming GM food (Cher and Rickertson, 2002; Bauer and Gaskell, 2002).

Perceived risks and benefits seem to be important when it comes to acceptance of GM food. When information consisting exclusively of the benefits is given to respondents, this results in more favourable attitudes, but even when both risks and benefits are mentioned, the benefits concerning environment, taste and health make people more positive to GM food (Frewer et al, 1996; Frewer et al, 1997; Hamstra, 1998; Hoban, 1998). However, benefits perceived as only favouring producers have a negative impact on public acceptance, and products associated with risks especially for the environment and physical illness are not accepted to the same extent as benefits to the consumer (Frewer et al, 1996; Hamstra, 1998). This is confirmed in an opinion study that shows that people so far do not see any consumer advantages with GM food products; moreover, the benefits of GM food are believed to remain solely with the industry (Alvensleben, 2001).

Whether attitudes to genetic engineering and food in general influence people's perception of GM food is rather unclear. Some studies suggest that attitudes to genetic engineering in general are an important determinant (Frewer et al, 1997), while other results show that general attitudes towards food production, nature and genetic engineering contribute only marginally to the evaluation of GM products (Hamstra, 1998).

Earlier studies also show that the evaluation of GM food differs between different types of applications. Transgenetic animals are accepted to a lesser extent than plants and micro-organisms, which are more widely accepted (e.g. Gaskell and Bauer, 2001; Durant et al, 1998; Hamstra, 1998; Hampel et al, 2000; Urban and Pfenning, 2000). It is important to note, however, that the biggest difference is not between different kinds of GM food applications, but rather between GM food and other applications of gene technology, for example medical applications (Gaskell and Bauer, 2001; Bauer and Gaskell, 2002; Durant et al, 1998; Hampel et al, 2000). Moral values and beliefs about nature also play a role in the evaluation of GM food. When GM food is perceived as unnatural or immoral, acceptance is low (e.g. Frewer et al, 1996; Hamstra, 1998; Hoban, 1998).

Between 1998 and 2000, a large number of focus group interviews on agricultural biotechnology were conducted in five European countries (Marris et al, 2001). The study is critical of earlier studies and rejects several of the findings discussed above as well as a number of what the authors frame as 'myths' about lay people's ideas concerning agricultural biotechnology. The authors state that such myths consist of the belief that there is a lack of knowledge among the general public, that the media influence public perceptions, that there is a difference in judgement regarding medical and agricultural applications of gene technology, and that there are differences in public perception between countries. According to the study, there are great similarities across countries, different groups and over time, and these similarities are based on salient dimensions of experience of ordinary people. This similarity is seen as evidence of the lack of media effects since media coverage differs between countries, and instead the authors emphasize the existence of commonly shared salient dimensions of the experience of ordinary people. They also put forward the idea that the shared character of public responses across countries represents the emergency of a common European public culture on scientific and technology trajectories.

Altogether, the empirical research shows that there is no single perception of 'the' GM food. Instead, evaluations differ from application to application and from institutional actor to institutional actor. For non-experts or so-called lay people, the situation is characterized by two aspects: the perception of social conflicts about GM food and the lack of direct experience. Both aspects lead to the question of how non-experts can acquire knowledge and form evaluations in order to decide about GM food-related topics in everyday life. Since they will use non-direct experiences if they decide to actively participate in decision processes concerning GM food (on whatever level of action), the crucial problem for them is that of trust in information sources.

Trust in information sources

The concept of trust

Scholars dealing with trust underline the fact that the concept of trust is directly linked to the concept of risk (Luhmann, 1979; Coleman, 1990; Giddens, 1990; Hardin, 2002). A risky situation denotes a possible benefit but at the same time a possible loss. Another crucial character of trust is the lack of knowledge or control. As the German sociologist Georg Simmel puts it, 'trust – the hypothesis about the future action of the other – is a medium state between knowledge and non-knowledge. A person with total knowledge does not need to trust whereas a person without any knowledge at all cannot trust' (Simmel, 1964, p38; Lewis and Weigert, 1985a). This quotation underlines another important feature of trust, its reference to future situations. Altogether one can say that trust is addressed to another social actor, that it expresses an expectation towards this actor which refers to a future action of this actor, that it is characterized by insufficient knowledge about the outcome of this future action and that it therefore includes the awareness of a certain risk.

The aspects of an open future and a perceived risk are decisive for trust situations. In other words, when there is nothing at stake, trust is not needed. A situation is risky because it and particularly the other actors involved are uncontrollable. For example, in the case of GM food the control of the safety and also the judgement of benefits are definitely not in the hands of the consumer. Modern societies are characterized by autonomous expert systems (Giddens, 1990), each with its own organizational structure, specialist language and logic of action. An individual is not able to control the effectiveness of these systems and their actors on his or her own, due to a lack of knowledge and insufficient other resources, like money and time.

The function of trust is therefore to anticipate the future: the consumer replaces the missing information by trust in order to tolerate the perceived uncertainty of the situation (Luhmann, 1979, 1988; Lewis and Weigert, 1985a, b; Earle and Cvetkovich, 1995; Seligman, 1997). The so-called trustee (i.e. the one who trusts) makes use of a piece of information or a judgement by another person in order to continue his/her own social acting. A trust action denotes the selective linking of others' actions with one's own actions at times when there is a concern about the uncertainty of the outcome (Kohring, 2001, 2003). The crucial point is that in the moment of decision (to eat a GM apple, to form and utter an attitude), this adoption is not based on situation-specific knowledge. Because trust is not based on situation-specific arguments or knowledge, most indicators for trust are symbolic – they are taken as a sign for trust (for instance, the taste of the apple mentioned above). Since in modern societies, even in the field of one's own expertise, no one knows everything, trust has become an eminent mechanism in social life (and trustworthiness an indispensable resource). Trust allows people to widely broaden their possibilities of social action, 'simply' by replacing information with trust. The alternative would be a time-consuming control of the situation or an overall withdrawal from any action. It is important to note that, in our under-standing, trust refers to expectations towards social actors and not to technological products, as for example food itself. To trust in things is a form of self-confidence. In this chapter, we are interested in the role that social trust relations, for example in specific information sources, play in the acceptance of information about GM food.

Now it becomes clear why today trust in information sources is more impor-tant than the approach of exerting control via the transmission of knowledge. The traditional view of the role of knowledge is that people would not accept biotechnology because of a deficit in knowledge. The 'therapy' then would be to provide people with more scientific or technological knowledge in order to heighten acceptance of biotechnology. But research has shown that it is not necessarily the case that people object to biotechnology because they are ignorant or uneducated (Midden et al, 2002). They may protest because of other reasons, and often experts themselves are critical of certain applications of a technology. The so-called deficit model of public understanding of science and technology ignores the fact that acceptance is a matter not merely of knowledge but of external evaluations regarding, for example, usefulness, political participation and ethics. But even if technological knowledge really did govern acceptance, the idea of transferring knowledge to 'lay people' would be a hopeless task, simply because people lack sufficient resources such as time, money and cognitive resources to receive and adopt the information. This overwhelming complexity is among other things reduced by trust, or alternatively distrust. Therefore, at least in modern western societies, trust is perhaps the most important key to the relationship between science, technology and the public. GM food is the most controversial among the applications surveyed in the Eurobarometers 1996, 1999 and 2002 (Gaskell et al, 2002), and it is the aspect of trust rather than knowledge that explains the encouragement of biotechnology.

Trust in journalism as an information source

Regarding trust in journalism, we draw on recent efforts in theory development and scale construction that are beyond the scope of this chapter (see Kohring 2001, 2003; Matthes and Kohring 2003). At the most general level, this work suggests that for almost all people the journalistic information in newspapers, television, radio and also the internet offers almost the only possibility to acquire knowledge, to consider several aspects of GM food and to form judgements and evaluations. Therefore the question of trust in journalism (trust in 'media' would be a less exact term, because advertising, public relations and entertainment is not meant here) is very important for the perception of GM food. The concept of journalistic selectivity is crucial for the issue of trust in journalism. Journalistic selectivity refers to the process of informing the journalistic publics about events in society which are of possible relevance to them. Four interdependent dimensions or factors of trust in journalism can be distinguished:

1   Trust in 'theme selectivity' means the selection of themes or subjects for coverage.
2   Trust in 'fact selectivity' refers to the selection of further information which contextualizes the already selected theme.
3   Trust in the 'correctness of descriptions' refers to the verifiable correctness of information (= credibility or believability).
4   Trust in 'explicit evaluations' refers to the explicit weighing of themes and information.

Taken together, journalism can be regarded as the crucial source of information about social and political life. Its societal function consists of selecting and conveying information about the complex interdependencies of modern society. Doing so, journalism enables social actors (personal and organizational) to orient themselves to their social environment(s) and to adjust their expectations regarding other social actors. Trust in journalism as an information source is therefore a necessary condition for trust in other social actors. Therefore, trust in social actors such as those in the field of GM food (industry, distributors, farmers, consumer organizations, politicians, Greenpeace and so on) is dependent on the degree of trust that people are willing to grant to journalistic organizations such as newspapers or radio stations. This is also true for the development and change of attitudes towards GM products, which is the main focus of this chapter.

The formation of attitudes on GM food

From the long history of research on persuasive communication we know that one of the factors influencing the persuasive impact of a message is the trustworthiness and credibility of the message source (see, for example, Hovland et al, 1953; Petty and Wegener, 1998). Within the framework offered by the elaboration likelihood model (ELM), the trustworthiness of a message source has predominantly or perhaps even exclusively been studied as a peripheral cue that allows for attitude formation without much effort (Petty and Wegener, 1999). This research has shown that attitudes are influenced more strongly by the trustworthiness of a source (or related source characteristics such as source expertise) under conditions of low elaboration likelihood than under conditions of high elaboration likelihood (Petty and Cacioppo, 1985). In the latter case, attitudes are influenced more strongly by what the source actually has to say or, in other words, the source's viewpoint and argumentation. The results of this research suggest that attitudes are based either on source trustworthiness or some other peripheral cue, or on arguments. In order to develop a comprehensive understanding of the role of trust in persuasion, we draw on the heuristic systematic model (HSM) by Chaiken (see, for example, Eagly and Chaiken, 1993, 1998; Chen and Chaiken, 1999), which provides a more clearly specified dual-processing approach.

The HSM on persuasion and attitude change describes how people form attitudinal judgements and react to new information. The HSM was developed to apply to validity-seeking persuasion settings in which people's primary motivational concern is to attain accurate attitudes that square with relevant facts. The model postulates that this goal can be achieved through two types of information processing, namely *heuristic processing* and *systematic processing*. Systematic processing (SP) refers to a comprehensive, analytic type of processing in which a person scrutinizes a great deal of relevant information. It also involves argumentation in a message being evaluated and related to other available information. This mode demands that a person has both the capacity to process information and the motivation to do so. The second mode, heuristic processing (HP), is conceptualized as a more limited mode of information processing that requires less cognitive effort and fewer cognitive resources. In this mode, people focus on simple decision rules, cognitive heuristics or schemata to formulate their judgements and decisions. Examples of heuristics are 'experts can be trusted' or 'consensual judgements can be trusted'. Attitudes based on HP are supposed to be less stable and less resistant to counter-information and less predictable with regard to behaviour than attitudes based on SP.

It is assumed that both processing modes can occur concurrently (Eagly and Chaiken 1993). They may act additively and interdependently. SP can be inhibited because it requires ability and motivation. HP needs at least the presence of heuristic cues and the cognitive availability of their associated heuristics. Finally, if people are unsure whether or not to put effort into forming or changing their views on a particular issue, heuristics may affect judgement by helping them to decide on the level of effort. SP produces a lot of relevant information and may therefore attenuate the effects of HP. However, HP may also act independently on persuasion.

In selecting a processing mode, two main motives exert influence. The first is the *least effort principle*, which asserts that people will prefer less effortful modes to more effortful modes. The second motive is the *sufficiency principle*, which assumes that people are motivated to make the effort that is necessary to accomplish the processing goal. This means that people will pay attention to a message to attain a sufficiently confident assessment of message validity. The sufficiency threshold is defined as the desired level of judgemental confidence that a person aspires to attain in a given judgement setting. It holds, among other things, that a person will stop processing when the sufficiency threshold has been reached. The sufficiency threshold can vary between situations and between persons.

On the basis of the two principles of least effort and sufficiency, we may derive some expectations. In the following, we will present these basic hypotheses and the experimental approach to put them to test. According to the HSM, the impact of any piece of information on attitudes depends on how much confidence a person has in his or her attitude. If a person has sufficient confidence, he or she will not be open to new information and hence it will not be likely that either cues or arguments will have an effect. If a person is insufficiently confident of his or her attitude, he or she will be open to new information and hence it will be more likely that a cue or an argument will affect his or her attitude.

Hence, according to this approach, as self-confidence decreases, the likelihood that source trustworthiness has an impact on attitudes increases in principle. However, the likelihood that arguments have an impact on attitudes increases as well. The fact that under these circumstances often no effect of source trustworthiness on attitudes is observed is explained in terms of the informative value of cues versus arguments. Because cues are usually less informative than arguments, the impact of cues is usually attenuated by the impact of arguments. If this is true, the impact of source trustworthiness on attitudes should be higher in cases of low confidence than in cases of high confidence, provided that no arguments are presented that overrule the cue effect. Consequently, we hypothesize *that the impact of source trustworthiness on attitudes towards genetically modified food is higher in the case of low judgemental confidence compared to high judgemental confidence.* This basic hypothesis was tested in the present experiment. In addition to this hypothesis, another independent variable was included as a further research question: the valence of the message. In one condition, a source was presented who pleads against GM food and in the other condition the source pleads for GM food. We added this variable in order to explore possible interactions between the perceived trustworthiness of the source and the direction of the evaluation held by the journalist. The judgemental impact of trust as a heuristic cue will become greater when the sufficiency threshold is at a high point, compared to a low point, of the confidence scale. Thus, if there is a serious health risk (negative evaluation of GM food), the perceived trustworthiness of the source could show more effect on attitudes.

Methods

Two experiments (using the same procedure) were conducted, one in Germany and one in Sweden. The participants were told that the study was about product innovations, and then they were asked to take a seat behind a PC and to work through the experiment via a computer program. A total number of 224 persons participated in the experiment, of whom 55 per cent lived in Germany and the other 45 per cent lived in Sweden, and 48 per cent were male and 52 per cent female. The mean age of the sample was $M = 25$ (SD = 4.79); the youngest participant was 18, the oldest 46. The participants were students from different departments.

In the experiment, the participants were confronted with a message about a GM apple (there were also information and questions about four other innovations). This message argued either for (risk triggering) or against (risk suppressing) market introduction of the GM apple. The message was given by a source of either high or low trustworthiness, respectively, which gives a two (judgemental confidence: low or high) by two (message direction: pro or con) by two (trustworthiness: low or high) factor between subjects design, with judgemental confidence being a quasi-experimental factor and message direction and trustworthiness being experimental factors. The dependent variable was the attitude towards consuming the apple.

Manipulations

Trustworthiness was manipulated by the information given about the author of the article (see Appendix). Pilot testing made sure that the sources of low and high trustworthiness respectively were consensually regarded as such. The experimental 'message valence' condition was different between the countries: the German participants received a positive message, whereas the Swedish participants received a negative message. The first part of the message was the same for both conditions. In the second part, a position either for or against the apple was presented (see Appendix).

Measures

Attitudes
In the first part of the experiment, attitudes towards five innovative products were measured by means of the question 'How do you feel about yourself using/consuming [the innovative product]?' Answers were given on a seven-point scale. After the introduction of the stimulus material, the attitude towards the GM apple was again measured by a semantic differential of five attitude items (Cronbach's alpha = 0.90). The difference between the two measures was taken as an attitude change variable.

Trust
Mainly based on a theoretically derived trust in media scale which measures the four dimensions of specific journalistic selectivity described above (Kohring 2001; Matthes and Kohring 2003), trust in the information source was assessed by asking participants to indicate the extent to which they agreed with a total of seven statements (see Appendix). Answers were also given on a seven-point scale. Exploratory factor analysis revealed a one-factor solution (eigenvalue = 3.78, explains 53.94 per cent of variance, Cronbach's alpha = 0.85).

Judgemental confidence
Judgemental confidence was measured by two different questions (both were on a seven-point scale; Cronbach's alpha = 0.70):

1   'How certain do you feel about your opinion on [the innovative product]?'
2   'To what extent do you doubt your opinion on [the innovative product]? [inverse]'

The assignment to the quasi-experimental condition of 'judgemental confidence' was based on a median split on the scale of these items (median = 5) because in several pilot studies the manipulation of judgemental confidence turned out to be unsuccessful.

Table 5.1 shows the number of participants per condition.

Table 5.1 *Number of participants per cell*

		Low JC	High JC
Positive message	Low trust	20	30
	High trust	31	19
Negative message	Low trust	39	22
	High trust	29	34

Results

First of all, an Analysis of Variance (ANOVA) with the manipulation of source trustworthiness as independent variable and trust in information source as dependent variable revealed a significant main effect of source trustworthiness ($F = 14.33$, $p = 0.000$). This means that our manipulation of the trustworthiness of the information source succeeded. Participants who received information that underlined the source's trustworthiness reported a higher level of trust, $M = 3.69$ (SD = 0.99), than participants who received information that undermined the source's trustworthiness, $M = 3.19$ (SD = 0.99). This allows us to check for the effects of source trustworthiness, judgemental confidence and message valence on attitude change regarding the genetically modified apple. Therefore, an ANOVA was conducted with judgemental confidence, source trustworthiness and message valence as independent variables and the difference between pre- and post-attitude towards consuming the GM apple as dependent variable.

As outlined above, we expected that the impact of source trustworthiness on the attitude change towards the genetically modified apple would be higher in the case of low judgemental confidence compared to high judgemental confidence. Surprisingly, this hypothesis cannot be confirmed: there is no significant interaction between trustworthiness and judgemental confidence. Nevertheless, the data reveal some interesting results. The interaction effect between source trustworthiness and message valence is significant, $F (1, 216) = 3.91$, $p = 0.049$. Tests of the simple effect of source trustworthiness within each level of message valence revealed that source trustworthiness did not affect attitude change in case of the negative message, $F < 1$, n.s., but did affect attitude change in case of the positive message, $F(1, 216) = 3.90$, $p = 0.050$. As can be seen in Table 5.2, the positive message resulted in negative attitude change when source trustworthiness was low and positive attitude change when source trustworthiness was high. In other words, when an incompetent and biased journalist pleads for genetically modified food, he achieves exactly the opposite from what he seems to want (this is a boomerang effect).

Table 5.2 *Effect of source trustworthiness and message valence on attitude change*

	Low source trustworthiness	High source trustworthiness	Row totals
Positive message	−0.24 (1.10)	0.20 (1.07)	−0.02 (1.10)
Negative message	0.02 (1.06)	−0.05 (1.11)	−0.02 (1.08)
Column totals	−0.10 (1.08)	0.06 (1.10)	
	Sample total		−0.02 (1.09)

Note: Table shows the means and standard deviations of the attitude change variable.

In sum, the hypothesized interaction between judgemental confidence and the trustworthiness of the information source cannot be confirmed. One explanation might be that due to the median split procedure the difference between low and high judgemental confidence was not large enough to achieve a difference in attitude change. The direct measure of judgemental confidence led to a slightly skewed distribution as the median of judgemental confidence is 5.00 on a seven-point scale. This calls into question whether we could separate high and low judgemental confidence properly.

Complexities in message reception

In this chapter, we have discussed the role of trust in journalism in the formation of attitudes on GM food. To examine this relationship, we gave a brief overview of empirical studies regarding the public perception of this application. Taken together, these studies indicate that consumers tend to focus on the disadvantages rather than on the benefits of GM food products.

One crucial characteristic of GM food is the fact that most potential consumers have to rely on non-direct experiences to develop their attitudes and to act on GM food-related aspects of social life. Therefore, trust in information sources such as journalism is a key variable when it comes to the acceptance of GM products. We define trust as a mechanism that helps people to reduce the complexity of social life by anticipating future action and tolerating the risk of delegating control. As an information source we chose journalism, which we regard as the most important origin of information for consumers.

The heuristic systematic model (HSM) was used as a conceptual framework in order to derive some initial hypotheses on the role of trust in persuasion processes. Specifically, we argued that the impact of source trustworthiness on attitudes towards genetically modified food should be higher in the case of low judgemental confidence compared to high judgemental confidence. Furthermore, we explored the impact of positive versus negative viewpoints. We found an interaction effect of source trustworthiness with message valence, but, contrary to our assumption, independent of the degree of judgemental confidence. Trustworthiness had an impact on attitude change only when the valence of the message was positive. At first glance, this difference might be interpreted as a cultural effect, that is, the German subjects show a different pattern than do the Swedish. However, the fact that the prior attitudes in both countries were the same speaks against this explanation. This finding can also be explained by reasoning that in this context it is more risky to accept a positive message than it is to accept a negative message. Accepting the positive message means that the participant has to consider actually eating the GM apple and therefore taking the risk of negative health consequences. Contrary to this, accepting the negative message implies that the participant does not consider eating the apple and hence is not taking the risk of any negative consequences. The interaction effect of valence and source trustworthiness occurs because a risky request to act raises the sufficiency threshold, which in turn triggers the processing of trust cues. As previously discussed, trust is only relevant in situations perceived as risky. This may also explain why a positive message given by an untrustworthy journalist leads to even more negative attitudes towards the GM apple.

These first results point to some unresolved issues, each of which warrants further inquiry for future research. First of all, in the foregoing we treated the two types of information (information about the source trustworthiness and the message as information from the source) as independent sets of trust cues. However, this might be an overly simple impression of the mechanisms involved. Not only is the information *from* the source interpreted in the light of the information *about* the source, as we have already argued, but the information *about* the source is also interpreted in the light of the information *from* the source. This interaction effect means that the message, the acceptance of which should be a function of trust in the information source, itself influences trust in the information source. For example, in the experiments described above, the source was a journalist. Since a journalist is expected to be independent, the journalist may trigger suspicion if he or she presents one-sided information. In our experiments, both the information about the source and the information from the source provided people with multiple cues of the source's trustworthiness. As a consequence, we have to consider the differentiation between trust effect and message effect on attitude formation. Therefore, future research should try to measure the pure effect of trustworthiness manipulation on trust in information sources. The first manipulation check of trustworthiness should be placed before the presentation of the message, and a second one after that. Additionally, since risk perception is a central condition for the relevance of trust, we should directly measure risk perception and risk acceptance.

Altogether, the results of this study have clearly underlined the relevance of trust in information sources regarding risky future decisions in which people can only act when delegating control to other social actors. An obvious indicator for this relevance is our observation that a positive message uttered by an untrustworthy source leads to negative attitude changes. Furthermore, it is also crucial to study the conditions under which this key resource of modern societies evolves. In this respect, we have learned that the case is even more complex than we could have anticipated.

References

Alvensleben, R. von (2001) 'Beliefs associated with food production methods', in Frewer, L. J. and Schifferstein, H. (eds) *Food, People and Society: A European Perspective of Consumer's Food Choices*, Springer, Berlin

Bauer, M. W. and Gaskell, G. (eds) (2002) *Biotechnology: The Making of a Global Controversy*, Cambridge University Press, Cambridge

Chen, S. and Chaiken, S. (1999) 'The heuristic-systematic model in its broader context', in Chaiken, S. and Trope, Y. (eds) *Dual-process Theories in Social Psychology*, Guilford, London

Cher, W. S. and Rickertson, K. (2002) *Consumer Acceptance of GMO: Survey Results from*

Japan, Norway, Taiwan and the United States, Working paper: AEDE-WP-0026-02, Ohio State University, Columbus, OH

Coleman, J. (1990) *Foundations of Social Theory*, Harvard University Press, Cambridge, MA, and London

Durant, J., Bauer, M. W. and Gaskell, G. (eds) (1998) *Biotechnology in the Public Sphere: A European Sourcebook*, Science Museum, London

Eagly, A. H. and Chaiken, S. (1993) *The Psychology of Attitudes*, Harcourt Brace Jovanovich, Fort Worth, TX

Eagly, A. H. and Chaiken, S. (1998) 'Attitude structure and function', in Gilbert, D. T., Fiske, S. T. and Lindzey, G. (eds) *The Handbook of Social Psychology*, McGraw-Hill, Boston, MA

Earle, T. C. and Cvetkovich, G. T. (1995) *Social Trust: Toward a Cosmopolitan Society*, Praeger, Westport, CT, and London

Frewer, L. J., Howard, C., Hedderley, D. and Shepherd, R. (1997) 'Consumer attitudes towards different food-processing technologies used in cheese production – The mediating influence of consumer benefit', *Food Quality and Preference*, vol 8, pp271–280

Frewer, L. J., Howard, C. and Shepherd, R. (1996) 'The influence of realistic product exposure on attitudes towards genetic engineering in food', *Food Quality and Preference*, vol 7, pp51–67

Gaskell, G., Allum, N. and Stares, S. (2002) *Europeans and Biotechnology in 2002: Eurobarometer 58.0, A report to the EC Directorate General for Research from the project 'Life Sciences in European Society'*, QLG7-CT-1999-00286

Gaskell, G. and Bauer, M. W. (eds) (2001) *Biotechnology 1996–2000: The Years of Controversy*, Science Museum, London

Giddens, A. (1990) *The Consequences of Modernity*, Polity Press, Cambridge

Hampel, J., Pfenning, U. and Peters, H. P. (2000) 'Attitudes towards genetic engineering', *New Genetics and Society*, vol 19, pp234–249

Hamstra, A. (1998) *Public Opinion about Biotechnology: A Survey of Surveys*, European Federation of Biotechnology, Task Group on Public Perceptions of Biotechnology, The Hague

Hardin, R. (2002) *Trust and Trustworthiness*, Russell Sage, New York

Hoban, T. J. (1998) 'Trends in consumer attitudes about agricultural biotechnology', *AgBioForum*, vol 1, no 1, pp3–7

Hornig Priest, S. (2000) 'US public opinion divided over biotechnology?', *Nature Biotechnology*, vol 18, pp939–942

Hovland, C. I., Janis, I. L. and Kelley, H. H. (1953) *Communication and Persuasion: Psychological Studies of Opinion Change*, Yale University Press, New Haven, CT

Kohring, M. (2001) *Vertrauen in Medien – Vertrauen in Technologie* (Trust in media – trust in technology), Akademie für Technikfolgenabschätzung (Academy for Technological Assessment), Stuttgart

Kohring, M. (2003) 'Vertrauen in Journalismus. Theorie und Empirie eines mehrdimensionalen Konstrukts' (Trust in journalism. Theoretical and empirical analysis of a multidimensional construct), unpublished dissertation, University of Jena

Lewis, J. D. and Weigert, A. J. (1985a) 'Social atomism, holism, and trust', *Sociological Quarterly*, vol 26, pp455–471

Lewis, J. D. and Weigert, A. J. (1985b): 'Trust as a social reality', *Social Forces*, vol 63, pp967–985

Luhmann, N. (1979) *Trust and Power*, Wiley, Chichester, New York, Brisbane and Toronto

Luhmann, N. (1988) 'Familiarity, confidence, trust: problems and alternatives,' in Gambetta, D. (ed) *Trust: Making and Breaking Cooperative Relations*, Blackwell, New York and Oxford

Marris, C., Wynne, B., Simmons, L. and Weldon, S. (2001) *Final report of the PAVE research project*, www.pabe.net

Matthes, J. and Kohring, M. (2003) 'Operationalisierung von Vertrauen in Journalismus' (Operationalization of trust in journalism), *Medien and Kommunikationswissenschaft*, vol 51, pp5–23

Midden, C., Boy, D., Einsiedel, E., Fjaestad, B., Liakopoulos, M., Miller J. D., Öhman, S. and Wagner, W. (2002) 'The structure of public perceptions', in Bauer, M. W. and Gaskell, G. (eds) *Biotechnology: The Making of a Global Controversy*, Cambridge University Press, Cambridge

Petty, R. E. and Cacioppo, J. T. (1985) 'Source factors and the elaboration likelihood model of persuasion', *Advances in Consumer Research*, vol 11, pp668–672

Petty, R. E. and Wegener, D. T. (1998) 'Attitude change: multiple roles for persuasion variables', in Gilbert, D. T., Fiske, S. T. and Lindzey, G. (eds) *The Handbook of Social Psychology*, McGraw-Hill, Boston, MA

Petty, R. E. and Wegener, D. T. (1999) 'The elaboration likelihood model: Current status and controversies', in Chaiken, S. and Trope, Y. (eds) *Dual-process Theories in Social Psychology*, Guilford, London

Seligman, A. B. (1997) *The Problem of Trust*, Princeton University Press, Princeton, NJ

Simmel, G. (1964) *The Sociology of Georg Simmel* (edited by Kurt Wolff), Free Press, New York

Urban, D. and Pfenning, U. (2000) 'Attitudes towards genetic engineering between change and stability: results of a panel study', *New Genetics and Society*, vol 19, pp251–268

Appendix

Trust items

1　'I have the impression that this journalist usually writes about topics that have my interest.'
2　'I have the impression this journalist usually tells the truth.'
3　'I have the impression this journalist usually makes proper judgements.'
4　'I have the impression this journalist usually looks at an issue from various perspectives.'
5　'I have the impression this journalist is trustworthy.'
6　'I have the impression this journalist is competent on the issue of biotechnology.'
7　'I have the impression this journalist only wants the best for his readers.'

Manipulation of source trustworthiness

Low trustworthiness

The author of this article is working as a trainee journalist for a small local newspaper. Mainly he writes about sports and entertainment. As a second job, he works for a local biotechnology firm doing layout work. He wrote the following article because a colleague became ill and he had to cover the science news at short notice.

High trustworthiness
The author of this article is an experienced science editor for an important national newspaper. For his critical background coverage of the BSE crisis, he received the prestigious 'Media Award for Consumer Protection'. For the following article, the author has looked in depth at the issue of biotechnology – for example by visiting conferences.

Manipulation of message valence

First part for both conditions
Is the consumer ready for the techno-apple?

Everyone knows the apple, this tasty fruit from a family with more than 25 varieties. Apples can be bought at every supermarket and every local market. Usually the consumer has the choice between different kinds of apple, each having its own characteristic 'bite'. The apple is a very versatile, but a common, everyday product, which enjoys a host of loyal fans.

Almost everyone knows tooth decay as well, from personal experience or from stories by other people. In the western world, almost 100 per cent of the population suffers in some degree from caries, which is the official name of tooth decay. The most likely cause of this is the presence of certain bacteria in the mouth, which play a role in the processing of sugars. Young children are particularly affected by caries. Good dental care comprises several activities, basically aimed at increasing mouth hygiene.

What is the link between the apple and tooth decay, you may wonder? Well, scientists using genetic engineering have developed a new apple. This new apple contains bacteria that may help to keep the teeth healthy. This is the latest development in a series of applications of genetic engineering to reach a state in which they are ready for the market.

Second part of the positive message condition
The question is how the consumer will react to this techno-apple. If you ask me, the genetically engineered apple is a desirable product which should be welcomed on the market.

Second part of the negative message condition
The question is how the consumer will react to this techno-apple. If you ask me, this genetically modified apple should not be admitted to the market.

Part 2

The Efficacy of Public Opinion

6

Public Mobilization and Policy Consequences

Jürgen Hampel, Petra Grabner, Helge Torgersen, Daniel Boy, Agnes Allansdottir, Erling Jelsøe and Georgios Sakellaris

After a period of initial liberalization, the European regulatory handling of agricultural biotechnology became more restrictive during the second half of the 1990s, culminating in 1999 in a de facto moratorium on new GM crops in Europe. A widely cited explanation for this policy shift was 'public outrage' resulting from risk perception, lack of trust in government, media reporting and non-governmental organization (NGO) campaigns. Empirically, it remains unclear whether public outrage existed or was significant for policy. Surveys showed considerable variation in risk perception across Europe, but this was not the most important variable determining support for biotechnology. Overall trust in relevant institutions did not differ between the US and the European Union (EU). Triggers for public debate differed across countries and time, and issues varied widely. In some European countries, public debate started before or long after the onset of NGO activities; in other countries, political actors themselves started a debate on biotechnology. A policy shift can be observed in some countries but not in others. In addition, the major addressees of demands have not been political institutions but retailers. Due to these inconsistencies, the proposed linkage between public perception, NGO activity and policy shift remains questionable.

In contrast to traditional research on mobilization emphasizing visible activities, we propose a different concept that takes account of survey results, media and NGO strategies, but also includes the perspective of the addressees of mobilization. We discuss a possible mechanism that results in strategic decisions aimed at preventing pending mobilization.

Policy shift and the moratorium

In her seminal paper comparing biotechnology policies in the US, the UK and Germany, Sheila Jasanoff concluded that the three governments shared the aim of wanting to make biotechnology happen (Jasanoff, 1995), although by different means. There is strong evidence that the European Commission had a similar aim (Cantley, 1995). Despite public controversies, functional elites from politics, science and industry tried to stay on the biotechnology train in order not to miss economic and technological opportunities (Budd, 1993). In the field of medical biotechnology, commercial activities became uncontested in Europe. This was not the case for agricultural applications of biotechnology.

Although NGOs and industry had struggled for decades, the issue was only transiently salient for the general public. In the early 1990s, countries with very restrictive regulations on biotechnology, such as Germany, exploited any opportunity for relaxation the EU framework offered, and in the UK the first genetically modified (GM) food products were sold in the early 1990s without raising controversy. By the mid 1990s, the time seemed ripe for the large-scale import of US-grown genetically modified agricultural products (widely accepted in their home country) to Europe. However, the import of GM soya, and later of maize, triggered a wave of resistance throughout Europe (Lassen et al, 2002). Although several surveys over time had shown a generally hesitant welcome for GM food in most places, media analyses indicated a dramatic increase of attention combined with a predominantly negative framing of the issue after 1996 (Bauer et al, 2001, p38).

On the regulatory level, many countries were increasingly reluctant to implement new GM crops.[1] The EU novel food prescription, passed soon after the first import of GM soya beans, made labelling of GM products mandatory. Eventually, some EU member states would no longer support the European Commission's cautious but increasingly permissive regulatory policy (Bandelow, 1999) and refused the approval of new products. Member states were unable to reach agreement. So in 1999 the European Commission had to accept a de facto moratorium on new GM crops until the Release and Marketing Directive 90/220 was revised. Even after the adoption of the new Directive 18/2001, EU member states were reluctant to take up the processing of proposals according to the new regulatory framework; in other words, they were reluctant to return to business as usual. New demands on labelling, segregation and coexistence demanded new efforts at regulatory harmonization.

Obviously, in the wake of the pending imports of GM crops, a policy shift had taken place in several member states and, subsequently, on the European level (Torgersen et al, 2002a; Grabner et al, 2002; Seifert, 2000, 2002). Over the same period, the US implemented agricultural biotechnology on a large scale without significant public debate.

Possible explanations for the policy shift

This policy shift calls for an explanation; a prominent one is that after the early 1990s, NGO campaigns together with public outrage forced European policy makers to implement increasingly restrictive regulation of agricultural biotechnology (Bernauer and Meins, 2003). Bernauer and Meins attribute the growing influence of NGOs to the multi-level system in the EU and their access to DG Environment, the European Commission (EC) department responsible for biotechnology regulation. This is in contrast to the single-level system in the US and the close association between the Food and Drink Administration (FDA) and biotechnology companies. Furthermore, in Europe, NGOs have succeeded, through campaigning, in separating the interests of upstream parts of the food industry (biotechnology and seed companies and farmers) from the downstream parts (food processors and retailers). Together, these factors have increased the collective action capacity of anti-biotechnology NGOs.

This convincing analysis by Bernauer and Meins, however, makes little reference to the link between public outrage, brought about through a combination of enhanced risk perception and lack of trust in regulatory agencies, NGO aims and activities, and the ensuing policy on a national and European level. One is left with the impression of a black box through which NGOs translate their increased collective action capacity into an overall biotechnology-critical policy. Many questions need to be answered. What event, or events, triggered the increase in public attention? Was there a coordinated NGO activity everywhere? What was the assumed public outrage about? What was the importance of the risk argument? How did NGOs exert their pressure, and how did policy react? Finally, to what did the policy shift pertain?

Following some remarks on the relevance of the proposed variables, we look at events post-1996 in several European countries.[2] The six questions detailed above will guide us in our discussion of the policy shift in order to learn more about the role of public outrage. Finally, we will explain mobilization as an alternative concept to public outrage.

The concept of public outrage

Bernauer and Meins (2003) put increased risk perception, lack of trust in the regulatory agencies and NGO campaigns at the centre of their explanation of policy shift. Similar explanations are frequently encountered among functional elites of regulators, scientists and industry as well as NGO representatives (Torgersen and Bogner, 2005). Policy is only seen to react to pressure from NGO activism and negative public opinion. We refer to this view as the 'outrage concept'.

With respect to public opinion, there are consistent differences between the United States and the European Union on an aggregate level, with Europeans being more concerned about biotechnology than Americans. However, European surveys over a decade have shown risk perception to vary considerably within a country over time and even more so across countries (Durant et al, 1998; Gaskell and Bauer, 2001; Gaskell et al, this volume). If public outrage were a main determinant for policy, one would assume that levels of risk perception would somehow correspond with government policy on agricultural biotechnology. Analyses have shown, though, that public support for biotechnology, or rather the lack of it, depends considerably on non-risk issues such as moral acceptability or utility (Gaskell et al, 2001a). There are indeed indications that in some EU countries, levels of support corresponded vaguely to a relatively more restrictive or supportive policy (Torgersen, 2002); a robust correlation, however, cannot be established. Regarding trust in institutions related to food biotechnology, survey analysis has shown virtually no differences between the US and the EU (Gaskell et al, 2001b) despite differing attitudes to GM food. In addition, trust varied widely within Europe; it seems to be more determined by differences in national attitudes towards government than by specific (bio)technology-related issues (for an analysis of trust in information see Kohring et al, this volume). Hence, the proposed attitude variables fall short in attempting to explain the observed policy shift.

Another factor mentioned by Bernauer and Meins (2003) is NGO campaigns. However, their presence is not necessarily reflected in the political impact they have. Most NGO activists have experienced futile campaigns yielding few results. Rather, we must look for the repercussions or 'ripples' (Kasperson et al, 2001, p20, in his outline about 'stigma') they elicit and search for triggers that kicked off debates.

The role of public outrage in policy shift

In the following, we will discuss, addressing five themes, the observed policy shift in order to learn more about the role of public outrage. First, we will address the question of whether there was a single trigger that initiated the debate across Europe. Then we will discuss whether the policy shift can be understood as a result of coordinated NGO action. Third, we will look at the content of the controversy and discuss whether food risk really was the central issue of the debate. Fourth, we will ask who the addressees of the protest were and how they reacted, and fifth, we will discuss how sustainable the policy shift was. Finally, we will develop an explanatory framework that aims to explain our observations.

GM soya beans: the trigger for public outrage?

The event that is widely held as being the decisive trigger of the GM controversies (Lassen et al, 2002) was the attempted import of genetically modified soya beans from the US to the EU in November 1996. When the first ships with the new high-technology crops reached European harbours, there were reactions from what could be called a European public. Media analysis showed a huge increase in reporting about biotechnology after 1996 in many European countries (Bauer et al, 2001), the import of GM crops from the US being a prominent issue.

A closer look at public reactions across Europe suggests, however, that there was no universal pattern. In some EU member states such as Greece and Denmark, this mobilization started late in 1996 (Sakellaris and Chatjouli, 2001; Jelsøe et al, 2001). In other European countries, however, the import of GM soya beans produced only limited reactions. A little later, in 1997, a second event created significant media attention for biotechnology: the birth of Dolly the cloned sheep (Einsiedel et al, 2002). On the surface, this had nothing to do with GM crops, but in France and Italy the societal debates about biotechnology – including GM crops – only took off after this second trigger event (Boy and de Cheveigné, 2001; Allansdottir et al, 2001). Reactions were also triggered by events at national rather than international level. For example, the Austrian public had already been mobilized in spring 1996 when, as part of Austria's first release experiment, the GM plants had been sown before the company had received permission (Grabner and Torgersen, 1998). There, the arrival of genetically modified soya on European shores from the US only promoted an ongoing debate.

The hypothesis that the import of GM soya beans served as a universal trigger for societal conflicts on agricultural biotechnology in all European member states does not explain the variation of the development of debates on biotechnology across Europe. It could be said that there was no single trigger event for the whole of Europe, although GM soya played an important role. Specific conditions in the various European countries heavily influenced public reactions to agricultural biotechnology. In addition, it was not only the import of soya beans that served as an international trigger for debates on agricultural biotechnology, but also the announcement of the birth of the first cloned mammal, Dolly the sheep (Einsiedel et al, 1992).

Coordinated NGO action

If there was no universal trigger, why did agricultural biotechnology suddenly receive so much negative press coverage in many European countries? Was this coincidence, or was an internationally coordinated NGO campaign responsible?

In 1996, Greenpeace, the biggest international environmental NGO, started to campaign against agricultural biotechnology all over Europe. However, its attempts were only partly successful. Greenpeace became the dominant actor in very diverse countries such as Germany and Greece. In other EU member states, despite active campaigning, other – mostly domestic – NGOs were more influential in the national debates. This was particularly striking in France, where Greenpeace campaigns in November 1996 remained without any major effect. Rather, it was the national Confédération Paysanne, originally a leftist farmers' trade union, which took up NGO issues and strategies (Boy and de Cheveigné, 2001) and became the dominant actor. In Denmark, a coalition of domestic NGOs outperformed Greenpeace by far in dominating the growing controversy. Similarly, in Austria a national NGO was at least as important as Greenpeace. Initially in Germany, despite its being a country with strong NGOs, there was hardly any political mobilization of the public against biotechnology.

However, there were some surprises. While NGOs, according to the outrage concept, exert pressure through public opinion and force a change in policies, in some countries governments acted without visible influence from NGOs. In France, the Conservative government took a more restrictive course without widespread NGO mobilization of the public. After the government changed, in May 1997, the prime minister's decision not to authorize the cultivation of GM maize – initially a French proposal – in February 1997 'was the one event which most catalysed the ensuing controversy on GM crops' (Marris, 2000, p26). The French government then linked the fate of GM crops to the outcome of a citizens' conference organized in June 1998, which resulted in moderate support for agricultural biotechnology and two marketing permits that the government later withdrew (Boy and de Cheveigné, 2001). This seems to indicate that, ironically, it was the public (if one may consider a lay panel as a surrogate public) that opted for a less restrictive policy, while government resumed a more restrictive line. Likewise, in Italy, activities in the arena of formal policy making were mirrored, but not preceded, by growing resistance movements. The Italian Environment Minister topped an increasingly restrictive policy with a ban on GM maize in March 1997 with comparatively little pressure to do so from outside (Allansdottir et al, 2001). These French and Italian instances show that it is not easy to differentiate between a situation where NGOs put pressure on government in order to change policy, and situations where more restrictive regulation is a genuine part of the agenda of politicians. NGOs were clearly in the driving seat in many countries, and policy would not have developed the way it did without NGO campaigns.

A third argument comes from survey work: the critical European public attitude towards GM food preceded the events of late 1996 (Gaskell et al, 2002). It is justifiable to say that the latter only boosted rejection, mediated and highlighted by NGOs. The development of the biotechnology debates in Europe indicates that the capacity of NGOs to initiate a mobilization process, that is, to set the agenda, is limited. Rather, NGOs succeeded in stirring up the policy agenda. While NGOs clearly played a role, there are obviously reasons for the observed policy shift other than internationally coordinated protest activities.[3]

GM food risk as the universal issue

The outrage argument suggests that risk is the major factor for public outrage, and food-related risks have proven to be the most tangible ones. Indeed, in most countries, protest activities centred on postulated risks from genetically modified food. Campaigns went far beyond risk and addressed topics such as the environment, consumer rights and the freedom of choice. In addition, more locally specific topics were of high importance. In countries such as France and Italy, globalization issues and the fight against international companies and for a national (food) culture added another layer.

This was seen especially in France, where, after 1998, anti-GM groups, in particular the Confédération Paysanne of José Bové, combined resistance to agricultural biotechnology, the threat of 'McDonaldization' for the French food culture and issues associated with the WTO (Boy and de Cheveigné, 2001). Aspects of autonomy of culture and cuisine were at least as strong arguments as the risk to human health to be assessed by natural science. In Austria and other countries that had more recently joined the EU, another aspect of campaigns was the conflict between newly EU-derived regulation and familiar national regulation. It resulted in tensions about the remaining national sovereignty and provided ample opportunity for politicians to seek the villain in hostile Brussels.

In summary, rather than publics in different countries being outraged by the same general issue, we find different topics in different countries and at various times. Nationally derived themes such as EU versus national regulation or the cultural competition between America and Europe played a major role. The main role of NGOs was to bring very distant issues under the umbrella of biotechnology and link them to risk arguments, with the result that a large variety of arguments got onto the agenda and remained there for a while.

In the national laws as well as within the framework of European regulation, protection from risks is central. It seems as if part of the importance of the risk argument stems from the fact that other issues addressed in the campaigns could not be legitimately conveyed to the regulatory system, either nationally or at the EU level. Hence, postulating risks, especially from food, was the only way for NGOs to successfully challenge biotechnology regulation (for an elaboration of the argument see Torgersen et al, 2002a).

The linking of biotechnology to other issues nevertheless was a necessary element in the campaigns. In a similar way to the struggle about AIDS (Rosenbrock and Schaeffer, 2002), the issue remained salient as long as it stayed in the phase of 'exceptionalism'. As soon as normalization held sway, biotechnology disappeared from the agenda, as with many applications in the medical field. In order to keep it on the agenda, it had to be linked to various topics that had a potential to be viewed as 'exceptional' for various reasons. This was subject to national contingencies, and therefore differed from one country to another. Consequently, demands and possible solutions differed as well. Hence, biotechnology became a sounding board for very diverse societal concerns (Torgersen et al, 2002a).

The addressees of protests

According to Luhmann (1998, p853), protest movements only exist (apart from religious systems) in functional systems that have established their own centre, for example in the political system. In fact, studies have shown the political sector to be the addressees of protest activities pertaining to political issues (Rucht, 1995). Accordingly, we may assume that in the conflict on GM food as well, the addressee of NGOs is politics. However, in this case a remarkable shift took place over time. The political sector continued to be an addressee in countries where this proved effective, that is, where important actors within this sector took up the issue and gained from the protests, such as in France, Greece or Italy. In most places where there were no influential accession points within the system, however, the protest looked for other targets.

Towards the end of the 1990s, most international NGOs concentrated their activities on food retailers. They turned out to be the strategic weak point of the biotechnology sector, since in most countries there are only a few supermarket chains with fierce competition and a low profit rate, and they depend on consumer trust.[4] Thus, they are highly susceptible to NGO activities. In Austria, NGOs had already joined forces with three big retail chains in a working group on GM-free food in 1997. In March 1999, retail chains in France, Belgium, the UK, Ireland and Italy announced that they would not market GM products under their own brand names. This increased the pressure on domestic food retailers in other countries. In Germany, Greenpeace gained enormously in profile by organizing a consumer network and initiating activities to 'observe the market'.

NGOs were successful in keeping genetically modified food away from the average European consumer. Ironically, this meant GM food could not serve as a trigger for action. The mutual control of retailers resulted not only in their being able to control the producers, but also in a moratorium for such products. Thus, the interests of producers and retailers were successfully divided and there was no common 'industry interest' any more. Bernauer and Meins (2003) used this division as a main argument in their explanation for the more restrictive regulation in the EU as compared to the US. However, such an alliance must have been fragile as interests diverge even without GM products.

NGO arguments gained political importance not so much through direct NGO pressure on regulators but through (often involuntary) alliances with retailers and some producers. Also, established industry channels were used to influence policy makers. Hence, by being able to use part of industry's more traditional means of lobbying, NGOs gained access, albeit indirect, to policy that would normally have been closed to them.

Patterns of reaction to critique

At first glance, the political system reacted to the perceived societal pressure whereby mobilization activities were successful. To meet the critique, governments devised measures that conveyed the impression of 'giving in'. In some instances, new bodies were established, for example in Britain (Gaskell et al, 2001c), or critics were invited onto existing committees. The Greek case may provide an extreme example, where opposition succeeded in imposing a rather restrictive biotechnology policy. It culminated in the appointment of a former leader of Greenpeace Greece as the Vice-Minister for the Environment responsible for issues of biotechnology (Sakellaris and Chatjouli, 2001). Some governments, however, implemented stricter regulations without pressure from outside.

Actors in favour of biotechnology tried to cope with what they perceived as societal pressure. The problem of counter-activities was often that strategies and interests differed according to actors. For example, in such campaigns it was not easy to reconcile the views of government, scientists, food retailers, the food producing industry and various kinds of farmers.

At the public discourse level, governments pursued a variety of counter-strategies to balance the influence NGOs seemed to have gained. Those aimed at 'educating' the public, i.e. at replacing what was seen as scaremongering in conjunction with tabloid newspapers by, in the elites' eyes, unbiased scientific information mostly failed to significantly influence public opinion (Gaskell et al, 2001a).

Attempts to actively counter-mobilize the public in favour of biotechnology by common business strategies proved to be of limited value as well. Monsanto's US\$ 2 million advertising campaign in Britain and France had the reverse effect and attitudes against GM crops hardened even more. Among the more successful initiatives was the German government's BioRegio contest in the mid 1990s. It linked biotechnology, competitiveness and job creation with the aim of stimulating local innovation networks. At the same time, government tried to keep agricultural biotechnology out of public and political controversy, to gain time and to prevent activities that might endanger measures to promote industrial and research competitiveness. The Swiss scientific community made even more successful steps towards counter-mobilization when they fought, with silent but potent help from industry, against a referendum that threatened to put heavy restrictions not only on GM food but also on animal experimentation for medical research (Bonfadelli et al, 2001). The issue of GM food was deliberately kept at a low profile in order not to jeopardize the effect that could be elicited by stressing the point of industrial and scientific competitiveness (see Grabner et al, 2001). Hence, counter-strategists seemed to be more successful if they tried, as far as possible, to keep the reference to GM food minimal, taking into account the fact that negative attitudes were deeply entrenched.

However, whether governments only reacted to the pressure or had a will of their own often remains a matter of interpretation. In some cases, counter-strategies were proactive: in Denmark, government started to deliberate on how to deal with GM soya in spring 1996, at a time when the topic was not yet salient (Jelsøe et al, 2001). The regulatory discourse, which preceded any conflicts, had a significant contribution from the Danish parliament and focused on labelling and organic farming (Lassen et al, 2002). The Danish regulators were quite successful in closing the debate but, just as in Italy and France, the burgeoning public controversy on cloning that followed the announcement of Dolly the sheep brought the topic of biotechnology, including GM food, firmly back onto the agenda again.

Although NGO arguments were nowhere entirely and openly dismissed, European countries differed in the degree to which critical voices were taken seriously and their arguments influenced policy making. In some countries, any reference amounted to lip service only.

Sustainable policy shift

Even prior to 1996, European countries' biotechnology policies were anything but uniform. Although virtually all European governments embraced the motto 'make biotechnology happen', the means differed considerably. Even Austria, considered to be the most recalcitrant and disobedient to EU regulatory harmo-nization concerning GM products, can be seen as adhering to the make-it-happen paradigm. By sacrificing the relatively unimportant agricultural biotechnology sector, untenable anyway in a country with the highest share of organic agriculture in the EU, medical biotechnology acquired the chance to go undisputed (Seifert and Torgersen, 1997).

After 1996, not all countries in Europe turned 'hostile' to GM crops. For example, the Netherlands struggled to pursue its supportive policy (Gutteling et al, 2001). Germany, without publicly backing GM crops, tried to keep on the biotechnology track too, although the topic was very controversially discussed within the German government coalition, with Social Democrats in favour of biotechnology and the Greens opposing it. Among the member states that adopted a more restrictive policy, such as Denmark and Italy, many had already been less supportive than the European average before 1996. Others, like Greece, had had no particular position on GM crops at all and developed their own policy for the first time (Sakellaris and Chatjouli, 2001). The UK took measures that would partly give in to critics while still considering agricultural biotechnology an asset that should not be abandoned, and therefore devised measures to reconcile critical voices and industry interests (Gaskell et al, 2001a). The most significant shift could be observed in France, where policy changed from being highly supportive for GM crops before 1997 to becoming somewhat inconsistently restrictive (Boy and de Cheveigné, 2001; Marris, 2000).

France as a major player, together with some other member states, moved the centre of gravity in the EU towards more restrictions, so that by the end of the 1990s an outside observer might have got the impression that there was a general, deliberate and consistent policy shift. The new Release and Marketing Directive 2002/18 explicitly cited the precautionary principle and apparently imposed new far-reaching demands for new permits, which could be taken as an indication of a generally restrictive policy. Taking into account the campaigns of international NGOs seemingly coordinated across Europe, the negative reporting of tabloid newspapers in a relatively large number of countries and the cautious statements of individual policy makers virtually everywhere, one could come to the conclusion that policy, indeed, has been driven by NGOs via public mobilization.

However, the ends apparently had not changed. Commission officials fre-quently stated that the new Directive only served to clarify certain aspects and that the substantial difference to the old Directive was small indeed (Marris, 2001). The justification as to why the Commission considered the new Directive and additional regulation on labelling and traceability necessary followed the same rationale as previously. It aimed

> to address the concerns of Member States and to build consumer confidence in the authorization of GM products. The revised Directive (2002/18) and the adoption of the two proposals for Regulations are expected to pave the way for a resumption of GM authorizations in the European Union. (Crop Biotech Update 2002)

Similar to measures taken in many member states, the new Directive tried to deal with some of the critics' concerns in order to pave the way for a new round of GM products.

The difference lies in the means. While the old Directive 90/220 more or less followed the rhetoric of 'exploiting chances while preventing risks', the new Directive puts more emphasis on 'dealing with uncertainties' and the more reflexive governance approach that has been hallmarked in the European Commission's White Paper 'Science and Society' (2001). The new argumentation acknowledged the role of civil society and the legitimacy of different preferences without giving up the overall aim making biotechnology happen. There is little evidence to support the view that the policy shift also included the ends, and not only the means.

To summarize:

1   Although the attempt by Monsanto to import GM soya into Europe was important, it cannot be described as the single trigger event that sparked the debate about GM crops and food in Europe.
2   The capacity of NGOs to set the agenda is limited. To be successful, efforts aimed at public mobilization only seem to work if the public has grown susceptible as a result of other, independent events. Rather than being in the driving seat, NGOs often jumped on the bandwagon.
3   Instead of a general issue salient in all countries, nationally derived topics played a major role for as long as they remained 'exceptional', and biotechnology became a sounding board for very diverse societal concerns.
4   Apart from disrupting the association of upstream and downstream producers, NGOs succeeded in gaining indirect access to policy makers through industry lobbying.
5   Although NGO arguments were not openly dismissed anywhere, countries differed in the degree to which NGOs influenced policy making.
6   Like measures in member states, the new EU Directive tried to deal with some concerns in order to pave the way for new GM marketing proposals. The rationale was revised without giving up the aim of making biotechnology happen.

Public outrage or mobilization

The concept of public outrage, in the form of increased risk perception, lack of trust in institutions and the presence of NGO campaigns, falls short in explaining the policy shift in European agricultural biotechnology policy after 1996. As an alternative to 'outrage', we propose an interpretative concept of mobilization.

We understand mobilization to be a process where members of the public are induced to actively support, by various means, the aims of the pertinent (NGO) campaign and contribute to bring about a policy shift according to the aims of the campaigner. Mobilization is a social process where attitudes are central. In our understanding, it therefore refers not only to the measurable activities of mobilized people, and to the level and framing of media reporting, but also to the mental processes that enable individuals, or enhance their readiness, to take action without necessarily or immediately leading to action.[5] According to our understanding, visible activity is a special case of mobilization.

Because visible mobilization can seriously impede the addressee, it has to be avoided. Potential addressees therefore observe their environment to detect developments that may lead to mobilizing activities. From their perspective, the perception that mobilization is likely to occur may have the same effect as visible acts of mobilization. Therefore, mobilization does not necessarily have to be visible in order to elicit consequences.

Actors with an interest in mobilizing the public can only succeed if they touch upon pre-existing social representations (Wagner et al, 2001, 2002) within relevant parts of the public (Torgersen et al, 2002). The pattern of attitudes prevalent after 1996 in many European countries provided a resource for critical groups to tap into and to achieve tacit support from elements of the public.[6] Measures of public attitudes through quantitative surveys over years have consistently shown that, across the whole of Europe, the public has held ambivalent or even negative views on agricultural biotechnology, and that the general support for this technology has declined between 1996 and 1999 (Gaskell et al, 2001a, 2003).

But surveys measure attitudes and not activity. Even if people agree in an interview that they will take action, this cannot be taken for granted. The same surveys showed that the overall salience of the issue was lower than one would have suspected. According to the data of Eurobarometer 58.0 from 2002, more than half of the respondents had not talked about biotechnology before the interview. Biotechnology is obviously not a subject of everyday communication, so it is no surprise that visible indications of public mobilization could hardly be observed. There were few mass events such as demonstrations, strikes, real consumer boycotts[7] or similar activities in Europe.[8]

Since the membership of a big environmental NGO is usually large but very varied and not always interested in the issue of a particular campaign, it is necessary to produce events that find resonance in the media (see Wolfsfeld, 1997; Kriesi, 2001). Therefore, NGOs need trigger events – not necessarily the same in every country – as well as suitable media coverage in a mobilization-promoting way. Activities were restricted to events that were 'staged' to elicit attention and subsequent media reporting (Seifert, 2002).

Through media coverage, arguments and their interpretation of events are brought to the attention of a wider public, elicit attention and become amplified (Renn, 1992), which then may lead to action.[9] Media report an event mostly if this taps into existing or emerging representations and 'meets a demand'. They amplify its relevance and, at the same time, enhance their own performance (Kohring, 1997). If an event is designed, or framed in the media in retrospect, in such a way that it sends a message coinciding with a pattern of widely held interests, perceptions, beliefs or value judgements among the general public, then mobilization may ensue. It is a matter of resonance between parts of the public, interest-mediating organizations such as NGOs or others (Rucht, 2001), media and parts of the political system. 'Under mobilization, activated people by and large endorse the demands of a particular group and eventually carry on the message in different forms of social communication' (Torgersen and Hampel, 2002b, p22). NGOs are successful in 'mobilizing' the public only when important parts of it are ready to be mobilized.

In the late 1990s, there had to be a point in time that was favourable for fighting GM crops and food.[10] Several scandals had revealed what ignorance of public distrust could entail. In particular, the regulatory crisis around bovine spongiform encephalopathy (BSE) shortly before had shown the political and economic consequences of an irritated public. In the UK, media reaction to the so-called Pusztai affair[11] had made it clear that there is no use in attempting to contain the debate (e.g., to scientific criteria only) in mitigating the conflict once it has reached a certain level (Durant and Lindsay, 1999). Most governments' traditional counter-strategies of reassuring the public by means of expert advice had proved futile. Surveys have shown that NGOs commanded more trust than most governmental experts (Gaskell et al, 2001a) adhering, for the most part, to the imperative to make biotechnology happen.

Representing general societal values, it was important for NGOs to be seen to be speaking for the public. Kitschelt (1991, p334) in his evolutionary approach assumes that social movements find viable collective strategies in a process of trial and error. In the case we have described, they brought existing attitudes to light. Social movements do not invent strategies but, by suggesting appropriate framings and providing arguments, they have amplified and reified social representations and turned them into salient issues. Instead of 'creating' mobilization, NGOs enhanced, steered and exploited the process. All this has rarely resulted in mass action. It is therefore difficult to assess how 'real' the mobilization was.

Mobilization as a social construct

We have already argued that a potential addressee will – preferably proactively – avoid mobilization because it reduces the addressee's capacity for action. In order to be relevant, therefore, it is of little importance whether mobilization really 'exists' or not. It is more important that relevant political actors think that mobilization does, or probably will, occur. To paraphrase the Thomas theorem (Merton, 1995), mobilization 'happens' if relevant social actors agree that it exists. Upon suggestion from the media, industry, NGOs, and so on, relevant regulators might assume that a certain pattern of public attitudes will probably turn, or has already turned, into mobilization. The same may be the case if there are similar events in other countries or in related policy fields. They would proactively devise measures to prevent any pending mobilization. This is supported by the observation that sometimes governments take decisions that appear to be an answer to massive and powerful public protest despite the obvious lack of it. In such a case, mobilization may only 'exist' in the press, in regulatory discourses and in the minds of political actors; it may be imagined and, yet, politically relevant.

This gives room for further considerations: in the absence of visible action and extensive or sensational media reporting, mobilization might have occurred without policy makers having taken notice of it; or they might have grossly underestimated it. Thinking one step further, actors in favour of implementing agricultural biotechnology such as the seed company Monsanto could have based their attempt to ship GM soya to Europe on the assumption that the possible mobilization their advisors might have warned of was only imagined. They could have interpreted proactive moves against them by some governments as an attempt to intercept a potential mobilization. However, in the eyes of Monsanto, there were no clues that mobilization was real. At the time of the pending import of the US-grown crops, there was no open and massive public protest as an indicator of reality; neither were there powerful actors that had taken up the issue. However, very soon Monsanto found out that mobilization was real indeed, with devastating results for them.

Demobilization

In order to cope with the procedural character, it is important to look at mobilization also in the context of demobilizing strategies. Since it was in the interest of regulators and industry to prevent a sustained mobilization of the public and to regain consumers' trust, they devised a range of strategies. In contrast to more aggressive moves towards 'winning the hearts of the consumers' through advertising or to initiatives aimed at the public understanding of science, a strategy of 'duck and cover' and keeping the issue out of the headlines proved to be more rewarding.

Therefore, as an alternative to an understanding that sees the observed policy shift as the result of the collective action potential of anti-biotechnology NGOs turned into political pressure, this shift can also be seen as a move to prevent sustained public mobilization. Similarly, we may understand the decision of retail chains not to put GM products on their shelves, if only for a period of time, as part of a 'duck and cover' strategy to gain time until the issue of GM food loses its status of exceptionality.

From the perspective of today, this strategy has both succeeded and failed. It has succeeded in removing the issues from the headlines. Towards the end of the 1990s, the frequency of reports on food and biotechnology had already declined rapidly (Bauer et al, 2001).[12] The public was apparently exhausted and the issue had lost its salience, not least due to the absence of GM food on Europe's grocery shelves. It failed, however, with respect to a change in public perception: the image of GM food does not seem to have significantly improved; rather, it has stabilized on a rather low level (Gaskell et al, 2003).

In Europe, the biotechnology landscape has since focused on medical rather than agricultural applications (Ernst & Young, 2001), forging public attitudes into industry structures. On the regulatory level, the moratorium is slowly fading out under the new European Directive. However, new issues such as traceability and coexistence of GM and non-GM agriculture have entered the regulatory arena, again assigning a new quality of exceptionality to the issue of GM crops and food. Mobilization, it seems, has gone to sleep but may rise at any time.

Notes

1 In contrast to Bernauer and Meins (2003), who consider the European policy on agricultural biotechnology to have constantly grown more restrictive during the 1990s, we consider the events of 1996/97 as a 'watershed' (Torgersen et al., 2002a) with respect to both public opinion and policy. We agree with Bandelow (1999) that European policy between 1992 and 1996 had slowly grown more permissive and, after 1996, became more restrictive.

2 This chapter is one outcome from a series of investigations made under the EU-funded projects 'Biotechnology in the European Public'; 'European Debates on Biotechnology' and 'Life Science in the European Society', where a group of international researchers (including the authors) looked at the development of public opinion, media coverage and policy on biotechnology in Europe.

3 Bernauer and Meins (2003) reject the hypothesis that the more restrictive policy in the EU was due to protectionist intentions, since the rejection of biotechnology in agriculture affected European companies as well, and the import of GM soy and maize would not have touched major domestic European agricultural interests anyway.

4 Such as Sainsbury and Marks & Spencer (in the UK), Carrefour (in France), Superquinn (in Ireland), Migros (in Switzerland), Delhaiz (in Belgium) and Effelunga (in Italy).

5 This is in part-analogy to the martial meaning of mobilization, where the potential for combat is increased without implying that anybody is already involved in fighting. Unlike military mobilization, however, social mobilization as an enhanced readiness to engage is not easily visible.

6 In the light of such attitudes, it becomes understandable that those who wanted to support biotechnology, or to 'make it happen', abstained from ringing the bell by eliciting a broad public debate. So, contrary to frequent declarations of intent, many governments meticulously avoided biotechnology becoming a topic of public debate unless they could sit in the driving seat.

7 With the exception of the 'Einkaufsnetzwerk' that Greenpeace organized in Germany; there, consumers signed a list indicating that they would not buy genetically modified food.

8 Closest to a traditional understanding of mass mobilization came the situation in France, where the Confédération Paysanne organized demonstrations, etc.

9 Studies on New Social Movements therefore often take media coverage as an indicator for the salience of a topic and for the mobilization of the public. Analysts assess mobilization according to the number of events reported or people actively taking part in them (Rucht, 1995, 2001). While we would not agree that public debate is identical to media reporting and mobilization akin to the frequency of coverage, the latter is an important indicator.

10 Food scandals such as that around bovine spongiform encephalopathy (BSE) had paved the way for consumers to become highly aware both of potential risks and of discrepancies in experts' assessments, and thus eroded trust in mainstream expert advice. This made it much easier to depict such advice as being interest-driven. In fact, this was a generic phenomenon that had effects on debates about topics as different as gene transfer and allergenicity, environmental impacts on agriculture and undesired effects on beneficial insects.

11 Arpad Pusztai, a British toxicologist, had informed the press without seeking permission from laboratory officials over his preliminary and non-peer-reviewed findings indicating possible adverse effects of feeding GM potatoes to animals. When

it was alleged that he had not conducted the experiments appropriately, he was suspended and eventually lost his job. Some 'counter-experts' collected signatures for an open letter in defence and elicited a huge press campaign (Parliamentary Office of Science and Technology, 2000).

12 For example, a database search reveals that the number of pertaining articles from the British quality newspapers the *Observer* and the *Guardian* went down from 574 in 1999 to 326 in 2000 and 182 in 2001. This indicates a closing of the issue cycle on biotechnology and food, at least in the UK.

References

Allansdottir, A. et al (2001) 'Italy: From moral hazards to a cautious take on risks', in Gaskell, G. and Bauer, M. (eds) *Biotechnology 1996–2000: The Years of Controversy*, Science Museum, London, pp215–228

Bandelow, N. C. (1999) *Advocacy-Koalitionen und politischer Wandel am Beispiel der Gentechnologiepolitik*, edition sigma, Berlin

Bauer, M. W., Kohring, M., Allansdottir, A. and Gutteling, J. (2001) 'The dramatisation of biotechnology in elite mass media', in Gaskell, G. and Bauer, M. W. (eds) *Biotechnology 1996–2000: The Years of Controversy*, Science Museum, London, pp35–52

Bernauer, Th. and Meins, E. (2003) 'Technological revolution meets policy and the market: Explaining cross-national differences in agricultural biotechnology regulation', *European Journal of Political Research*, vol 42, no 5, pp643–683

Bonfadelli, H. et al. (2001) 'Biotechnology in Switzerland: From street demonstrations to Regulations', *Biotechnology 1996–2000: The Years of Controversy*, in Gaskell, G. and Bauer, M. (eds) Science Museum, pp282–291

Boy, D. and de Cheveigné, S. (2001) 'Biotechnology: A menace to French food', *Biotechnology 1996–2000: The Years of Controversy*, in Gaskell, G. and Bauer, M/ (eds) Science Museum Press, London, pp181–190

Budd, R. (1993) *The Uses of Life: A History of Biotechnology*, Cambridge University Press, Cambridge

Cantley, M. (1995) 'The regulation of modern biotechnology: A historical and European perspective', in Brauer, D. (ed.) *Biotechnology*, vol 12, VCH, New York, pp505–681

Crop Biotech Update (2002) *EU-Stalemate on GM Labeling and Traceability*, 30 October

Durant, J., Bauer, M. W. and Gaskell, G. (1998) *Biotechnology in the Public Sphere: A European Sourcebook*, Science Museum, London

Durant, J. and Lindsay, N. (1999) *The Great GM Food Debate*, Report to the House of Lords Select Committee on Science and Technology, Science Museum, London

Einsiedel, E. et al. (2002) 'Brave new sheep – The clone named Dolly', in Bauer, M. W. and Gaskell, G. (eds) *Biotechnology – The making of a global controversy*, Cambridge, Cambridge University Press, pp313–347

Ernst & Young (2001) *Integration*, Ernst & Young's Eigth Annual European Life Sciences Report, Ernst & Young, London

Gaskell, G. and Bauer, M. W. (eds) (2000) 'The years of controversy', in Gaskell, G. and Bauer, M. (eds) *Biotechnology 1996–2000: The Years of Controversy*, Science Museum, London

Gaskell, G., Bauer, M. and Durant, J. (eds) (1998) *Biotechnology in the Public Sphere*, Science Museum, London, pp3–12

Gaskell, G. et al (2001a) 'In the public eye: Representations of biotechnology in Europe', in Gaskell, G. and Bauer, M. (eds) *Biotechnology 1996–2000: The Years of Controversy*, Science Museum, London, pp53–79

Gaskell, G. et al (2001b) 'Troubled waters: The Atlantic divide on biotechnology policy', in Gaskell, G. and Bauer, M. (eds) *Biotechnology 1996–2000: The Years of Controversy*, Science Museum, London, pp96–115

Gaskell, G. et al (2001c) 'United Kingdom: Spilling the beans on genes', in Gaskell, G. and Bauer, M. (eds) *Biotechnology 1996–2000: The Years of Controversy*, Science Museum, London, pp292–306

Gaskell, G., Thompson, P. and Allum, N. (2002) 'Worlds apart? Public opinion in Europe and the USA', in Bauer, M. W. and Gaskell, G. (eds) *Biotechnology: The Making of a Global Controversy*, Cambridge University Press, Cambridge, pp351–375

Gaskell, G. et al. (2003) *Europeans and Biotechnology in 2002, Eurobarometer 58.0* (2nd edition: 21 March), A report to the EC Directorate General for Research from the project 'Life Sciences in European Society' QLG7-CT-1999-00286

Grabner, P. et al (2001) 'Biopolitical diversity: The challenge of multilevel policy-making', in Gaskell, G. and Bauer, M. (eds) *Biotechnology 1996–2000: The Years of Controversy*, Science Museum Press, London, pp15–34

Grabner, P. and Torgersen, H. (1998) 'Gentechnik in Österreich – Technikkritik versus Modernisierung' in Wächter, Ch. (ed.) *Technik Gestalten. Interdisziplinäre Beiträge zu Technikforschung und Technologiepolitik*, Profil, Munich, pp209–223

Gutteling, J. et al. (2001) 'The Netherlands: Controversy or consensus?' in Gaskell, G. and Bauer, M. (eds) *Biotechnology 1996–2000: The Years of Controversy*, Science Museum Press, London, pp229–236

Jasanoff, S. (1995) 'Product, process or programme: Three cultures and the regulation of biotechnology', in Bauer, M. (ed) *Resistance to New Technology: Nuclear Power, Information Technology and Biotechnology*, Cambridge University Press, Cambridge, pp311–331

Jelsøe, E. et al (2001) 'Denmark: The revival of national controversy over biotechnology', in in Gaskell, G. and Bauer, M. (eds) *Biotechnology 1996–2000: The Years of Controversy*, Science Museum Press, London, pp157–171

Kasperson, R.E. et al (2001) 'Stigma and the social amplification of risk', in Flynn, J., Slovic, P. and Kunreuther, H. (eds) *Risk, Media and Stigma*, London and Sterling, VA, Earthscan

Kitschelt, H. (1991) 'Critique of the resource mobilization approach', in Rucht, D. (ed) *Research on Social Movements: The State of the Art in Western Europe and the USA*, Campus and Westview Press, Boulder, CO, pp323–347

Kohring, M. (1997) *Die Funktion des Wissenschaftsjournalismus: Ein systemtheoretischer Entwurf*, Westdeutscher Verlag, Opladen

Kriesi, H. (2001) *Die Rolle der Öffentlichkeit im politischen Entscheidungsprozess: Ein konzeptueller Rahmen für ein international vergleichendes Forschungsprojekt*, Berlin, WZB working paper P01-701

Lassen, J. et al (2002) 'Testing times – The reception of Roundup Ready soya in Europe', in Bauer, M. W. and Gaskell, G. (eds) *Biotechnology: The Making of a Global Controversy*, Cambridge, Cambridge University Press, pp 279–212.

Luhmann, N. (1998) *Die Gesellschaft der Gesellschaft*, 2 vols, Suhrkamp, Frankfurt am Main

Marris, C. (2000) Swings and roundabouts: 'French public policy on agricultural GMO since 1996', *Notizie di Politeia*, vol 16, no 60, pp22–37

Marris, C. (2001) *Public Views on GMOs: Deconstructing Myths*, EMBO reports, vol 2, no 7, pp545–548

Merton, R. K. (1995) 'The Thomas theorem and the Matthew effect', *Social Forces*, vol 2, no 74, pp379–424

Parliamentary Office of Science and Technology (ed) (2000) *The Great GM Food Debate: A Survey of Media Coverage in the First Half of 1999*, POST Report 138, May

Renn, O. (1992) 'The social arena concept of risk debates', in Krimsky, S. and Golding, G. (eds) *Social Theories of Risk*, Praeger, Westport, CT, and London, pp179–195

Rosenbrock, R. and Schaeffer, D. (eds) (2002) *Die Normalisierung von Aids: Politik – Prävention – Krankenversorgung. Ergebnisse sozialwissenschaftlicher Aids-Forschung*, vol 23, Berlin, edition sigma

Rucht, D. (ed) (1995) *Research on Social Movements: The State of the Art in Western Europe and the USA*, Campus, Frankfurt, and Westview, Boulder, CO

Rucht, D. (2001) 'Protest und Protestereignisanalyse: Einleitende Bemerkungen', in Rucht, D. (ed.) *Protest in der Bundesrepublik. Strukturen und Entwicklungen*, Campus, Frankfurt and New York, pp7–25

Sakellaris, G. and Chatjouli, A. (2001) 'Greece: losing faith in biotechnology', in Gaskell, G. and Bauer, M. (eds) *Biotechnology 1996–2000: The Years of Controversy*, Science Museum Press, London, pp204–214

Seifert, F. (2000) 'Österreichs Biotechnologiepolitik im EU-Mehrebenensystem – Zu Effectivität öffentlichen Widerstandes im supranationalen Gefüge', in Barben, D. and Abels, G. (eds) *Biotechnologie und Globalisierung – Politische Gestaltungsmöglichkeiten transnationaler Technologieentwicklung*, Sigma, Berlin, pp313–332

Seifert, F. (2002) *Gentechnik – Offenlichkeit – Demokratie. Der österreichische Gentechnik-Konflikt im internationalen Kontext*, Profil, Munich

Seifert, F. and Torgersen, H. (1997) 'How to keep out what we don't want – An assessment of "Sozialverträglichkeit" under the Austrian Genetic Engineering Act', *Public Understanding of Science*, vol 6, no 2, pp301–327

Torgersen, H. (2002) 'Austria and the transatlantic agricultural biotechnology divide', *Science Communications*, vol 24, no 2, pp173–183

Torgersen, H. and Bogner, A. (2005) 'Austria's agri-biotechnology regulation: Political consensus despite divergent concepts of precaution', *Science and Public Policy*, vol 32, no 4, pp277–284

Torgersen, H. et al (2002a) 'Promises, problems and proxies: 25 years of European biotech debate and regulation', in Bauer, M. W. and Gaskell, G. (eds) *Biotechnology: The Making of a Global Controversy*, Cambridge University Press, Cambridge, pp21–94

Torgersen, H. et al (2002b) *The Gate/Resonance Model: The Interface of Policy, Media and the Public in Technology Conflicts*, ITA manuscript http://www.oeaw.ac.at/ita/pdf/ita_01_03.pdf

Wagner, W. et al (2001) 'Nature in disorder: The troubled public of biotechnology', in Gaskell, G. and Bauer, M. W. (eds) *Biotechnology 1996–2000: The Years of Controversy*, Science Museum, London, pp80–95

Wagner, W., Kronberger, N. and Seifert, F. (2002) 'Collective symbolic coping with new technology: Knowledge, images and public discourse', *British Journal of Social Psychology*, vol 41, pp323–343

Wolfsfeld, G. (1997) *Media and Political Conflict: News from the Middle East*, Cambridge University Press, Cambridge

7

The Coming of Age of Public Participation

Edna Einsiedel and Mercy Wambui Kamara
with additional assistance from Daniel Boy, Urs Dahinden,
Carmen Diego, and Nicola Lindsey and Arne Mortensen

For the past several decades, the grand narratives of biotechnology as a key pillar in the knowledge-based economy or in national innovation strategies have pervaded policy documents in many countries. The visions promoted in many of these policy papers have centred on the rapidly advancing knowledge and its impact on individual organisms and ecosystems, with consequences from agriculture and food production, to medicine, forestry, and environmental resources and protection. As the knowledge base has grown exponentially, societal reflections have lagged behind. The experience of biotechnology in various countries has demonstrated that such reflections and the mechanisms that provide for these have occurred during commercialization, when early products came to market. By then, such reflective activities undertaken by different publics took place against a backdrop of controversies. These reflections, afterthoughts and responses have occurred in many forms – from letters to the media, to demonstrations on the streets, networking with like-minded groups, to political pressure on politicians and regulatory officials.

Responses by public officials had often been reactive rather than proactive. Only in the past 15 years has there been a greater interest and more concerted effort in enjoining publics to participate. By examining the trajectory of biotechnology and its applications through the lens of public participation, we may gain insights into whether technology decisions are 'opening up', whether values such as accountability and transparency, pillars without which public participation remains hollow, are being practised, and whether institutional mechanisms are developing to provide opportunities for greater public involvement.

Much participation has been initiated by organized groups or has been requested by governments or other stakeholder sponsors. In both instances, the range of participatory activities is diverse. These activities have also been mediated by the local political and cultural contexts in which they take place as well as the globalized context in which biotechnology applications have developed.

When we look at the rise of ethical debates on applications of biotechnology, we see a trajectory of an institutionalization process occurring in a number of European Union (EU) countries and, indeed, internationally.[1] And in parallel to this emerging attention to ethical and moral issues, the role and importance of public involvement and participation have increased. It is timely and interesting to look at the development and nature of the trajectory of public participation on biotechnology and, in particular, to ask whether any institutionalization of public participation has occurred. If so, what forms has public participation taken, in which arenas? To what extent have these different forms been institutionalized and formalized in the policy-making process? What are the forms – structural or procedural – that are developing or have been developed to accommodate this interest in public participation? Which actors have been influential or have participated and which ones have been excluded? And what factors may have led to such institutionalization? We pose these questions in this chapter.

This analysis is based on a cross-country examination of different political cultures and participation practices in Canada, Denmark, France, Portugal, Switzerland and the UK. These six countries provide a varied range of cultural and political contexts as well as diversity of experiences with engaging publics on the issue of biotechnology.

We begin with an explanation of what we mean by 'institutionalization'. If institutions are 'socially constructed, routine-reproduced program or rule systems' (Jepperson, 1991), institutionalization refers to the process by which such programmes, systems of rules or routinized practices are created. Thus, in the context of public participation, the conduct of a town hall meeting or a series of town hall meetings can be considered a form of public consultation. But the routinization of such a practice as part of a range of other practices designed to obtain public input through established norms, policies or legislation would encompass the process of institutionalization. We expect that the more generic process of considering public views occurs in a variety of ways and its occurrence or non-occurrence will be dependent on the particularities of political cultures, the activities of actors and the occurrence of specific trigger events within a country.

We use the term 'public participation' to refer to a broad range of approaches – formal and informal – that allow members of the public to provide input on technology decisions.

The trajectory of biotechnology and its applications and the role of publics

The history of modern biotechnology is typically traced to the 1973 scientific studies which announced the successful efforts to transfer genes from one species to another. The startling implications of such processes led to a consensus among scientists for a moratorium, followed by the development of guidelines developed through the US National Institutes of Health imposing restrictions on the science.

The earliest debates occurred in the 1970s, primarily in the pages of the Boston media and in the halls of the Boston city council focusing on the issue of safety (of workers primarily and of the population secondarily). The issue of laboratory safety was also echoed in a few other countries, primarily in Denmark, but the early discussions in that country were further centred on the theoretical implications of the new biology (Jamison and Lassen, 2004).

Controversy was further inflamed during the 1980s in connection with the environmental implications of field trials (Krimsky and Wrubel, 1996; Jelsøe et al, 1998). Control and regulation of such experiments as well as concerns over the products being developed (genetically engineered (GE) strawberries with an antifreeze gene from a fish) were dominant themes. Academics and environmental organizations were prominent in these debates, as were the media, which found the elements of conflict intriguing, on top of a 'new technology' story which featured 'transgression lines'. Not surprisingly, the additional newsworthy element of attention-grabbing pictures (protesters clad in gas masks and anti-contaminant suits in the middle of experimental strawberry fields) proved irresistible.

From the early 1980s through to the 1990s, genetically modified (GM) food and crops became the focus of controversy, particularly in Europe. The elaboration of this controversy developed as civil society organizations, most notably environmental groups, successfully marshalled the issue into the media. Subsequently, a broader range of actors became involved, including supermarkets, consumer and farming organizations, scientists, industry organizations and politicians. The issue of food risks was further exacerbated by the mad cow crisis in the UK and other food safety issues in other European countries.

The evolution of biotechnology was not occurring in a vacuum. The historical scientific controversies, particularly around the development of the nuclear industry, provided some of the early lessons in terms of societal questions regarding controversial technologies, conflicts over applications of science in such areas as the military (atomic weapons) and agriculture (pesticides). The growth of social movements was in direct response to issues raised from these scientific applications, such as environmental movements, or provided a base from which to challenge scientific applications from perspectives of safety or equity (e.g. consumer organizations and the women's movement).

The questioning of science was also spurred by much academic writing on risk (Beck, 1992), the nature of expertise, the limits to scientific knowledge and the interests that drive knowledge production (Wynne, 2000), as well as increasing recognition of uncertainty. These ideas began to be echoed in policy documents in some countries, most particularly the UK (see, for example, Parliamentary Office of Science and Technology (POST) documents on Science and Society, on Science in Policy, the Role of Uncertainty in Policy Making, and on Public Dialogue).

The patterns of experiences in specific countries did not follow a similar script, however. While there are some common features and experiences, their impacts appear to play out in different ways and with different timelines.

The institutionalization of public participation?

In the light of these considerations, we pose three questions. First, can we discern some general patterns in the participation of various publics on the issue of biotechnology? Second, what features of institutionalization have emerged? And third, what factors could have led to or hindered the institutionalization of public participation in the countries in question: Canada, Denmark, France, Portugal, Switzerland and the UK?

Phases of public participation

We identify three phases on the road to greater public participation. The first phase can be considered as an informal phase, which is characterized by some modes of public participation spearheaded by environmental and consumer organizations. Indeed, from the early part of the GM debate, in most of our case countries, environmental and consumer organizations became highly successful in putting biotechnology issues (especially GM food) on the public agenda. This was carried out through a range of tactics which included direct actions, demonstrations, media campaigns, lobbying of government or industry and, in some cases, through public information and education campaigns. While many of these organizations worked single-handedly or in collaboration with other environmental or consumer organizations, in some cases these organizations and activities were supported and joined by technology assessors within academia. For example, in the UK in 1997, Greenpeace in collaboration with academics at Lancaster University carried out some focus group interviews that looked at public concerns over genetically modified food. Equally, in 1998, the NGO 'The Genetic Forum' organized a citizen jury, 'Citizen Foresight', which was organized in collaboration with the University of East London (Wynne, 2000, 2001; Grove-White et al, 1997, 2000; Glover et al, 2002; http://www.ids.ac.uk/ids/govern/citizenvoice/pdfs/citsjurygm.pdf).

The second phase, which is a spin-off effect of the more informal public involvement activities, is characterized by two elements: formal recognition of the importance of public participation through legislative acts and policy statements, and more informal 'experiments' with different approaches to public engagement. The first element consists of legally binding stipulations through acts of parliament to directly involve the public, environmental, consumer or other interested and affected non-governmental organizations (NGOs) and non-binding policy pronouncements. The legally binding form of public involvement came to occur and operate within structures overseen by appointed or administrative officials who were given overall responsibility for administering and coordinating GM policy (or risk assessment procedures). In Denmark, for example, through the Danish Gene Act, NGOs and the general public were given the right to access and comment on all release applications, with comments and concerns to be forwarded to and overseen by the Danish Environmental Protection Agency.

In addition to legally binding stipulations for public participation, in this second phase we see a rise of government policy statements acknowledging the limits to scientific knowledge and expertise and, because of this, endorsing the need for a more inclusive, open and precautionary GM policy. Such statements further recognized the importance of ethical considerations and public values in the assessments of technology. Such formal incorporation of ethical questions in biotechnology assessments was evident in the establishment of ethical committees, as well as in the increased government funding for research and activities that were to explore such ethical issues.

The second type of public participation is the non-binding direct involvement of citizens in providing input, the outcome of which might be mediated by an advisory body, council or ministerial committees. These include stipulated periods of public comments, open public meetings, opinion polls or surveys, deliberative methods of public engagement (including consensus conferences, citizen juries, scenario workshops and other technology assessment processes which engage publics), public information or education activities. The use of non-binding approaches to public participation – particularly the consensus conference – appeared to acquire its own trajectory of dissemination as it was implemented in various countries, including Canada, the UK and France and increasingly so elsewhere. Not surprisingly, GM food and agriculture became the subject of many of these discussions. While in Denmark these non-binding direct deliberative activities became common, often in the other case countries they appeared to be one-off events (Kamara, 2004; Einsiedel et al, 2001; Einsiedel, 2001; Glover et al, 2002; Jelsøe et al, 1998, 2001).

The third phase, which includes the current period, has seen three changes. First is the increasingly diverse range of stakeholder organizations interested in influencing policy decisions. The developments on the biomedical front, from therapeutic cloning to stem cell policies, saw the increasing emergence of various patient organizations, this time supporting further biomedical research and development. These participation activities from various publics now covered a more complex spectrum of views and standpoints. For example, on the issue of stem cells, patient organizations were lined up to influence legislation that would encourage further research, while other organizations such as the pro-life movement, particularly in the US and Canada, and some church organizations, tried to push governments to more restrictive positions (de Cheveigné et al, in this volume). Second is the continuing opening up of established institutions to activities that enhance public participation (e.g. provision of more information, transparency and accountability routines) as an extension to legislative or policy calls for openness and participation. The third is the parallel and complementary informal and formal public participation events. With transparency, openness and public participation becoming buzzwords in government institutions, environ-mental or consumer organizations (both at the national and at the EU level) continued to hold their own parallel events and activities. The reason for this was that they saw the institutionalization of public participation efforts not as an attempt to consult and involve the public, but rather as a media stunt and top-down attempts at a fait accompli. Forums around world trade and globalization became focal arenas for expressing dissident public views – and discontents – on biotechnology.

While formal mechanisms for engaging the public are only evident in Denmark, in other countries, such as Canada, France and the UK, the public participation mechanisms favoured appeared to be ad hoc ones (e.g. public membership on advisory committees). At the same time, it is in the second phase and this third phase that features of institutionalization are beginning to emerge (Kamara, 2004; Einsiedel et al, 2001; Einsiedel, 2001; Glover et al, 2003). This trend was enhanced through various international agencies also emphasizing the role of publics and discussions of international regulatory protocols and agreements which incorporated stakeholder views and participation.

Features of institutionalization of public participation

In our cases, we observe that public participation has occurred in various forms and under the rubric of various policy and legislative tools. As participation has developed from the informal to more formal modes, we identify four features which we discern as evidence for some form of institutionalization. The first of these features is the stipulation and enactment of legally binding policy statements (by government), or acts of law which support and promote greater public involvement and participation. The second is the structural response or support, which is evident through the creation or establishment of new governmental advisory bodies, committees, councils or institutions tasked with the responsibility of overseeing or promoting greater public participation or information activities. Third is the resource base, evident through the disbursement of public funds earmarked for financing various public information or participatory activities. Such activities are typically initiated by the established public consultative bodies and, in some countries, by NGOs or the general public. Fourth is the initiation of public participation or enlightenment events by established institutions actually creating a forum or space for greater public input, information or empowerment. In the following, we shall briefly look at the four features in turn.

Policy statements and legal directives

Policy statements are explicit signs of intent or political willingness to engage the public. Sometimes this leads to structural and procedural initiatives such as the enactment of laws or the setting up of governmental bodies tasked with the responsibility of ensuring that these policy statements or legally binding policies are implemented. In Denmark, for example, following heated debates between Danish biotechnology industries and NOAH (the Danish Friends of the Earth), in a parliamentary debate in 1982 the Minister of Environment said that the Danish public was interested in and concerned about the effects of modern biotechnology and would welcome a public debate (about GM biotechnology) in Denmark. This statement and the subsequent debates were followed by the enactment of the Danish Act on Environment and Gene Technology. This granted NGOs the right to petition against genetically modified organism (GMO) release applications; the right to inform the Danish public about any release applications; and public access to release application documents, as well as an open and transparent parliamentary deliberation process. In the UK, we saw the publication of a Royal Society report (1985), *The Public Understanding of Science*, that stressed the need for greater scientific literacy about GM biotechnology among the public. Furthermore, there were explicit policy statements by the UK Minister for Science (1997) on the need to hold public consultation exercises on the House of Lords Science and Technology Committee report (2000) stressing that 'direct dialogue with the public should move from being an optional add-on to science-based policy-making and to the activities of research organizations and learned institutions, and should become a normal and integral part of the process'. In Canada, the government publicly committed itself to broader public participation and consultation, and the government department that is responsible for handling biotechnology policy was given a mandate to consult the public widely on biotechnology issues (Kamara, 1999, 2004; Einsiedel et al, 2001; Einsiedel, 2001; Glover et al, 2002).

Structural response

The implementation of such legally binding statements or policies cannot occur in a vacuum, however. It is because of this that we see governments setting up advisory bodies or committees to ensure successful implementation of public participation and an information policy. In Denmark, these twin tasks of public information and consultation have been carried out in both the Danish Board of Technology (DBT)[2] and the Danish Council of Ethics (DCE).[3]

To ensure the accountancy of public values, membership of expert committees broadened to include public representatives, as exemplified by public membership on such bodies as the Danish Council of Ethics (DCE), various UK Advisory committees (e.g. the Human Genetics Commission), the Canadian Biotechnology Advisory Committee, and ad hoc ministerial advisory committees on biotechnology. A more recent development is the establishment of a joint or liaison body by the government, the so-called BIOSAM, in May 1997. The body has the responsibility of promoting openness and informing the public about developments in biotechnology research and the use of biotechnology, and to ensure that, as early as possible, the government and the public are informed about biotechnology developments that could provoke ethical concerns in society.[4]

Furthermore, in 2001 the Danish government adopted a four-year action plan for biotechnology and ethics that is coordinated by an interdepartmental task force involving nine Danish Ministries, the so-called BioTIK-Task Force, which has the responsibility of initiating public dialogue and information activities.[5] In France, a National Commission of Public Debate was established in 1995 by the Parliamentary Office for Scientific and Technological Choices (OPESCT) to encourage and initiate public participation and information activities. Also, in 1998 a steering committee was appointed to oversee and organize the first French consensus conference. The UK has seen a string of committees including the establishment of the Genetic Manipulation Advisory Group (GMAG) in 1976 and the Advisory Committee on Novel Foods and Processes (ACNFP)[6] in 1989. In 1990, the Advisory Committee on Releases to the Environment (ACRE). was set up,[7] whose members included non-experts, interest groups and consumer representatives and committees – tasked with the responsibility of engaging closely with the public. In April 2000, the Food Standards Agency was set up and pledged to be 'more open and transparent', including holding open public meetings and consultation strategies. Two other committees, the Human Genetics Commission and the Agriculture and Environment Biotechnology Commission (AEBC), also followed similar objectives, and included 'lay' and NGO representatives in their memberships. Both were charged to look at the social and ethical issues relating to developments in biotechnology which have implications for agriculture and the environment, and to provide strategic advice to government in this area. Indeed, in the 2001 debate about UK farm trials, AEBC heard evidence from all stakeholders including lay members of the public, farming groups, and other non-governmental organizations. And in 1999, the government of Canada established the Canadian Biotechnology Advisory Committee (CBAC) – a body that is composed of experts as well as lay persons and non-governmental organizations and was charged with the responsibility of informing Canadian citizens about biotechnology developments, as well giving them a voice in the Canadian biotechnology decision-making process.[8]

Disbursement of funds

Pronouncements are cheap without the resources to walk the talk. In Denmark, public participation was promoted as part of a larger Biotechnology Development Programme. For example, in the 1987 programme, 3.3 million Danish crowns was earmarked for technology assessment and public information. This money came to finance most of the bottom-up public debate and information initiatives, funding NGOs' public debates, information and education activities. Other economic resources were channelled through the Danish Board of Technology or the Danish Ethics Council. An additional 16 million Danish crowns was earmarked by the Danish government for the BioTIK initiative to promote public debate and information.[9] In the UK, the Office of Science and Technology allocated over £4.5m a year to public understanding of science activities (e.g. museum exhibitions, National Science Week, etc.). More recently, the UK government earmarked £650,000 for nationwide public consultation events on GM food and crops.[10] In Canada, around $1m supported the national consultations on xenotransplantation, while the CBAC further supported semi-annual public opinion surveys, focus groups and media analyses as a way of keeping track of public views. Additional funds were made available through individual ministries. For example, a consultation on genetic testing was carried out through the Justice Ministry in 2004.

Public education and debates initiatives

These legal, structural and economic resources have supported and encouraged the more obvious forms of public participation. These include local or district public debates, museum exhibitions, national science weeks, public meetings, hearings, information campaigns, educational courses, books and videos, as well as the more systematic methods of public engagement such as citizen juries, referendums, 'people's panels' and consensus conferences. Under the auspices of the Genome Canada programme, a museum exhibit created as a public education initiative but primarily extolling the virtues of genomics, called 'The Geeee in Genome', was sponsored in six sites around the country in 2004. Denmark has held many consensus conferences on GM biotechnology, a method that came to be adopted in a number of countries; Switzerland has held and is known for its referendums, gene dialogues or public forums. The UK was noted recently as establishing for its citizens one of the best websites on biotechnology (see the SMART regulation initiative).

Perhaps the best-known episode of formal public participation was the UK's nationwide public discussion around GM issues, organized and financed by the UK government. Within the £650,000 budget that was earmarked for this purpose, between June and July 2003 an estimated total of over 600 regional, county and local meetings were organized across the country by local authorities and network groups. An event that was seen, or hoped, by many to have the potential to effect a sweeping change in British public policy gave the British people a chance to come forward and say what they felt about genetic modification and the commercial growing of GM crops in the UK. To the organizers, the event demonstrated widespread unease among the UK public about the safety of this technology, together with profound scepticism about its benefits. In a survey questionnaire, an overwhelming 86 per cent of the 37,000 people who responded said that they would not be happy to eat GM food and only 8 per cent said that they would be happy to eat GM food.[11] However, as a model for public debate this exercise raised more questions than it answered (Gaskell, 2004).

The road to institutionalization

What can we conclude about the nature and extent of public participation on biotechnology? From our case countries, it is clear that there have been different degrees and different forms of public participation practices, reflecting institutionalization to varying degrees. At one extreme, public participation practices in Portugal remain nascent while in Denmark public participation has been clearly institutionalized. From the cases we examined, it is clear that there is a cluster of similar circumstances common to all countries; at the same time, what happens within each country leads to different responses and, thus, different pictures of how institutionalization has or has not progressed.

Biotechnology, of course, is the technology that has prompted this examination of public participation. It is this technology around which governments in many countries – from industrializing to post-industrial states – have staked their competitive futures in a global economy. But the introduction of this technology and its associated applications has occurred within the larger context of societies that have seen the benefits and the significant risks of science and technology. The publics are now familiar with the limits to scientific knowledge and its uncertainties. Even on its own merits, biotechnology also raised a host of questions that went to the heart of what it means to be human, of the nature of identity, crossing boundaries and playing God. Its applications coalesced concerns about long-term environmental impacts, implications for biodiversity, access to technological benefits by developing countries, and domestic economic considerations in the context of a globalized economy. It was perhaps inevitable that these competing interests would clash. The interest in deploying biotechnology as a strategic tool in the post-industrial global economy, coming into conflict with those wanting to see technologies becoming more responsive to risk concerns, ethical and social considerations, and demands for democratic accountability.

In our case study, the evidence suggests that the institutionalization (or lack of it) of public participation was influenced and steered by a number of contributory factors. We categorize these in terms of initiating factors and responsive factors. The first of these initiating factors grew out of the 'risk society', and the increasing recognition of uncertainty, which, in turn, led to challenges to previously unquestioned technological introductions. These challenges were championed by social movements schooled via their experiences in promoting alternative visions for earlier technologies. These organizations included environmental, consumer and farmer organizations, armed with information technologies and savvy with the mass media. Their messages focused on uncertainty and complexity in risk assessment, the importance of accounting for ethical, environmental and equity considerations in assessing the worth of technologies, and the interests inherent in scientific work. At the forefront were their continuing questions about the safety and environmental impacts of GM food and crops.

The success of these messages, which were further disseminated via the mass media, contributed to the pervasive public ambivalence to GM food and agriculture, resulting in a policy impasse in Europe. The messages were carried across the Atlantic, and the Canadian and US publics, which earlier had been supporters of GM technology, also became increasingly cautious. Coalitions between international and local NGOs helped to further public anxieties although, on the whole, US publics remained generally most supportive, Canadians cautiously so, while Europeans remained disaffected. Participation by various publics in this sense was informal, generally expressed as reactions to controversy in the media and responses to issues raised by various activist groups (Gaskell et al, 2001).

The ongoing questions raised about GM agriculture in particular developed into large-scale controversies which were marked by sensational headlines, sensational tactics on the part of advocacy organizations, more sustained media attention to the issue and vociferous disagreements about risk. One effect of this was an increasing public distrust of institutions responsible for overseeing and regulating science and technology risks, in turn leading to a dramatic and long-lasting effect on the GM policy and decision-making process – the stalling of government and industrial efforts to make modern biotechnology happen. As the lay public were increasingly drawn into the GM debate, and policy formation, they became stakeholders in the decision-making process, and expressed a critical voice (Kamara, 2004; Einsiedel et al, 2001; Glover et al, 2003).

An example of the stalled efforts of government was the UK government's decision to review its GM policy and to reach a voluntary agreement with biotechnology companies to suspend commercial planting of GM crops for three years until farm trials were completed (in effect, establishing a moratorium). Another consequence was that, by 2000, 'openness and transparency' became policy issues.

In response to the growing public anxieties over GM food, regional and international institutions provided further arenas for policy mandates to extend public participation opportunities. In Europe, this was evident in the growing importance of the European Commission and the increasing role of EU-level decision-making processes. When Denmark enacted the first gene technology law in Europe, and indeed in the world, this became a trigger for a reactive GM policy at the EU level that was primarily meant to avoid cultural and legislative disharmonies across Europe. Fears that harmonious development of biotechnology in Europe would be hampered resulted in the enactment of the Deliberate Release Directive 90/220, a piece of precautionary legislation. This legislation, among others, highlights the role and importance of EU-level decision making.

The response in many EU countries (and later internationally) was that environmental, farmer and consumer organizations started to pool their efforts and activities as they recognized the importance of their combined force in lobbying for policies that would slow down if not stop biotechnological applications, particularly in the agricultural area, in addition to pushing for greater public inclusion and empowerment. It was hardly coincidental that Friends of the Earth Europe and Greenpeace Europe started to channel their lobbying activities through Brussels, and indeed move their offices there. The pooled efforts of NGOs were directed variously against the importation of GM soya beans from the US (which was simultaneously blocked in a number of EU countries by Greenpeace activists) and against the supermarkets in the UK, to force a retreat from the sale of GM products, with other European supermarkets following suit. This, in turn, led the European Commission to realize that market approval and commercialization would not be possible without labelling, leading to the amendment of Directive 90/220 in order to require informative labelling and, later, traceability of GM products.

The pooled efforts of NGOs found other targets. Objections to the US World Trade Organization case against the EU moratorium on the commercialization of GM crops and food were organized under the banner 'Bite Back' citizen campaign initiated by Friends of the Earth International with the support of Action Aid, Confédération Paysanne, Public Citizen, Research Foundation for Science, Technology and Ecology, and Greenpeace International, in addition to the backing of more than 680 international groups. In May 2004, they handed their first 1,000,000-citizen objection to the WTO.[12] Within four months, the European Commission launched a public consultation of stakeholders on how to enhance transatlantic economic trade.[13]

These public consultation initiatives at the EU level were expected to over-come citizens' or NGOs' objections to marketing applications by, among other things, taking account of ethical and public concerns. Indeed, at the start of this century, the EU Commission issued its 2000 Communication[14] based on the precautionary principle, which underlined the need for and importance of public opinion and the need to consider this opinion both in risk assessment and in EU-level decision making.[15] Similarly, in its 'Science and Society' Action Plan, the Commission underlined the importance of ethics, public awareness, dialogue and participation in EU science and technology assessment and decision-making processes.[16] In addition to the EU Commission stipulations, another good example of EU-level influence is the Århus Convention 1998,[17] which emphasized access to information, public participation in decision making, and access to justice in environmental matters.[18] Finally, in 2003,[19] the European Union enacted Directive 2003/35/EC of the European Parliament and of the Council of 26 May 2003, which provided for public participation and to be aligned with the Århus Convention.[20, 21] Because all member states have an obligation to enforce these EU-level stipulations or conventions (which include greater transparency and openness, ethical considerations, provision of consumer information and choice, and public participation), it could be argued that this explains why the gap between state and civil society in countries such as the UK, Portugal and France has, slowly but surely, narrowed. As governments embark on adopting such stipulations, people have also become increasingly aware of their rights and have increasingly taken an interest in decision processes on issues that are of direct interest to them. Indeed, in these countries, NGOs have become not only more visible, but also vocal and influential in their relation to citizens and public officials. This is highly visible in areas such as the environment and public health. In particular, the interest in considering ethical issues and the subsequent rise in institutionalization of ethics structures and processes (ethics committees, more stringent ethics boards, national ethics advisory committees, animal welfare committees) further contributed to the opening up of biotechnology questions for discussion. And it was this development that provided further impetus for exploring mechanisms for greater public input.[22]

International agreements provided yet another arena for participation oppor-tunities. A good case in point is the Cartagena Protocol on Biosafety,[23] and in particular article 23, which promotes and requires greater public awareness and participation within the signatory countries in the design and implementation of their national biosafety frameworks. In Canada, for example, the Canadian government publicly committed itself to broad-based consultations to seek the views of Canadians in order to inform its decision on signing and ratification of the Cartagena Protocol, as well as in ensuring inclusiveness, transparency and accountability. Following the conclusion of Cartagena protocol negotiations in January 2000, the Government began consultations with Canadian Provinces, Territories, and stakeholders including lay people and environmental groups. In such deliberations and through the internet, members of the public were invited to submit comments on a form or to submit them directly to government depart-ments. As a result of the stipulations of the Cartagena protocol, among others, there is some evidence of institutionalized forms of public information and participation among interested parties and conventional stakeholders in decision making on living modified organisms' biosafety issues (Glover et al, 2002).

Finally, trigger events also contributed to the consideration of the social-ethical dimensions and to push public concerns to the forefront, making more salient the need to provide opportunities for publics to express their concerns. These events included the early importation of GM soya into Europe, which was then stopped by NGOs at the docks, the cloning of Dolly the sheep and subsequent cloning events, genetic testing issues (raising public alarm over issues such as privacy and confidentiality, etc.), and a series of food safety crises including 'mad cow disease' and the related emergence of 'new-variant' Creutzfeldt–Jakob disease (nvCJD) in humans in the UK and internationally. In the public mind, the mad cow events, though technically unrelated to biotechnology, were all merged and were connected to an increasing lack of confidence in the Government's ability to ensure the safety of the food system and products. Other food safety crises such as the foot-and-mouth disease outbreaks in pigs, cattle and sheep further inflamed anxieties about food safety and the broader issue of the intensification of farming and its consequences for human health and the environment. One effect of these crises was the call for greater openness and transparency as well as the need to involve publics in decision-making processes. Indeed, in the BSE inquiry,[24] published in the UK in 2000, and in the House of Lords report *Science and Society*,[25, 26] we see calls for greater dialogue, openness and transparency. In the same way, by 2002, even after the BSE debates had calmed down, interest remained high in engaging publics. The year 2002 saw the newly created Department for Environment, Food and Rural Affairs (DEFRA) launch a public debate on the science and economics of GM crops, followed by an on-line public discussion on issues of liability post-commercialization.[27]

But what determined the political response, particularly the initiation of specific institutionalization mechanisms? The existing political culture of the given country was one important determinant. In Denmark, for example, the twin pillars of 'consensus-building' and 'public enlightenment culture' contributed to the early and leading adoption of public consultation and public education processes. On the other end of the continuum is Portugal, where, because of its tradition of centralism and secrecy in public administration, a key feature of political and regulatory culture is the non-inclusive approach to many of the public issues involving science and technology. A consequence of this is the absence of participatory initiatives in areas related to biotechnology. The UK, Canada and France have similar reliance on strong scientific expert systems but this has been changed in the first two countries with more public participation initiatives, while France has remained heavily reliant on its centralized administrative authorities. The strong conservative strain in Swiss politics with its emphasis on stability rather than social innovation and a strong tradition of representative politics made for an interesting counterpoint to the direct democracy practice of referenda. Only in one instance, when a referendum initiative on gene technology research threatened to put restrictions on such research, was there widespread debate among different stakeholders in various public arenas, including the media.

The existence of controversy was another factor encouraging a push towards calls for more public participation and for initiatives that actually made such participation happen. The ongoing controversy in the UK over GM food and crops, accompanied by high-volume media coverage, and the continuing interest by the Blair government in making biotechnology happen created the ideal environment for political opportunities for participation to take place.

Whither institutionalization?

We have shown that the institutionalization (or lack of it) of public participation in the context of assessing GM technologies has been a process influenced by:

- the political culture of the given country (Jasanoff, 1995);
- the spin-off effects of the more informal participatory activities that were initiated by citizen or NGO groups – be it in the form of direct actions, demonstrations, media campaigns or direct lobbying of government or industry – echoing to a certain extent some of the earlier forms of activism common in the 1970s and 1980s against nuclear energy (Wynne, 2000, 2001);
- increasing regional and international-level decision making such as through the EU or international conventions, which provided further opportunity structures for public participation; and
- the effects of the internet and the mass media, which provided fora for information dissemination, networking and collaboration, and public education by all key actors involved, from industry to NGOs and regulatory agencies, and accessible to the general public.

In the same way, we have delineated four features or factors that can be considered as evidence of such institutionalization. These are:

- stipulation or enactment of legislative mandates or policy directives;
- structural response through, for example, establishment of governmental bodies or institutions tasked with the responsibility of overseeing and supporting greater public participation;
- economic support, through earmarked funding for public participation and information; and
- the actual public activities and events, be they public comments, multi-level consultations or public education/information campaigns.

If we were to use these delineated features as 'evidence' or lack of 'evidence' for institutionalization of public participation on biotechnology, then Denmark could be considered to be the only country that has clearly institutionalized public participation on the GM issue. The UK and Canada have both had policy directives and have also initiated a number of public participation activities. In the UK, where controversy has been higher, the policy pronouncements have been highly visible, as have been some initiatives (e.g. 'GM Nation'). The forms of institutionalization are different in the UK, with continued reliance on expert committees but accommodating 'public' membership. A similar pattern is occurring in Canada alongside a longer tradition of multi-stakeholder consultations and participation. Switzerland has an Office of Technology Assessment which has experimented with deliberative forms of consultation but this is a relatively new development. France remains steeped in its culture of centralism with heavy reliance on bureaucratic and technical expertise. Portugal can be considered as still experimenting and struggling with a development that may continue to challenge the country's elite and centralized policy culture.

While it seems clear that there is an increasing trend towards some institutionalization of public participation, what is unclear, however, is the effect of this development on influencing the trajectory of modern biotechnology. Many argue that these opportunities for public participation remain as instruments to mollify and placate, all the while seeing governments proceed – albeit more slowly in some instances – towards their original goal to make biotechnology happen in their jurisdictions. For example, while the European GM moratorium and its strict GM policies (e.g. mandatory labelling and traceability requirements, coexistence laws or regulations, etc.) can be considered a result and effect of having heard public concerns, the original goal remains intact. In Denmark, the country that has made the most strides towards institutionalization, between 1990 and 1999 there was an annual increase in the number of GMO release research projects approved and carried out. And in the UK, while public participation, openness and transparency become and continue to be the UK government's explicit policy, the UK government, and in particular Prime Minister Tony Blair, has continued to be a keen supporter of GM food and crops. Indeed, at the EU level, the UK government has voted yes in six out of the seven EU-level applications for the commercialization of GM products.

The recent UK public participation and consultation activities have attracted a number of criticisms. For example, the Government's willingness to embrace true democratic process was questioned as a result of the small budget that was allocated for public participation and consultation activities. The small budget made it impossible for the process to benefit from the range of mechanisms and processes that could be targeted at different audiences or focused on specific issues. In the same way, some groups have termed the public consultations as no more than a mere PR stunt, a top-down order of a fait accompli intended, as it were, to justify a purely technocratic risk assessment procedure. A similar dissatisfaction has been expressed at the EU level, in the main by NGOs that see the EU Commission as caving in to the pressures of commercial interest as well as to the Bush administration against the concerns and interests of the EU public. And in Canada, Canadian organizations have expressed frustration with the public participation and consulting mechanisms, which they see as faulty while meant to weaken true democratic processes and extensive public participation.

In sum, while there is clearly a trend towards greater interest in public participation, the pace at which this has occurred has differed from one country to another. Indeed, the forms of institutionalization of public participation have not been uniform and, given the differences in political cultures, this is not surprising. The impacts of such early steps remain to be determined. In the end, it may be the continuing blend of institutionalized mechanisms for publics to participate and the absence of such institutionalization – thus expanding the possibilities for individuals or groups to exert pressure on established political structures of decision making without the constraints of formal modes of legitimating – that will allow the greatest number and most diverse range of voices to be heard.

Notes

1 Lindsey et al (2001)
2 www.tekno.dk
3 www.etiskraad.dk
4 www.biosam.dk
5 www.biotik.dk/english/
6 www.foodstandards.gov.uk/science/ouradvisors/novelfood/
7 www.defra.gov.uk/environment/acre/about/index.htm
8 http://cbac-cccb.ca/epic/internet/incbac-cccb.nsf/en/h_ah00002e.html
9 www.biotik.dk/english/
10 Heller (2003)
11 Heller (2003)
12 www.bite-back.org/index.php
13 www.europa.eu.int/comm/trade/issues/bilateral/countries/usa/pr290904_en.htm
14 www.gdrc.org/u-gov/precaution-4.html
15 www.europa.eu.int/comm/dgs/health_consumer/library/pub/pub07_en.pdf   accessed 9 October 2004
16 http://europe.eu.int/comm/research/science-society/action-plan/action-plan_en.html accessed 9 October 2004
17 http://www.unece.org/env/pp/documents/cep43e.pdf
18 http://europa.eu.int/eur-lex/pri/en/oj/dat/2003/l_041/l_04120030214en00260032.pdf
19 http://europa.eu.int/comm/environment/aarhus/
20 http://europa.eu.int/comm/environment/aarhus/
21 http://europa.eu.int/eur-lex/pri/en/oj/dat/2003/l_041/l_04120030214en00260032.pdf
22 Lindsey et al (2001)
23 www.biodiv.org/biosafety/default.aspx
24 www.bseinquiry.gov.uk/report/volume1/toc.htm accessed 12 October 2004
25 www.parliament.the-stationery-office.co.uk/pa/ld199900/ldselect/ldsctech/38/3801.htm
26 http://physicsweb.org/articles/world/16/10/1/1
27 www.defra.gov.uk/

References

Beck, U. (1992) *Risk Society: Towards a New Modernity*, Sage, London
Einsiedel, E. F. (2001) 'Citizen voices: public participation on biotechnology', *Notizie di Politeia*, vol 17, no 63, pp94–104
Einsiedel, E. F., Jelsøe, E. and Breck, T. (2001) 'Publics at the technology table: the consensus conference in Denmark, Canada, and Australia', *Public Understanding of Science*, vol 10, pp83–98

EU (2000) EU's Communication on Precautionary Principle. Commission adopts Communication on Precautionary Principle. Brussels, 2 February 2000, http://www.gdrc.org/u-gov/precaution-4.html accessed 8 October 2004

EU (2001) COM /2001/714 of 4 December 2001, Commission's Action Plan on Science and Society

Gaskell, G. (2004) 'Science policy and society: The British debate over GM agriculture', *Current Opinion on Biotechnology*, vol 15, pp241–245

Gaskell, G., Bauer, M., Allum, N., Lindsey, N., Durant, J. and Lueginger, J. (2001) 'United Kingdom: Spilling the beans on genes', in Gaskell, G. and Bauer, M. (eds) *Biotechnology 1996–2000: The Years of Controversy*, Science Museum, London

Glover, D., Keeley, J., Newell, P. and McGee, R. (2002) 'Public participation and the Cartagena Protocol on Biosafety: A review for DfID and UNEP-GEF', IDS Publications http://www.unep.ch/biosafety/development/devdocuments/PublicParticipation IDS.pdf accessed 11 October 2004

Glover, D., Keeley, J., Newell, P. and McGee, R. (2003) 'Public participation and the Cartagena Protocol on Biosafety: A review for DfID and UNEP-GEF, Part II: The Case Studies', IDS Publications http://www.ids.ac.uk/ids/env/PDFs/NBFpercent20 Casepercent20Studies.pdf accessed 11 October 2004

Grove-White, R., Macnaghten, P., Mayer, S. and Wynne, B. (1997) *Uncertain World: Genetically Modified Organisms, Food and Public Attitudes in Britain* (in association with Unilever), IEPPP, Lancaster University, Lancaster, UK

Grove-White, R., Macnaghten, P. and Wynne, B. (2000) *Wising Up: The Public and New Technologies. A Research Report by the Centre for the Study of Environmental Change*, Lancaster University, Lancaster, UK

Heller, R. (2003) *GM Nation? The Findings of the Public Debate*, Clarity, 42 Bloomsbury, London

IDS (2001) *Bringing Citizen Voice and Client Focus into Service Delivery: Case Study*, Citizen's Jury on GM foods (Citizen Foresight Project), IDS, Sussex http://www.ids.ac.uk/ids/govern/citizenvoice/pdfs/citsjurygm.pdf accessed 11 October 2004

Jamison, A. and Lassen, J. (2004) 'Assessing genetic technologies in Denmark', in Häyrinen-Alestalo, M. and Kallerud, E. (eds) *Mediating Public Concern in Biotechnology*, NIFU Rapportserie 2/2004, Oslo, Norway, pp23–48

Jasanoff, S. (1995) 'Product, process, or programme: Three cultures and the regulation of biotechnology', in Bauer, M. (ed) *Resistance to New Technology*, Cambridge University Press, Cambridge, pp311–331

Jelsøe, E., Lassen, J., Mortensen, A. T., Frederiksen, H. and Kamara, M. W. (1998) 'Denmark (national profile)', in Durant, J., Gaskell, G. and Bauer, M. (eds) *Biotechnology in the Public Sphere: A European Sourcebook*, Science Museum, London

Jelsøe, E., Kamara, M. W., Lassen, J. and Mortensen, A. T. (2001) 'Denmark: The revival of national controversy over biotechnology' in Bauer, M. and Gaskell, G. (eds) *Biotechnology 1996–2000: The Years of Controversy*, Science Museum, London

Jepperson, R. (1991) 'Institutions, institutional effects, and institutionalism', in Powell, W. and DiMaggio, P. (eds) *The New Institutionalism in Organizational Analysis*, University of Chicago Press, Chicago, pp143–164

Kamara, M. W. (1999) *Making Biotechnology Happen*, Teksam Forlag, Rapport serien no 78, June

Kamara, M. W. (2004) 'The golden age of genetic engineering: A challenge to science?', PhD dissertation, Roskilde University, Denmark

Krimsky, S. and Wrubel, R. (1996) *Agricultural Biotechnology and the Environment: Science, Policy, and Social Issues*, University of Illinois Press, Urbana

Lindsey, N., Kamara, M. W., Mortensen, A. T. (2001) 'Changing frames: The emergence of ethics in European policy on biotechnology', *Notizie di Politeia*, vol 17, no 63, pp80–93

UNECE (1998) Convention on Access to Information, Public Participation and Decision Making and Access to Justice in Environmental Matters, Århus, Denmark (2001) *Science-et-cité*, in http://www.science-et-cite.ch/

Wynne, B. (2000) 'Public consultation', in *Towards A Democratic Science: An e-conference for the British Council*, vol 1, River Path Associates, Wimborne, Dorset, UK

Wynne, B. (2001) 'Expert discourses of risk and ethics on genetically manipulated organisms: The weaving of public alienation', *Notizie di Politeia*, vol 17, no 62, pp51–76

8

Issue Salience and Media Framing over 30 Years

Martin W. Bauer and Jan M. Gutteling

Media coverage of modern biotechnology is the focus of this chapter.[1] The mass media are an important player and arena in the development of a new technology (Bauer, 2002a). They create the symbolic environment that fuels technological optimism and pessimism, as it may be, and thus contribute to a public sphere of technological controversies. Are the mass media an extension of interested actors, and therefore a mere epiphenomenon of the establishment, or are they making a contribution *sui generis* to technological debates? We will address this key issue by splitting it into three separate questions.

First, are mass media a powerful lever to influence public perceptions of controversial issues? The empirical evidence is not unequivocal. We will review some key media effect hypotheses and evaluate the evidence for mass media influence on public perception of modern biotechnology.

Second, we will address the question of mass media autonomy. Are mass media autonomous in their coverage and framing of biotechnology, or are they the conveyor belt of techno-scientific actors? This is not only a theoretical, but also a pressing empirical question. We will discuss this within the context of news values, which also allows us to address grievances between scientists and journalists.

Finally, if the mass media do have a limited but defined influence on public perception, and if they are not an appendage of the powers that be, but indeed social actors, it is warranted to map the trajectory of the coverage of biotechnology in its own terms. How much and in what manner have the mass media covered biotechnology over the past 30 years, and to what extent do different contexts present a different coverage?

The role of the media in the formation of public opinion

The widely believed idea that mass media exert an overpowering influence on public opinion spawned the tradition of mass media effects research in the first half of the 20th century. The mass media were modelled on a *hypodermic needle*, injecting the passive and empty public with information (see, for example, Katz, 1963). This notion is based on a stimulus–response theory: the public is exposed to information (stimulus) and reacts uniformly, directly and in a way that is consistent with the content of the message (response). This model is also known as the 'magic bullet theory'. At first, mass media effect studies seemed to confirm these original notions. The results indicated, alarmingly, that attitudes of young people were influenced by watching movies. The impact of radio was illustrated spectacularly by the broadcast of *War of the Worlds* by Orson Welles on 30 October 1938. The resulting panic has been controversial ever since; according to some sources more than a million listeners panicked over the lively description of an invasion by Martians (see McCombs and Becker, 1979; Cantril et al, 1947). A similar situation occurred in Sweden in 1973 after a radio broadcast about a simulated accident in the nuclear power plant of Barseback (Rosengren et al, 1974).

Media effects research focused on immediate persuasion. This perspective changed in the early 1970s when long-term effects like agenda setting, spiral of silence, knowledge acquisition and cultivation of perceptions became a new focus. The agenda-setting function refers to the media's capability, through repeated news coverage, of raising the importance of an issue in the public's mind (McCombs and Shaw, 1972). The agenda-setting approach claims that the press 'may not be successful much of the time in telling people what to think, but it is stunningly successful in telling its readers what to think about' (Cohen, 1963, p13). Typically, agenda-setting studies compare public agendas and media agendas at different times in order to measure co-variance. Altogether, the results of different studies seem to confirm the agenda-setting hypothesis from mass media to public perceptions, unless certain conditions reverse the causality from the public to the mass media (Protess and McCombs, 1991; Brosius and Kepplinger, 1990).

Many accounts of the relation between media coverage and public attitudes towards controversial technologies have been published since the 1960s and 1970s, when public opinion began to change over major technological develop-ments (see, for example, Gutteling and Wiegman, 1996). Many blame the media for taking a biased position towards technology, implying a causal relation between the media's negative position and shifts towards negative attitudes of large parts of the population. So-called biases were reported over risks and hazards in particular. The media tend to emphasize dramatic and exceptional aspects such as errors, accidents, expert disagreements and conflicts. Sometimes a result of sci-entific research is published prematurely and/or without proper peer review. Thus, issues are being simplified, distorted and inaccurately interpreted (Covello et al, 1987). Other studies indicate that media reportage depends on single sources, so that verification is impossible (Friedman et al, 1987; Rubin, 1987). Even with coverage meeting expected standards of accuracy, it may still have undesirable effects on the way the public perceives scientific information (Mazur, 1981).

Besides polemical studies of a 'media bashing' nature, many empirical and conceptual accounts take a genuine interest in the media's function in the formation of public opinion. For example, recent experimental studies show that positive news of biotechnology tends to stimulate more negative thought among readers, listeners and viewers than negative news items (Peters, 2000). Here, we will explore three mid-range hypotheses of media effect and assess field study evidence in relation to biotechnology. In assessing the coupling of mass media and public perceptions in a public sphere, empirical effect studies enter a polemical field but steer the middle ground. By empirically assessing the media impact on perceptions and attitudes, they equally avoid armchair cultural critique and moral panic over the subversive or demoralizing mass media. However, how do these models differ from each other? News calls our attention to some issues at the expense of others because of limited space and attention span, agenda setting. The quantity of coverage idea suggests that negative public attitudes co-vary with increased media coverage, but gets limited empirical support. The knowledge-gap hypothesis focuses on the structural inequalities of information flow and issue knowledge in society and the mitigating function of public controversy. Cultivation analysis is defined by its long-term focus on world-views: how audiences come to see the world according to their media consumption pattern.

Quantity of coverage

Mazur (1981) published probably the first model of media coverage and public perception over controversial technologies. He observes that 'the rise in reaction against a scientific technology appears to coincide with a rise in quantity of media coverage, suggesting that media attention tends to elicit a conservative public bias' (Mazur, 1981, p106). Mazur suggests that an increase in the quantity of coverage on a controversial technology leads to a negative public bias against a new technology. This hypothesis has been frequently cited, but rarely empirically tested. Our project allowed this model to be tested in a multinational context. Gutteling (2005) found that the intensity increase in biotechnology coverage after 1997 is not related to negative changes in public attitudes across countries, once the changes are controlled for readership of this press material.

Knowledge gaps and the function of public controversy

The knowledge-gap hypothesis states that 'as the infusion of mass media information into a social system increases, segments of the population with higher socio-economic status tend to acquire this information at a faster rate than the lower status segments, so that the gap in knowledge between these segments tends to increase rather than decrease' (Tichenor et al, 1970, pp159–160). This hypothesis questions the information functions of mass media in democratic societies by confronting evidence of a structurally uninformed public. Increased information flow will normally not result in an equally informed public. The better educated are able to use the media more efficiently than the less well educated. And as a result, knowledge gaps between social groups will increase. The knowledge-gap hypothesis is well supported by empirical studies, and receives support over biotechnology. Bonfadelli (2005) reports considerable variation in knowledge of biotechnology across and within countries, and shows that knowledge gaps increased with increases in media coverage after 1997.

The initial gap hypothesis was refined with a social function of public controversy: gaps tend to increase in pluralistic social settings and in the absence of controversy, whereas gaps are seen to decrease in more homogeneous settings and in the face of controversy (Donohue et al, 1975). Indeed, consistent with these predictions, Bauer and Bonfadelli (2002) showed that before 1996 the level of public controversy is negatively correlated with knowledge gaps over biotechnology: countries with more activity in the political sphere – including parliamentary debates, public hearings, public demonstrations and protests, referenda – saw smaller knowledge differentials on biotechnology between the educated and the uneducated public. On the other hand, the more polarized the public sphere is in terms of left–right political positioning, the larger are these knowledge differentials. Public controversy over biotechnology can be educational and compensate for existing educational disparities in public discourse.

Cultivation of the images and perceptions of biotechnology

The cultivation hypothesis is defined as follows:

> *Cultivation analysis examines the extent to which cumulative exposure to television contributes to viewers' conceptions of social reality, in ways that reflect the most stable, repetitive, and pervasive patterns of images and ideologies that television (especially entertainment programming) presents. (Morgan and Shanahan, 1997, p1)*

Mass media, in particular television, dominate our symbolic environments and make specific and measurable contributions to our beliefs about the world, about things and events that are not within our direct experience. The guiding notion is a long-term trickle: socialization and enculturation (Gerbner et al, 1980). In public debates over new technology, it is important to follow the trajectory of category distinctions as an index of such beliefs. It is not predictable which semantic code of a new technology will prevail in public opinion. Mass media messages frame everyday discourse by providing a pervasive language and powerful imagery with cumulative effects. For biotechnology, Bauer (2002b) showed for Britain that the increasing differentiation of media coverage between 'green' agricultural and 'red' bio-medical biotechnology throughout the early 1990s was related to an increasing gap between attitudes towards red and green biotechnology by 1999; in Britain, red biotechnology came to be viewed positively, green biotechnology negatively. Here the attitude distance between red and green biotechnology is an index of a categorical public perception of biotechnology. Comparative analysis did not, however, confirm consistent cultivation effects across European countries, but showed the convergence of media coverage and public perceptions among readers of the elite press over time. The extent to which the elite press reports differently on red and green biotechnology is directly related to the difference between public attitudes towards red biotechnology and attitudes towards green biotechnology (Bauer, 2005).

News values and the relative autonomy of the mass media

After having explored the evidence for limited but definite effects of mass media coverage on public perception, we will, in this section, explore the evidence for the relative autonomy of mass media vis-à-vis external inputs. On any day, many more events occur than the media are able to report. Therefore, at several stages in the process of news production, information is being processed: it is traced, collected, translated, edited, shortened or expanded, and transferred. After the final editorial process, the public receives this information about the news event. News production can be understood as the process through which complex issues are reduced to journalistically manageable dimensions, resulting in a particular focus on an issue. This implies that framing leads to selection; for example, journalists rely heavily on the information of particular sources (Gutteling et al, 2002), and observe each other in order that they do not miss a good story. These processes result in media outlets individually and collectively highlighting some aspects of biotechnology at particular times, but also ignoring others completely.

Ideas about the power of the mass media are both a source of public confidence and a source of public concern. Communication professionals mostly take an instrumental view of mass media as a lever to perception management. This is a source of concern for those who consider the mass media, or sections of it, to be a factor in moral decline and political subversion. Both positions tend to overestimate the influence of the mass media on public perceptions. The instrumental view of mass media is very much evidenced in the field of science communication and in technological controversies, where the lack of coupling between mass media and its scientific sources creates much dissatisfaction. The fact that newspapers or television programmes do not report science in the way scientists would like creates a climate of moralistic indignation over bias, inaccuracy and sensationalism. The problem arises from divergent professional perspectives: what is 'inaccurate' from a scientist's point of view might make a 'good story' from the point of view of the professional journalist. Good science is hardly news (see, for example, Covello et al, 1987; Friedman et al, 1987; Rubin, 1987).

A literature has built up analysing and trying to deal with this tense relationship between scientists and journalists (Weingart, 1998; Peters, 1995; Friedman et al, 1986). For scientific actors wanting to enhance their media presence, much of the advice they receive concerns the barriers to mass media access, such as jargon used, appearance, accessibility, and concern for working routines of media professionals. For journalists there is a balancing act between access to valuable

Table 8.1 *Examples of 'news values' implicitly or explicitly guiding news selection*

Author	News values
Galtung and Ruge (1965) Foreign news values	• Being sudden, short time span • Great in scale and intensity, big numbers • Clear and unambiguous • Surprises, but culturally close to home; continuity with existing images (modern news production in general) • Reference to elite people • Negativity
Hansen (1994) Science specific	• Relevance to daily life • 'Weird and wacky' • Human interest stories • Significant new development (breakthrough) • Controversy: part of wider social and political problems
Neidhardt (1993) General values applied to science reportage	• (Time) surprisingly new; extraordinary, non-conventional, aberrant event (established facts are not news) • (Topical subject) superlative, big numbers, catastrophe • (Social) binary conflict, contrasts; controversy, balancing experts

information in order to land a scoop and keeping an independent judgement on any story. This independence is often supported by the professional culture of journalism, which is different from thinking about and doing research as a scientist. Cultures support an ethos and bring a definition of the situation, norms, everyday routines and practices. 'News values' is a concept that is used to highlight the relative autonomy in news production: whether a story gets selected for inclusion in the news depends on whether the story matches the 'news values', an internal criterion. We can then ask: what are the news values for science? Table 8.1 gives an overview of such news values. The discussion might distinguish general news values (Galtung and Ruge, 1965) from specific news values for science. The original idea of news values is based on the model of foreign news, which has to be a sudden, surprising and short-term event, clear and great in scale, and with a negative story line. Hansen (1994) identified the relevance for daily life, the human interest angle, the breakthrough, the weird and wacky, and the controversial development as elements of scientific news values. Neidhardt (1993) brought this to the point of three dimensions: a scientific story must be extra-ordinary and non-conventional, large in scale or referring to catastrophic events and controversial to make the news.

Explaining the grievances of science communication with news values has several advantages. First, it can be demonstrated how good journalistic practice necessarily leads to a perceived bias on the part of scientists. For example, news media operate with the dramatization of binary conflicts, thereby presenting position and counter-position in equal terms, while excluding any middle position.

This translates differences in arguments into polar differences between persons and often exaggerates minority opinion. One of the positions may actually have little or no scientific legitimacy. This regularly violates the expectations of scientific communities. Second, news values get us out of a moralistic discussion of mis-information and 'bias'. The analysis of bias requires an indisputable standard of comparison, which is often impossible to provide. However, news values explain the apparent bias with operational factors in the culture of journalism, a systemic part of the production of news and not a personal disposition of any-one in particular. Furthermore, they distance our judgement of good reporting from expectations of the scientific community. This leaves open the question of professional ethics, whether a journalist lives up to the standards expected from news values, and whether there may be a tension between news values and other quality standards of reporting (see Bader, 1992 for an example discussion of standards for science journalism).

Changes in salience and framing of biotechnology over the years

If the media are not an appendage of the powers that be, but an actor in themselves with relative autonomy in the construction of news and with potential influence in the formation of public opinion, then the media are also not the conveyor belt of techno-scientific information to influence public perceptions. This warrants our efforts to describe in some detail the trajectory of mass media coverage of biotechnology. This is what we will do in our final section.

Our database covers the years 1973 to 2002 and comprises countries across Europe, as well as Japan, the US and Canada. Our database of the opinion-leading press contains nearly 20,000 articles from 18 countries as shown in Table 8.2 (see Appendix). This allows us to estimate total coverage and to analyse the content of a systematic sample of articles. We analyse the media content using indicators of salience and framing. The *salience* of biotechnology is the number of articles in a single elite newspaper. The framing of biotechnology news is indicated first by *evaluation*, second by references to *risks or benefits*, and third by the *themes* of biotechnology. Thirty-five topics of biotechnology were coded and then collapsed into nine themes, namely Medical, Basic Research, Animal and Agricultural, Economic, Regulatory and Policy, Ethical, Personal Identification, Safety and Risk, and a residual category of new issues that emerged during the debate. For each article three themes were allowed. For our methodology of media analysis see the relevant chapters in Durant et al (1998), Gaskell and Bauer (2001) or Bauer and Howard (2004).

Opinion-leading press coverage of biotechnology 1973–2002

The mass media cover a wide field of activity. We restricted our data corpus to one or two 'opinion-leading' outlets in each country. This makes sense for several reasons. First, we assumed that the elite press is an early indicator of public discourse and rising public awareness. For an emergent technology with, as yet, little impact on daily life the elite press is the likely arena for the issues arising. Other media outlets will follow their lead on that. Second, and more pragmatically, the elite press is a source that is easily accessible in most countries, historically as well as for purposes of current monitoring. Indeed, from about the mid-1980s onwards, most elite newspapers are available in accessible computerized format. Because we collected materials backwards to 1973, we needed to consider accessibility to archival materials.

One could argue that television is a more important source of information for the contemporary citizen, and therefore the more prototypical mass medium to study public salience and framing. This may be true once an issue has matured, but not over a longer observation period where the issue is still emerging. It is likely that television and other more popular news media follow the lead of the elite newspapers on an issue such as biotechnology. Furthermore, the collection of comparable data of television coverage over 30 years faces enormous technical and financial hurdles. And it may also be plainly wrong to attribute primacy to television, because people may wrongly remember television to be the main source of vicarious experiences (see Shrum, 1997).

Salience and the evaluation of biotechnology

Media intensity is an indicator of public salience of an issue. This might reflect the level of controversy over biotechnology, but also the workings of the national media system. Figure 8.1 shows the intensity and the evaluation of modern biotechnology in the newspaper coverage.

The salience figures are national annual averages which show the four phases of a global issue cycle of biotechnology: low early coverage until 1980; a steady increase between 1981 and 1995; the massive explosion of coverage from 1996 to 2001; and the beginning of the end of the attention cycle after 2002. Two public events were responsible for the massive increase in public attention after 1996: the arrival of Monsanto's Roundup Ready soya in late 1996, which led to the GM food debate in Europe; and the presentation of Dolly the cloned sheep in February 1997, which led to the global stem cell debates. Both events increased media coverage massively – in particular in Germany, Italy, Austria, France and Britain, and synchronized public attention to biotechnology across Europe. In North America, Canada followed the pattern of Europe, while in the US this increase occurred later, in 2000. We have called these years the 'watershed years' of public opinion on biotechnology (Gaskell and Bauer, 2001). The annual averages reported in Figure 8.1 mask enormous differences in the intensity of coverage per country (see Table 8.2 in the Appendix). For example, by 2002 Japan carries 2444 articles,[2] the UK 1385, the US 1143, Germany 1068, while Greece reports only 46 articles, Norway 80 and Portugal 135 articles in a single elite newspaper. In some countries, biotechnology has become a daily news item, on the political as well as on the economic pages.

Our evaluation index is based on coder judgements on the (positive and negative) tone of voice in the articles. Average ratings are all above zero, indicating

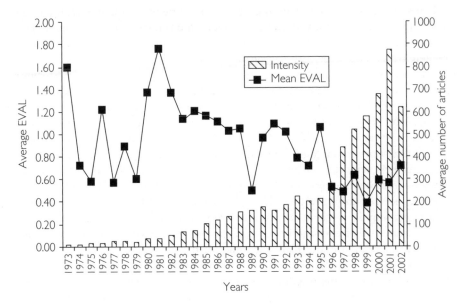

Note: Salience is based on estimated average annual figures from 18 countries; evaluation is based on national samples; total N = 19,000.

Figure 8.1 *The intensity of biotechnology coverage, and the rated evaluation of biotechnology*

an overall positive evaluation of biotechnology by the newspapers. Figure 8.1 shows the coincidences between evaluation and salience with a correlation of $r = -0.53$: when salience is higher, evaluation tends to be lower. News volume is driven by negative news. Between 1973 and 1983, when coverage is slowly picking up, the tone of voice varies but moves to a veritable hype period in the early 1980s. From 1983 to 1999, the evaluation turns and becomes less positive while the salience sharply increases. After 1999, while salience seems to diminish somewhat, the evaluation becomes more positive again.

Risk and benefits of modern biotechnology

Each press article was coded for making a risk or benefit argument, both, or making no reference to either risk or benefit. Before and after the watershed years, the risk–benefit discourse of biotechnology shifted. Overall, 14 per cent of the articles in 1997–2002 contained risk-only information (previously 10 per cent), 34 per cent benefit-only information (previously 43 per cent). Of all analysed articles, 20 per cent contained both risk and benefit information (previously 23 per cent), and 32 per cent contained neither risk nor benefit information (previously 24 per cent). This modest overall shift again masks considerable country variation.

When we look at the individual countries in more detail, we see that the newspapers under scrutiny in Greece, Switzerland, Norway and Denmark carry a relatively large number of articles with risk-only information. Denmark stands out here with 63 per cent of the articles containing only risk information. The UK and the US are the opposite here: in both countries only 5 per cent of the articles in 1997–2002 have risk-only information. Articles with benefit-only information were published relatively often in Austria, Canada, Finland, Japan, Poland, Portugal and Norway. In Poland, Portugal, Japan and Finland, benefit information prevails. The balanced risk–benefit argument is relatively prominent in Canada, Greece, Switzerland, Finland, Poland, Portugal and Norway. Canada and Greece stand out here with 47 per cent and 45 per cent of all articles having balanced accounts of biotechnology. Finally, the risk–benefit discourse is generally low in Austria, France, Italy, Sweden, the UK, Germany and the US, where between 45 per cent and 70 per cent are not coded on either risk or benefit arguments.

To summarize this variability in risk discourse on biotechnology, we create an index and compare the relative position of the countries for the two periods. The ranking is inverted, reflecting the degree of risk discourse in each country. Figure 8.2 compares the rankings for 1973–1996 with those of 1997–2002. The small correlation ($r = 0.40$; $n = 16$) between rankings suggests both stability and shifts over time. The Netherlands, France and Germany do not move their relative position: they fall onto the diagonal line; Norway, Switzerland, the UK, Poland and Portugal move very little. Countries above the diagonal moderate their risk

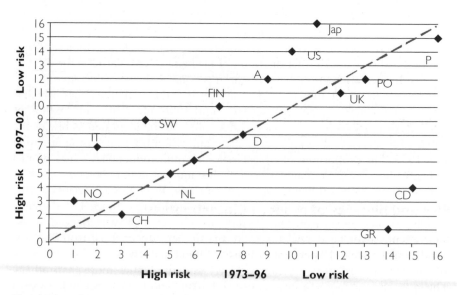

Note: High rank means higher risk discourse, low rank means lower risk discourse. The data are based on 16 countries, 1973–2002, N = 19,000).

Figure 8.2 *The ranking of risk discourse according to the index = benefit − (risk + mixed) for two time periods*

discourse, while countries below the diagonal accentuate their risk discourse of biotechnology relative to others. This is particularly the case for Greece and Canada. Greece ranks 14th out of 16 in the first period but moves to rank 1 in the second. Canada, with a ranking of 15 in the first period, moves to rank 4 in the second period.

With the exception of Greece and Canada, we can order 14 countries on a continuum of risk discourse that is consistent over time, from Norway, Italy and Switzerland with high levels of risk discussions, to Portugal, Poland, the UK, Japan and the US on the lower end of the scale. Our index decreases from an average of 18 (S.D. = 16) in the first period to 8 (S.D. = 11) in the second period. There is a trend towards more risk discourse with global debates over GM crops and foods and stem cell cloning in the second half of the 1990s, while on average our index remains positive: benefit coverage of biotechnology continues to prevail.

The thematic diversification and the limited resonance of the 'life science' idea

We coded a maximum of three different themes per article, and across the 18 countries we coded a total of 35,672 thematic references before and after the watershed years. A total of 30 per cent of all themes found in the first period, 1973–1996, refer to medical applications. These references were made in 56 per cent of all articles. After 1997, the proportion of medical issues diminishes to 23 per cent of all themes, distributed among 43 per cent of all articles. Clearly the medical theme attracts the attention of journalists in elite newspapers and reflects the general trend towards the medicalization of science news (Bauer, 1998). Figure 8.3 shows the shifting distribution of themes across articles for the two periods. In the early period, basic research is a major theme, while attention for this theme is far lower after 1997. The same is true for economic issues, which is the third important theme between 1973 and 1996, but ranks only sixth after 1997. Regulatory issues, new issues (that could not be identified as one of the expected themes), and in particular safety and risk attract increasing attention after 1997. The proportions of ethical issues, identification, policy issues, animal and agricultural issues remain lesser and constant over both periods.

Two observations on themes are worth making. First, there is relatively little variance of these themes within each country and across time. The thematic ordering is very stable, with some exceptions. Greece and Switzerland decrease their attention for basic research more than others. In contrast to the overall trend, Sweden sees a 10 per cent increase of attention to economic issues. Greece also increases regulatory issues and safety and risk issues more than others. The latter also get much more attention in Finland and France. Second, we see a shift and diversification of the main themes over time. From 1973 to 1996, 60 per cent of themes cover medical applications, basic research, economic issues and regulation, and in that order. After 1997, 56 per cent of themes cover medical issues, risk and safety, regulation and the other, new and unidentified issues. After the watershed years, economic arguments and basic research take a back seat,

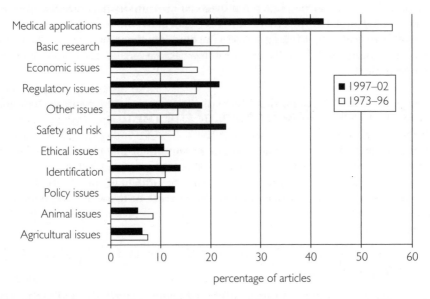

Note: Based on a maximum of three references per article from a single source in 17 countries between 1973 and 2002 (*N* = 19,049)

Figure 8.3 *Percentage of articles referring to some themes of biotechnology*

while safety and regulation take precedence. Overall, these themes become more equally distributed.

Looking at the linkages among these themes, we found that, after 1997, the story of biotechnology increasingly splits into two separate stories, one around 'red' biomedical, and another one around 'green' agri-food biotechnology. These two dramas are framed differently, evaluated differently in terms of risk and benefit, and mobilize different protagonists in the media. Over the watershed years, green biotechnology moved from a risk-and-benefit discourse to a discourse where risk dominated. Also, in comparing the red–green differentiation of public discourse, we found that the countries could be grouped into those where a discourse of prospects was evident on both developments of biotechnology (Poland, Italy, Germany, Canada and the US), those that saw prospects and concerns (France, Netherlands, Finland), those where green got a bad press and red was taken up with caution (the UK, Sweden, Greece, Switzerland, Austria), in Portugal red had a mainly positive press and green a mainly negative one, and finally Denmark, where both green and red biotechnologies were commented on as being 'risky business' (Bauer et al, 2001). This development of a red–green contrast in the elite press has been proven to have influenced public perception over time (Bauer, 2005), and thus might have contributed to the demise of the Life Science Project, the visionary bid of Monsanto and other international agri-chemical and pharmaceutical companies for a new industrial sector spanning farming, food production and health provision. The consolidation of a red–green split in public perception between GM food with unclear consumer benefits and global protests on the one hand and life-saving applications in the bio-medical area with less public protest on the other hand, made this integrated industrial vision increasingly untenable with little resonance in public opinion.

The impact of the media

In this chapter, we set out to look at three key questions that typify the discussion about the part the media play in the roll-out of technological developments. Although these issues are generic and applicable to virtually any technology, we applied theoretical notions and analysed what must be the most comprehensive corpus of media data relevant for the global discussion on modern biotechnology between 1973 and 2002.

The first question focuses on media power with respect to influencing the public perception of a technology such as biotechnology. Besides analyses that can be characterized as 'media bashing', many empirical and conceptual accounts take a genuine interest in the media's function in the formation of public opinion. In exploring three hypotheses of media effects, we concluded that there is evidence for limited but definite effects of mass media coverage on public perception. First, news sets the public's agenda onto some issues at the expense of others because of limited space and attention span. The quantity of coverage idea suggests that negative public attitudes co-vary with increased media coverage, but gets limited empirical support. The knowledge-gap hypothesis focuses on the structural inequalities of information flow and issues of knowledge in society and the mitigating function of public controversy. Cultivation analysis is defined by its long-term focus on world-views: how audiences come to see the world according to their media consumption pattern.

The second question is about the media being an epiphenomenon of power or an actor with relative autonomy. We looked at the idea of 'news values', a concept that highlights the relative autonomy in news production: whether a story is selected for inclusion in the news depends on whether the story matches the 'news values', an internal criterion, and is not necessarily input or source driven. This throws some light on the ongoing grievances between science and the media. What appears 'inaccurate' from a scientist's point of view might make a 'good story' from the point of view of the media professional.

Our third question addresses the actual media coverage of modern biotech-nology and its changes. We analysed and compared salience, evaluation, risk discourse and thematic focus across countries and over time. The analysis of salience shows four phases of global biotechnology coverage from 1973 to 2002: low early coverage until 1980; a steady increase between 1981 and 1995; the massive explosion of coverage from 1996 to 2001; and the beginning of the end of the issue cycle after 2002. Between 1973 and 1983, the tone of voice varies, but moves to the hype period in the early 1980s. From 1983 to 1999, the evalu-ation turns and becomes less positive while the salience sharply increases. After

1999, the evaluation becomes more positive again. The arrival of Monsanto's Round-up Ready soya in late 1996 and the presentation of Dolly the cloned sheep in February 1997 increased media coverage massively, in particular in Germany, Italy, Austria, France and Britain, and synchronized public attention to biotechnology across Europe. In North America, Canada followed the pattern of Europe, while in the US this increase occurred only in 2000, with the stem cell debate. In spite of these general trends, intensity differences between countries persist. So, in some countries biotechnology has become a daily news item, on the political as well as on the economic pages, while in others it has remained a weekly story.

The watershed years 1996–1997 also mark the transition of the biotechnology discourse in some countries, where overall analysis mainly indicates stability. The transition is very evident in Greece and Canada, where the risk discourse after the watershed really picks up. Countries like Norway, Italy and Switzerland are characterized by high levels of risk discussions but hardly change after 1996–1997, while Portugal, Poland and the UK do not change much either and stay at relatively low levels of risk discourse. These findings must be seen in the light of the fact that the prevailing coverage of modern biotechnology is positive.

The thematic analysis of the media coverage indicated that medical applications are by far the most important issue in biotechnology, as seen from the perspective of journalistic news value. Approximately half of all articles on biotechnology are about medical applications, clearly reflecting a general trend for medicalization of this strand of news. After the watershed, the biotechnology drama splits in two: the red medical biotechnology, including genomics and stem cell research, on the one hand, and the green agri-food and crop biotechnology on the other.

In summary, we conclude that the mass media have a limited and varied, but definite impact on public perception of biotechnology. The public is not an empty shell, but follows mass media coverage in terms of agenda, knowledge and basic conceptions of the issues. The mass media on the other hand are relatively autonomous in the production of news, and are not an extension of science. The documented variation between countries, despite a global context of news production, on coverage of modern biotechnology supports the notion of news values. On a country level, the news media represent a relatively autonomous actor. We did not find evidence to support fears for the media as a spin doctor of the scientific establishment, or to support the conveyor belt hypothesis of techno-scientific information through which public perceptions can be easily managed or manipulated. Both the relative autonomy of the mass media vis-à-vis interested actors and the relative autonomy of the public vis-à-vis the mass media suggest that moral panics over misinformation as well as overconfident spin doctoring for science and technology might be sustainable only by ignoring the evidence.

Notes

1   The analyses were performed in the context of the international collaborative research project LSES (see www.lse.ac.uk/depts/lses) thanks to funding of the EU and various

national funding agencies. We would like to acknowledge our colleagues from the LSES project who participated in the media analysis

2   Atsuko Tusji (a journalist working on *Asahi*, personal communication, June 2004) attributed the massive coverage in Japan in part to the fact that the newspaper employs more than 20 staff science writers, a much higher number than other newspapers. In Britain, the competition between several elite papers, each anxious not to miss a good story which the others carry, might explain in part the high public salience of the issue throughout the period

References

Bader, R. (1992) 'Was ist publizistische Qualität am Beispiel des Wissenschaftsjournalismus', manuscript, FU Berlin, January

Bauer, M. W. (1998) 'The medicalisation of science news – From the "rocket-scalpel" to the "gene-meteorite" complex', *Social Science Information*, vol 37, pp731–751

Bauer, M. W. (2002a) 'Arenas, platforms and the biotechnology movement', *Science Communication*, vol 24, pp144–161

Bauer, M. W. (2002b) 'Controversial medical and agri-food biotechnology: A cultivation analysis', *Public Understanding of Science*, vol 2, no 11, pp1–19

Bauer, M. W. (2005) 'Distinguishing RED and GREEN biotechnology: Cultivation effects of the elite press', *International Journal of Public Opinion Research*, vol 17, pp63–89

Bauer, M. W. and Bonfadelli, H. (2002) 'Controversy, media coverage and public knowledge', in Bauer, M. W. and Gaskell, G. (eds) *Biotechnology: The Making of a Global Controversy*, Cambridge University Press, Cambridge, pp149–175

Bauer, M. W. and Howard, S. (2004) *Biotechnology and the Public (Media module) – Europe, North America and Japan, 1973–2002*, Integrated Codebook, LSE report, May

Bauer, M. W., Kohring, M., Gutteling, J. M. and Allansdottir, A. (2001) 'The dramatisation of biotechnology in the elite mass media', in Gaskell, G. and Bauer, M. W. (eds) *Biotechnology 1996–2000: The Years of Controversy*, Science Museum, London, pp35–52

Bonfadelli, H. (2005) 'Mass media and biotechnology knowledge gaps within and between European countries', *International Journal of Public Opinion Research*, vol 17, pp42–62

Brosius, H. B. and Kepplinger, H. M. (1990) 'The agenda-setting function of television news: Static and dynamic views', *Communication Research*, 17, pp183–211

Cantril, H., Gaudet, H. and Herzog, H. (1947) *The Invasion from Mars*, Princeton University Press, Princeton, NJ

Cohen, B. C. (1963) *The Press and Foreign Policy*, Princeton University Press, Princeton, NJ

Covello, V. T., Von Winterfeldt, D. and Slovic, P. (1987) 'Communicating scientific information about health and environmental risks: Problems and opportunities from a social and behavioral perspective', in Covello, V. T., Lave, L. B., Moghissi, A. and Uppuluri, V. R. R. (eds) *Uncertainty in Risk Assessment, Risk Management, and Decision Making*, Plenum Publishing Corporation, NY, pp39–61

Donohue, G. A., Tichenor, P. J. and Olien, C. N. (1975) 'Mass media and the knowledge gap: A hypothesis reconsidered', *Communication Research*, vol 2, no 1, pp3–23

Durant, J., Bauer, M. W. and Gaskell, G. (eds) (1998) *Biotechnology in the Public Sphere: A European Sourcebook*, Science Museum, London

Friedman, S. M., Dunwoody, S. and Rogers, C. L. (1986) 'Scientists and journalists – Reporting science as news', AAAS, Washington

Friedman, S. M., Gorney, C. M. and Egolf, B. P. (1987) 'Reporting on radiation: A content analysis of Chernobyl coverage', *Journal of Communication*, 37, pp58–79

Galtung, J. and Ruge, M. (1965) 'The structure of foreign news', *Journal of Peace Studies*, 1, 64–90

Gaskell, G. and Bauer, M. W. (eds) (2001) *Biotechnology 1996–2000: The Years of Controversy*, Science Museum, London

Gerbner, G., Gross, L., Signorielli, N. and Morgan, M. (1980) 'Aging with television: Images on television drama and conceptions of social reality', *Journal of Communication*, vol 30, no 1, pp37–47

Gutteling, J. M. (2005) 'Mazur's hypothesis on technology controversy and media', *International Journal of Public Opinion Research*, vol 17, pp23–41

Gutteling, J. M., Olofsson, A., Fjæstad, B., Kohring, M., Goerke, A., Bauer, M. W. and Rusanen, T. (2002) 'Media coverage 1973–96: Trends and dynamics', in Bauer, M. W. and Gaskell, G. (eds) *Biotechnology: The Making of a Global Controversy*, Cambridge University Press, Cambridge, pp95–128

Gutteling, J. M. and Wiegman, O. (1996) *Exploring Risk Communication*, Kluwer Academic Publishers, Dordrecht

Hansen, A. (1994) 'Journalistic practices and science reporting in the British Press', *Public Understanding of Science*, 3, pp111–134

Katz, E. (1963) 'The diffusion of new ideas and practices', in Schramm, W. (ed) *The Science of Human Communication*, Basic Books, NY, pp77–93

Mazur, A. (1981) 'Media coverage and public opinion on scientific controversies', *Journal of Communication*, vol 31, pp106–115

McCombs, M E, and Becker, L. B. (1979) *Using Mass Communication Theory*, Prentice-Hall, Englewood Cliffs, NJ

McCombs, M. E. and Shaw, D. L. (1972) 'The agenda-setting function of mass media', *Public Opinion Quarterly*, 36, pp176–187

Morgan, M. and Shanahan, J. (1997) 'Two decades of cultivation research: An appraisal and meta-analysis', *Communication Yearbook*, vol 20, pp1–45

Neidhardt, F. (1993) 'The public as a communication system', *Public Understanding of Science*, vol 2, pp339–350

Peters, H. P. (1995) 'The interaction of journalists and scientific experts: Co-operation and conflict between two professional cultures', *Media, Culture and Society*, 17, pp31–48

Peters, H. P. (2000) 'The committed are hard to persuade: Recipients' thoughts during exposure to newspaper and TV stories on genetic engineering and their effects on attitudes', *New Genetics and Society*, vol 19, pp365–381

Protess, D. L. and McCombs, M. E. (1991) *Agenda Setting: Readings on Media, Public Opinion, and Policymaking*, Lawrence Erlbaum Associates, Hillsdale, NJ

Rosengren, K. E., Arvidson, P. and Sturesson, D. (1974) 'The Barseback "panic": A radio programme as a negative summary event', *Acta Sociologica*, vol 18, pp303–321

Rubin, D. M. (1987) 'How the news media reported on Three Mile Island and Chernobyl', *Journal of Communication*, vol 37, pp42–57

Shrum, L. J. (1997) 'The role of source confusion in cultivation effects may depend on processing strategy: A comment on Mares (1996)', *Human Communication Research*, vol 24, pp349–358

Tichenor, P. J., Donohue, G. A. and Olien, C. N. (1970) 'Mass media flow and differential growth in knowledge', *Public Opinion Quarterly*, vol 34, pp159–170

Weingart, P. (1998) 'Science and the media', *Research Policy*, vol 27, pp869–879

Appendix

Table 8.2 *Distribution of the corpus of newspaper articles across countries during the periods 1973–1996 and 1997–2002, and intensity of coverage*

Countries	Newspaper	Sample characteristics			Salience	
		1973–1996	1997–2002	Total sample	Salience	Based on period
Complete sample						
US	NYT and Washington Post	1700	1000	2700	17752	73–02
UK	The Times (73–87), Mirror (97–02), Independent (88–02)	539	562	1101	14380	73–02
Germany	FAZ	588	1243	1831	8022	73–02
Italy	Corriere della Sera	340	1200	1540	7857	73–02
France	Le Monde	623	780	1403	7735	73–02
Austria	Presse	302	647	949	5376	73–02
Switzerland	NZZ	211	500	711	4471	73–02
Sweden	Dagens Nyheter	734	600	1334	3628	73–02
Netherlands	Volkskrant	1119	600	1719	3131	73–02
Denmark	Information, Politiken	n/a	315	315	1931	73–02
Finland	Helsingin Sanomat, Savon Sanomat	375	1063	1438	1646	73–02
Greece	Kathemini, Eleftherotypia, Ta Nea, To Bima	65	324	389	401	73–02

continued

Table 8.2 *continued*

Countries	Newspaper	Sample characteristics			Salience	
		1973–1996	1997–2002	Total sample	Salience	Based on period
Partial sample						
Japan	ASAHI	350	700	1050	18067	85–02
Canada	Globe and the Mail	82	217	299	1868	92–99
Portugal	Publico	303	675	978	1202	92–02
Norway	Aftenposten, VG	418	1064	1482	n/a	93–02
Poland	Polityka, Gloswiekkopolski, Rzeczpospolita, Trybuna Ludu & Trybuna	208	158	366		73–99

Note: Countries are presented ordered by estimated overall salience. The upper part of the table comprises countries for which data are available from 1973–2002. The lower part of the table comprises countries for which partial databases are available. In countries where more than one newspaper is analysed, the intensity figures are based on (the equivalent of) one single newspaper.

9

The Politics of Bioethics[1]

The Case of Human Embryonic Stems Cells

Torben Hviid Nielsen[2]

The ideas in this chapter were first published in 'Five Framings – One Entity? The Political Ethics of Human Embryonic Stem Cells', *Science Studies*, 2005, vol 18, no 1

The 1998 summer issue of *Technology Review* disclosed and pre-announced the ongoing research on human embryonic stem cells under the front-page heading 'Biotech Taboo . . . The troubled hunt for the ultimate cell . . . that could be used to grow any type of human replacement tissue' (Regalado, 1998, front page and p34). Yet a year and a half later, the front page of the 1999 Christmas issue of *Science* promoted stem cells as the 'Breakthrough of the Year . . . capturing the Promise of Youth' (Vogel, 1999, front page and pp2238–2239). In November 1999, a committee under the American Association for the Advancement of Science (AAAS) found that stem cell research 'raises ethical and political concerns, but these are not unique to stem cell research' (AAAS, 1999, piv). Yet two years later a subsequent committee under the National Research Council (NRC) stated that 'the stem cell debate has led scientists and nonscientists alike to contemplate profound issues, such as who we are and what makes us human beings' (NRC, 2001, pxi). Human embryonic stem cells have, together with cloning, attained the dubious status of the most promising as well as the most controversial among the many emerging biotechnologies.

The derivation of a scientific discovery

Geron Corporation, Menlo Park, California, which had licensed the cells worldwide, had also coordinated and orchestrated the first public announcement of the derivation of human embryonic stem cells as a 'scientific discovery' and 'progress in basic research' very thoroughly. Two press releases from the company provided the key background information for the printed press's front-page news 'Scientist Found Cells at Root of Human Life' on 6 November 1998 (*The New York Times*, 1998). The press releases referred back to two prestigious scientific publications: an article in *Science* by Professor James A. Thomson and colleagues from the University of Wisconsin, who had isolated human embryonic stem (hES) cells from the inner cell mass of human embryos at the blastocyst stage (Thomson et al, 1998), and another article in *Proceedings of the National Academy of Sciences* by Professor John D. Gearhart and colleagues from Johns Hopkins University, Baltimore, who had isolated human embryonic germ (hEG) cells from foetal tissues obtained from terminated pregnancies (Shamblott et al, 1998).

An essential translation and reframing had, however, taken place on the passage from the scientific periodicals via the press releases to the front-page news. Stem cells, especially from bone marrow, had been known and used for cancer treatment since the 1950s. And embryonic stem cells had been derived from mice in 1981 (Evans and Kaufman, 1981) and primates in 1995 (Gearhart et al, 1995). The 'novelty' presented in the scientific publications was thus neither the existence of stem cells as such, nor of embryonic stem cells, nor even of human embryonic stem cells, but merely the successful derivation of human embryonic stem cells. And the derivation was presented as (technical and practical) know-how more than (scientific and systematic) knowledge.

Neither of the two articles has the aura of a new theoretical insight, nor do they proclaim any controversial breakthrough. The definition of the cell lines and the operational criteria for their derivation are conveyed unchanged from the previous experiments with mice and primates. A summary and documentation of research protocols with references to preceding studies is thus the dominating content of the two articles. Description and documentation of practical procedure in the laboratories has precedence over conceptual clarification and explanations. Large passages of the two articles resemble a mix of cookbook and manual, conceptual trivialities and complicated technicalities: those were the ingredients and this is how we proceeded at the lab bench. By way of a not untypical example:

> *Cells were grown in DMEM (GIBCO/BRL) supplemented with 15% fetal bovine serum (HyClone), 0.1 mM nonessential amino acids (GIBCO/ BRL), 0.1mM 2-mercaptoethanol (Sigma), 2 mM glutamine. . . Cultures were grown in 5% or 8% CO_2, 95% humidity and were routinely passaged every 7 days after disaggregation with 0.05% trypsin/0.53 mM EDTA (GIBCO/BRL) or 0.25% trypsin at 37° C for 5–10 min. . . Cells prepared for cytogenetic analysis were incubated in growth media with 0.1 μg/ml of Colcemid for 3–4 hr, trypsinized, resuspended in 0.075 M KCl, and incubated for 20 min at 37° C, then fixed in 3:1 methanol/acetic acid. (Shamblott et al, 1998, p13727)*

In brief, the articles do not claim to have found any new and unexpected substance, but rather to have demonstrated that the existence of an expected substance can be kept and maintained in a certain form: isolated, cultivated and expressed. The two research teams had successfully adapted, replicated or copied in human cells what had previously been attained in cells from mice and primates. The research teams thus constituted human embryonic stem cells as a new object for science analogous to the way Gregory Mendel constituted genetics (and Crick and Watson later DNA) as objects for science (Foucault, 1971), but theoretical implications and practical applications were not part of the agenda.

The triangle of collaboration between the private company Geron, the partly public universities and their partly outsourced research teams was a response to the political reality, that the US since 1996 had had a de facto ban on public funding of research 'in which a human embryo or embryos are destroyed, discarded, or knowingly subjected to risk of injury or death greater than that allowed for research on fetuses in uteri'. Congress had taken the decision ad hoc as the Dickey–Wicker amendment to the Department of Health and Human Services annual budget – and against the recommendations of the National Institute of Health and the Clinton administration. Yet as only the use of public funding was forbidden, a paradoxical consequence became, in the words of one of the Clinton administration's key advisors, Dr Ronald M. Green,

> [that] although much of the previous animal research on ES cells that had led to Thomson's achievements was federally financed, the commercial benefit would now be in private hands. (Green, 2001, p9)

Geron had been founded by Dr Michael D. West back in 1990. Following the publication of the derivation of embryonic stem cells from primates in 1995, Geron had funded the research of Thomson and Gearhart as well as Professor Roger Peterson, University of California, San Francisco (considered by many to be the most promising candidate to succeed (Regalado, 1998, p38)). Investments in funding for licences turned out to be an immediate financial success. Two applications for patents were filed well in advance of the scientific publication and were subsequently approved. On the very day of announcement, stocks rose from $6 to $23, and one month later, convertible debentures worth $15 million were sold to venture capitalists.

The two scientific publications closed with reservations characteristic of the genre. In the words of Thomson and colleagues, 'Substantial advances in basic developmental biology are required to direct ES cells efficiently to lineages of human clinical importance' (Thomson et al, 1998, p1147). Yet the patent applications present themselves as being as certain and convinced as the scientific articles are modest. They are both 'continuation-in-part' of earlier applications, but much longer and more detailed, and the 'Scientists' are completed in the standard formula as 'Inventors'. Gearhart's application (US Patent 6,245,566 filed 31 March 1998 and approved 21 June 2001) has the largest number of formal 'Claims' – 36 – all concerning methods of producing and/or maintaining 'human pluripotent embryonic germ cells'. The 11 claims in Thomson's application (US Patent 6,200,806 filed 26 June 1998 and approved 13 March 2001) are presented in another 'logic'. The first eight are different variants of 'a purified preparation of pluripotent human embryonic stem cells', the next two are methods of isolating such cell lines, and the last claim is finally the very cell line developed by the method.

In short, both claim protection for process as well as product, method as well as result. The pursuit of a maximum of legal protection appears to be the rationale behind the comprehensive claims – and a possible explanation of the contrast to the modest reservations in the scientific publications.

The criteria for patentability may have influenced even the choice of the key concept 'derivation'. 'Isolation' and 'establishment' (partly used as synonyms) were the key terms in the articles reporting the use of identical procedures and techniques on mice in 1982 and primates in 1995. But 'derivation' was also the key concept in the 1997 article announcing the cloning of the sheep Dolly, where it referred to the very different reality of a 'viable offspring', that is, the birth of an entire living animal (Wilmut et al, 1997). And these examples appear to be only illustrations of a general trend. During the 1990s, the use of the terms 'isolation' and 'establishment' versus 'derivation' in the prestigious scientific periodicals changed accordingly. 'Isolation' and 'establishment' were most frequently used in the beginning, but latterly 'derivation' has taken over. And this significant change took place just after the middle of the decade, around the time when Dolly and the human embryonic stem cells both were derived (see Figure 9.1).[3]

The new trend need not be permanent, but the relative increase of the term 'derivation' at the expense of 'isolation' and 'establishment' is both significant and meaningful. The concept 'derivation' is increasingly used to describe two quite different phenomena: the isolation, cultivation and expression of embryonic stem cells as well as the cloning of viable offspring, that is, two of the most promising and controversial of the many new biotechnologies. We do not know the degree to which the tendency reflects substantial changes in research priorities, mere changes in editorial criteria or even merely a change of habitual wording.

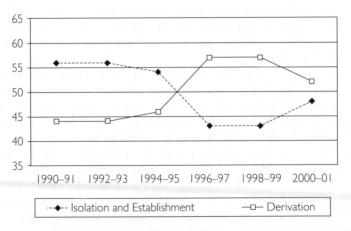

Relative occurrence of 'Isolat#' and Establish#' versus 'Deriv#' in titles of *Nature, Science* and *Proc. Natl. Acad. Sci.*

Figure 9.1 *'Isolation' and 'Derivation'*

The typical response from a handful of researchers in the field, when asked about the change, was that they had not previously been aware of any such change, that it nevertheless seemed plausible that it had happened, but that it did not require any special explanation. 'It is quite simply the concept we use.' We don't know why, but we do know that the concept 'derivation' has a prehistory from patenting in organic chemistry, where the 'derivation' of a substance was considered sufficient to satisfy one of the three crucial criteria for an invention. Although a substance of nature, a derivation was considered an invention, since it would not have existed in that form without the intervention of science. And a derived substance can, in principle, be granted patent for the process as well as the product, the 'making' as well as the 'use'.

Restoration to immortality: The promise of a regenerative medicine

The second framing as a medical hope is often presented as just the other side of the framing as scientific progress or basic knowledge, as the step from 'pure' to 'applied' science.

All stem cells, including adult stem cells, produce the enzyme telomerase, which was isolated for the first time in 1989 and maintains the non-coding bits of DNA attached to the end of each chromosome. Telomerase 'resets' – with a bio-chemical explanation for philosophers – 'the cell's chromosomal clock and prevents the timed death suffered by most differentiated cells' (Green, 2001, p35). Stem cells hence have the capacity for 'prolonged self-renewal' and are able to produce 'at least one type of highly differentiated or specialized descendant'. And embryonic stem cells have three additional capacities. They are *pluripotent*, that is, able to differentiate to all types of tissues in the body; they are *malleable*, that is, can be manipulated without losing the structure of the cell; and they are *immortal*, that is, able to continue differentiation apparently for ever (Weismann, 2000; Fuchs and Segre, 2000). The three unique capacities recurred in *Science*'s presentation of the human embryonic stem cells as the breakthrough of the year. 'If it lives up to its early promise, it may one day restore vigor to aged and diseased muscles, hearts, and brains – perhaps even allowing humans to combine the wisdom of old age with the potential of youth.' Human embryonic stem cells 'may one day be used to treat human diseases in all sorts of ways, from repairing damaged nerves to growing new hearts and livers in the laboratory; enthusiasts envision a whole catalog of replacement parts' (Vogel, 1999, p2238).

The potential of embryonic stem cells is thus an important part of the 'regen-erative medicine' that has enlarged the scope of medical therapy 'from simply halting the progression of acute or chronic disease to include restoration of lost organ functions'. And 'regenerative medicine would', writes Dr Thomas Okarma (Michael West's successor as Chief Executive Officer (CEO) of Geron), 'be a totally new value paradigm for clinical therapeutics', bypassing surgery's inter-ventions in the body and pharmaceuticals' side effects. Okarma can thus revolve the moral argument against the bioethicists. 'Not to develop the technology would do great harm to over 100 million patients in the US alone' (Okarma, 2001, pp3–13).[4] The real threat to morality is the sceptic bioethicist, who is willing to deprive one-third of the population of their cure, not the optimistic scientists.

Technology Review has depicted 'the human body shop' as a scenario behind the use of embryonic stem cells in regenerative medicine:

> *A decade from now and an elderly man gets the grim news that his heart is rapidly decaying and that the left ventricle – the chamber that squeezes blood out to the body – needs to be replaced. His physician takes a biopsy of the heart cells that are still healthy and ships the tissue to a lab that is really an organ factory. There, workers use that patient's own cells and special polymers to fashion and grow a replacement part – certified by the original manufacturer. In three months, the new ventricle is frozen, packaged and sent to the hospital, where the patient undergoes a standard surgical procedure: the insertion of a living implant created from his own tissue. (Garr, 2001, p73)*

The aura is high-tech, but the medical use of embryonic stem cells is depicted as *low intervention*. The stem cells are '*organic*', the body's own internal healing mechanisms, and '*personal*', one's own, and '*clean*', uncontaminated cells. The real 'magic', however, is the promise to *break the arrow of time*. 'The immortal Cell' presents a shortcut to 'The eternal Life'. Destiny and fate are no longer untouchable. Science and medicine promise to accomplish, here and now, what previously barely religion believed possible, and then only in the next world. 'There and then' might become 'here and now'. Life is about to become reversible or restorable, the permanent beginning or the continuous renewal (Alexander, 2003; Hall, 2003).

Medical hopes are high, but thus far 'proofs of principles' are the only reality. Experiments in vitro and with model animals have demonstrated that the principle *can* work, that is, new tissues can differentiate and old ones can be restored. The step from scientific principle to medical practice is, however, at the very least a question of degree and type of differentiation, density and intensity, compatibility, targeting, and possible side effects. The old blood-forming stem cells in bone marrow (HSC) are currently 'the only type of stem cell commonly used for therapy' (National Institutes of Health, homepage, 17 March 2003).

Overselling, promising too much too fast, is the severe shadow hanging over the medical hope. Even the pioneer scientists soon warned of a likely backlash. 'I'm not looking forward to the backlash three years from now when people say, "What happened to stem cells?"', said Thomson as early as 2002. 'We need to educate the public that science takes a long time' (Holden and Vogel, 2002, p2119). Yet Michael West was still keen to insist on the non-scientific, i.e. not invincible, nature of all obstacles. 'We have the basic discoveries within our reach to put regenerative medicine into the hands of physicians. We are missing only two components – an organized effort and time' (West, 2003, p220).

Playing God? Old ethical concerns in new voices

The framing as a new medical paradigm emphasized the good promises of health and the hope for cure of illness, but it did not succeed in setting the tone of the public discourse and thus dominating the political agenda. From the very beginning, the legitimacy of the scientific breakthrough was instead questioned by old ethical concerns. If science was about to replace religion as the explanation of life, then Christian (or Creationist) religion was soon to return with accusations aimed at the new technologies of 'playing God'. The most prominent international spokesmen were those of the Vatican, but the recently inaugurated US president, the Republican George W. Bush, followed along the line. One month prior to 11 September 2001, on 9 August, he addressed the nation, in a primetime broadcast from Crawford, Texas, 'to discuss . . . a complex and difficult issue, an issue that is one of the most profound of our time' (Bush, 2001).[5] And his speech touched upon the two arguments most frequently voiced by opponents and sceptics.

The first and foremost argument gains its immanent strength by ascribing *a special moral status to the embryo*. The Christian background is manifest in the President's description of the embryo as 'a sacred gift from our Creator'. Most believers in the argument regard the status of the embryo as emerging gradually (that is, increasing from (some time after) fertilization to the full born baby), but a more radical version considers the status as absolute and beginning from fertilization. The President's wording of the argument alludes to the absolute version. Paraphrasing the President, 'The beginning of Life [should also be] The end of Science'. But the President is politician enough not to engage directly in the controversial dispute between the two versions, splitting the religious communities.

The second moral argument alluded to by the President is a formal and generalized *maxim* on the proper relation between means and end. The maxim is usually referred back to Immanuel Kant's practical imperative, but the President's version is different.[6] In his wording, 'Even the most noble ends do not justify any means'. The version is open-ended and anticipates its own application. The question is whether a prolonged and/or healthier life (i.e. the 'most noble' end) can justify the destruction or 'killing' of embryos to harvest the required stem cells (i.e. 'any means').[7]

A strict interpretation and radical application of the two arguments prescribes a 'no' or a 'ban' to all research in and on human embryonic stem cells. The status is violated and the maxim infringed. Attributed an absolute status, the embryo resists its own use in science. The technologically unavoidable is morally untouchable, the required source itself morally problematic. And, although not exclusively, stem cells in research are definitely *also* used as means to an end. Ethics stands versus science and science versus ethics. No compromise seems possible. But the President did not take the radical consequence indicated by his rhetoric and supposed by his arguments. Instead, he concluded that:

> *we should allow federal funds to be used for research on these existing stem*
> *cell lines (more than 60 lines as a result of private research), where the life*
> *and death decision has already been made. (Bush, 2001)*

The unexpected conclusion was intended as a political balance with concessions
to the most influential interest groups and their lobbyists. The scientists were
offered (some) stem cell lines to work with, and the opponents (including the anti-
abortionists) were assured that no new demand for embryos would be created.
But the concessions soon turned into dissatisfaction on both sides. Scientists
complained that the available stem cell lines were too few (and not pure enough),
and the religious communities declined the conclusion as the use of moral double
standards.

As unsettled and thus postponed, human embryonic stem cells remained an
issue also during the next presidential campaign. The Democratic candidate, John
Kerry, promised to

> *overturn the ban on federal funding of research on new stem cell lines,*
> *. . . he will allow doctors and scientists to explore their full potential with*
> *the appropriate ethical oversight. Patients and their families should no*
> *longer be denied the hope that this new research brings. (Kerry and*
> *Edwards, 2002)*

Kerry's framing was the first of the two, that is, science as a necessary precondition
for useful medicine. The five arguments given in the press release stating his
position thus all circumvented the controversial ethical issues. The first argument
was political, an appeal to consensus: 'Stem cell research has broad bipartisan
support'. The last argument concerned competitiveness: the US is 'losing leadership in stem cell research'. But the three remaining arguments were all technical
critiques of Bush's decision as not only insufficient, but also unimplemented.
Fewer cell lines than originally promised are available, they are contaminated with
mouse cells, and other cells are not available. Apart from a few empty insertions,
ethical issues are unmentioned – apparently considered an argument of the
opposition so profound that the best tactic might be to avoid it.

Adult stem cells as Nature's own solution?

The attempt of the first two framings to avoid or overtrump the ethical considerations was only partly successful. The focal public debate became a partial
revival of old ethical concerns, a new version of the human embryonic research
debate. Novel and unique to human stem cells, however, was the way science itself
indicated new 'technical' solutions to the recurring ethical concerns. In two
subsequent steps, science partly regained the framing and the agenda; first, based
on the idea of adult stem cells as Nature's own solution, then by therapeutic
cloning as humankind's techno-fix to the ethical challenges.

The very same article in *Science* that promoted stem cells as the breakthrough of the year also pointed to another 'astonishing development that occurred in 1999 [and that] may ease the ethical dilemma':

> *In defiance of decades of accepted wisdom, researchers in 1999 found that stem cells from adults retain the youthful ability to become several different kinds of tissues: brain cells can become blood cells, and cells from bone marrow can become liver. (Vogel, 1999, p2238)*

If it could be demonstrated that adult stem cells had the same (or equivalent) potentials as embryonic cells, they would be 'nature's own solution' to the recurring ethical concerns, that is, a chance to obtain the advantages of stem cells without the use of embryonic cells. Even Thomson kept the theoretical possibility open. 'If it becomes possible to derive an ES cell line from a source other than an embryo, ethical controversies surrounding hES cells would greatly diminish' (Thomson, J. A., 2001). Eagerly monitored and partly funded by politicians who were sceptical towards research on embryonic stem cells, research teams speeded up their work with adult stem cells. In 2001, reports of examples appearing to prove the principle were published continually (Clarke et al, 2000; Coghlan and Young, 2001; Colter et al, 2001; Scolding, 2001), and on 21 June 2002 *Science* printed a chart to illustrate the plasticity that might be 'too good to be true . . .

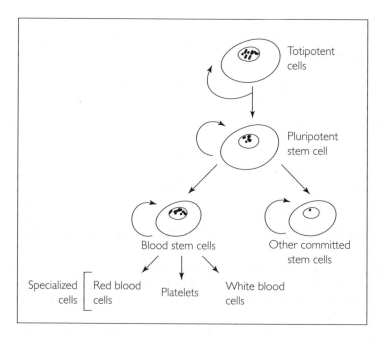

Source: *Science* 2002

Figure 9.2 *The possible plasticity of adult stem cells*

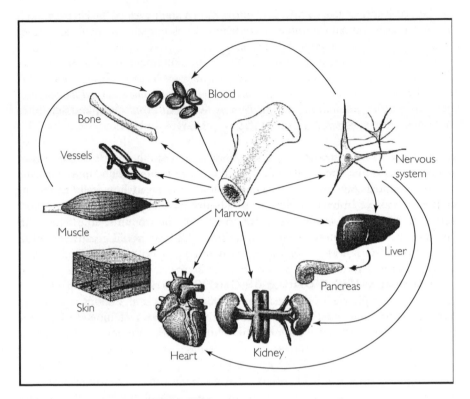

Source: National Institutes of Health, 2000

Figure 9.3 *The ontological hierarchy of stem cells*

that stem cells from a variety of tissues can produce progeny in different organs'
(Holden and Vogel, 2002, p2126).

Yet researchers and scientists did disagree no less, and no less seriously, than
the bioethicists. The National Institutes of Health's authoritative and widely used
Primer was thus a reproduction of the old 'accepted wisdom'. Stem cells were here
ranked in a one-way 'ontological' hierarchy which prescribed the moral dilemma
for anybody giving a special moral status to the embryo. The closer to the
biological origin, the greater the medical potentials – and the more suspect the
morality![8]

Theoretical arguments in favour of the hierarchical necessity were mostly
voiced by developmental biologists and embryologists. Stephen Jay Gould's
argument in favour of a 'progressive specification and differentiation' is typical:

> *The very structure of material reality imposes a principle of trade-offs in*
> *both nature and human affairs. . . We have, in short, traded regenerative*
> *capacity for the undeniable evolutionary advantages of maximal complexity*
> *. . . Unfortunately, von Bauer's law, and nature's broader structural rules*

of trade-off between complexity and flexibility, give us no alternative to embryonic stem cells for now. (Gould, 2001)

In brief, respected scientists conceptualized the potentiality of adult stem cells as either a closed 'theoretical impossibility' or an open 'empirical possibility', and the order of stem cells was correspondingly visualized as either 'an irreversible hierarchy' or 'an emanating star'. Different levels of abstraction and scientific traditions are at stake, yet neither of the two positions and hypotheses can be the whole truth. The still unsettled disagreement resembles the state of internal 'anomie' that often precedes a new paradigm, more than the everyday routines of an accepted 'normal science' (Kuhn, 1962). *Science*'s editorial stand that stem cells '[force] scientists to reconsider fundamental ideas about how cells grow up' (Vogel, 1999) might have implications even deeper than those hinted at. A new paradigm might be as badly needed in science as in medicine – and the former might be a precondition for the latter.

Therapeutic cloning as humankind's techno-fix?

In addition to adult stem cells as Nature's own solution, cloning and partheno-genesis were soon framed and presented as humankind's own techno-fix solution to the relentless ethical concerns.

On 25 November 2001, Advanced Cell Technology (ACT), Worcester, Massachusetts (now headed by Michael West, the former CEO of Geron) made it publicly known that they had created the first human embryo using cloning techniques. Two techniques had been used, both combining a human egg with the person's own cells to create an embryo that could provide stem cells. A technique à la Dolly replaced the genetic material of human eggs with that of adult cells. Eleven attempts used adult skin cells, eight cumulus cells. None of the eggs with skin cells survived to divide, whereas three eggs with cumulus cells divided once or twice before they died. The second and most successful technique was parthenogenesis, that is, a chemical stimulation of eggs to divide without fertiliza-tion. Twenty-two attempts were made, and six eggs lived and divided for up to five days, but all died before stem cells ready to be harvested were formed.

The moment and modus of going public was no less orchestrated than Geron's initial announcement of the derivation. Key players were actually identical (they had moved from Geron to ACT). The trinity of information was a blueprint, that is, scientific periodicals, press releases and the mass media. Yet a prepubli-cation in the January 2002 issue of the popular *Scientific American* (*Scientific American*, 2002) and a 'Rapid Communication' in the new web-journal *E-biomed: The Journal of Regenerative Medicines* (Cibelli et al, 2001) were substitutes for the prestigious *Science* and *Proceedings of the National Academy of Sciences*. The mass media generally reported the whole event as scientifically premature. Professor Weismann, a Nestor in stem cell research, even denounced the whole story as a 'non-event'. The necessary venture capitalists did not respond in any supportive way. And the ethics of cloning, not the intended revival of the framing as scientific progress, came to dominate the public debate. The very same techniques could also be the first steps towards reproductive cloning – an issue highlighted around Christmas the same year with a series of equally premature pronouncements of the first human clone already *in utero*. The suggested techno-fix was thus considered just another moral problem, hubris, playing – or taking the place of – God. Humankind's techno-fix creation was no less offensive than research on God's own creations.

The experienced staff at ACT had, of course, foreseen and was prepared to counter the ethical critique. Ronald Green[9] (the former founding director of the Office of Genome Ethics under the Clinton administration) had become chairman of ACT's own Ethical Advisory Board, and the conclusions of the board were printed together with the reportage in *Scientific American*:

> [U]nlike an embryo, a cloned organism is not the result of fertilization of an egg by a sperm. It is a new type of biological entity never before seen in nature . . . we preferred the term 'activated egg', and we concluded that its characteristics did not preclude its use in work that might save the lives of children and adults. (Scientific American, 2002)

The Ethical Advisory Board had expelled the ethical problem as a problem of (mis)understanding more than of substance – and as such to be solved on the level of concepts, neither in the labs nor on the political scene. Following the terms 'derivation' and 'regenerative medicine', the dispute over what constitutes an 'embryo', and the meaning of the term 'therapeutic cloning', the Ethical Board's conceptual manoeuvre is the fourth example of the 'power of definition' in this narrative (Wolpe and McGee, 2001). And ACT's Ethical Board was thus just one among many examples of the new role played by US bioethicists, who were increasingly hired and employed as a profession. The supply of educated bioethicists by far surpassed that of stem cell lines,[10] and in the absence of a comprehensive national law, they often serve as 'lawmakers' on the level of the firm. The old maxims of bioethics and the new profession of bioethicists seem to draw and to be drawn in different directions.

The political ethics of human embryonic stem cells

The five framings differ so profoundly that the question nearly poses itself as to how they can all refer back to the very same 'clonogenic cells capable of both self-renewal and multilineage differentiation'. Are the diversities of framings just a reflection of the unique and still partly unknown potentials inherent in the cells constituted only recently as objects for science? Are the multitudes of framings rather an expression of the many external interests involved in political decisions? Or might the disparity between the framings be a mere echo of the plurality and relativism of the postmodern optics?

Professions and experts have often claimed a kind of normative priority or even precedents on behalf of 'their' framing: for science as the necessary precondition for all the others; for medicine as the ultimate goal; for ethics due to its legitimacy to set limits for all the others; to adult stem cells as the ultimate solution; and to the techno-fix as the smartest solution. As a matter of description, however, none of the framings has had any such priority. They have all been part of the search for a truthful understanding and a fair evaluation, but none of them have prescribed unequivocal understandings and evaluations. A framing has not defined an agenda or determined an evaluation. Neither have the framings followed upon each other in a necessary succession. Nor have they existed in the pure form wherein they are here crystallized or idealized. On the contrary, politics and political decisions have over-determined, tinted and intermixed all the framings from the very beginning. To recapitulate: the scientific breakthrough was co-determined by the political requirements for funding and patents. The medical hope was embedded in general changes of lifestyle. Ethical recommendations have been altered according to political appointments. And adult stem cells and cloning/parthenogenesis were instantly presented to politics as possible solutions to the ethical concerns.

Sheila Jasanoff has mapped and emphasized substantial national differences in the American, British and German regulation of biotechnology (Jasanoff, 1995), but unrelated shifts of governments in the three nations during the early years of human embryonic stem cells have produced noteworthy shifts within the national regulations. The UK still represents national continuity, whereas the US has turned towards a more restrictive and Germany towards a more permissive regulation.

The British continuity is firmly rooted in the nation's customary scientific self-understanding and heavily institutionalized through the previous Warnock Committee, the subsequent Human Fertilisation and Embryology Act of 1990 and its corresponding executive body, the Human Fertilisation and Embryology Authority (Mulkay, 1997). Given this framework, Tony Blair's New Labour government could turn to the Chief Medical Officer for a delimited and authoritative examination. And neither government nor the parliamentary majority had problems with following the predictable recommendation that

> *research using embryos . . . to increase understanding about human disease and disorders and their cell-based treatment should be permitted subject to the controls of the Human Fertilisation and Embryology Act.*[11]

The only legal step needed was to agree to the Human Reproductive Cloning Act of 2001, which prohibited 'the placing in a woman of a human embryo which has been created otherwise than by fertilization', that is, by reproductive cloning.

Following the President's address, broadcast on 9 August 2001, the US had to implement a new advisory structure. An Executive Order of 28 November established the President's Council on Bioethics, headed by the well-known conservative bioethicist Professor Leon Kass (Kass, 2001). Seventeen additional members were appointed on 16 January 2002, addressed by the President the following day (Bush, 2002), and the Council's report 'Human Cloning and Human Dignity: An Ethical Inquiry' was ready in July the same year. The Council

was in full agreement not to accept 'cloning-to-produce-children', that is, reproductive cloning, but split regarding 'cloning-for-biomedical-research', that is,
therapeutic cloning. A majority of ten recommended 'a four-year moratorium',
whereas a minority of seven recommended 'regulation on the use of cloned
embryos for biomedical research' (President's Council on Bioethics, 2002).
Accordance between the President's policy and (the majority of) his ethical
advisors was thus re-established.

Following the shift from Helmut Kohl's CDU government to Gerhard
Schröder's SPD government, Germany underwent a similar, but reverse, shift
towards a more permissive policy. The Chancellor appointed the new Nationaler
Ethikrat on 25 April 2001 and addressed the Rat at its first meeting on 8 June
(Schröder, 2001), and the Rat's report *Stellungnahme zum Import menschlicher
embryonaler Stammzellen* was ready in the following summer. Fifteen members
voted for 'der vorläufige, befristete und an strenge Bedingungen gebundene
Import humaner embryonaler Stammzellen', whereas ten members voted in
favour of 'eine vorläufige Ablehnung des Stammzellimports' (Nationaler Ethikrat,
2002). Accordance between the Chancellor's policy and (the majority of) his
ethical advisors was thus re-established.

The arguments have been absolute and the rhetoric has been strong, but
bioethics has never been unambiguous, nor a superseding or decisive argument
in political decisions. On the contrary, politicians have recurrently appointed
ethicists (and thus also doctrines and advice) in accordance with their policies.
Bioethics has always also been political. The (Christian) argument based on
status and the (Kantian) maxim of means–ends have been powerful rhetorical
tools, but pragmatic or even utilitarian ethics have impacted political decisions
more forcibly. The attention of political bioethics has gradually but increasingly
turned from the status of the biological substances and general maxims towards
more comprehensive questions concerning society's justice and the individual's
identity. Focus has moved to possible consequences for society at large, that is, a
more hierarchical and competitive post-human world, and to the emergence of a
new, liberal and unintended eugenics. Not the sources of stem cells, but their
ultimate destiny 'what monsters we will soon be capable of creating' should be the
real cause of worry, writes Francis Fukuyama, a US neo-liberal and a member of
Bush's Council. 'The posthuman world could be one that is far more hierarchical
and competitive than the one that currently exists, and full of social conflicts as
a result' (Fukuyama, 2002, pp91, p218). And Jürgen Habermas, a German
philosopher in the tradition of the Frankfurter School, queries the identity of
individuals whose genetic make-up has been pre-selected or pre-manipulated as
a matter of 'Gattungsethik' (Habermas, 2002a, p9). 'Wir müssen uns heute
fragen, ob sich spätere Generationen gegebenenfalls damit abfinden werden,
sich nicht mehr als ungeteilten Autoren ihrer Lebensführung zu begreifen – und
auch nicht mehr als solche zu Rechenschaft gezogen zu werden' (Habermas,
2002b).

Policy decisions on stem cells have been pragmatic and balanced enough to
leave room for two apparently opposing critics: one aimed at the use of dual or
double standards and voiced mainly by religious communities, and another aimed

at the too restrictive regulations and voiced mainly by scientific communities and business.

The American 'moratorium' accepted the use of embryonic stem cell lines dating back to before the speech of the President 'where the life and death decision has already been made'. And the restrictive German law accepted the use of imported stem cell lines. Already existing and imported cell lines appear to be pragmatic loopholes if not inconsistency or double morality. Without loopholes, the second critic would, however, have been even more vociferous. It is thus conspicuous how the disappointed hopes have increasingly been explained and excused by the political regulations. The initial scientific framing is twisted to an argument blaming politicians giving too many concessions to the ethical concerns as the prime cause of the unfulfilled expectations. The disappointment is a question of delay, not of unsolvable problems; a matter of time, not of principles. Had science only had the freedom to follow its course, promises and expectations would also have been fulfilled. A hypothetical bogey has turned into a partial excuse.

Notes

1   Research for this article, including site visits at Geron Corporation and Advanced Cell Technology and a number of interviews, started during a sabbatical at the University of California, Berkeley, 2001–2002. The article also reflects dilemmas and experiences from the Norwegian Biotechnology Advisory Board www.bion.no, where the author served from 2000 to 2004. The author wants to thank Siv F. Berg, Ole Johan Borge, Troy Duster, Vidar Enebak, Karen Lebacqz, Ole Didrik Lærum, Rune Nydal, Dorothy Olsen, Gisli Palsson, Antonio Regalada, Gunnar Skirbekk and Henrik Treimo.
2   Torben Hviid Nielsen is Professor at the Centre for Technology, Innovation and Culture, University of Oslo, Norway. He contributed to the EU research projects 'Basic Ethical Principles in Bioethics and Biolaw' and 'Life Sciences in European Society'. From 2000 to 2004, he was a member of the Norwegian government's Biotechnology Advisory Board. Address: Centre for Technology, Innovation and Culture, University of Oslo, Oslo Research Park, Gaustadalleen 21, PO Box 1108 Blindern, No-0317 Oslo, Norway. Fax: +47 22 84 0601. Email: t.h.nielsen@ tik.uio.no.
3   The figures are generated by a data-search in 'Titles' in *Nature, Proc. Natl. Acad. Sci.* and *Science* from 1990 to 2001. 'Isolat#', 'Establish#' and 'Deriv#' were used as truncations. The absolute number of hits was 1137, with 266 in 1990–91, 214 in 1992–92, 209 in 1994–95, 161 in 1996–97, 162 in 1998–99 and 125 in 2000–2001.
4   The estimated figures originate from an overview by Daniel Perry (Perry, 2000) covering the 'potential US patient population for stem cell-based therapies'. The more than 100 million potential patients is the sum of 58 million with cardiovascular diseases, 30 million with autoimmune diseases, 16 million with diabetes, 10 million with osteoporosis and 8.2 million with cancer.
5   Secretary of Health and Human Services Tommy G. Thompson's testimony before Congress is a more technical and detailed follow-up (cf. Thompson, 2001).
6   Immanuel Kant's own wording of the 'practical imperative' is: 'Handle so, dass du die Menschheit, sowohl in deiner Person als in der Person eines jeden anderen, jederzeit zugleich als Zweck, niemals bloß als Mittel brauchst' (Kant, 1965, p52). Two observations are of special relevance in the context of bioethics. The maxim is directed

towards the use of Persons *solely as a means*. Although often assumed, the maxim does not prescribe that Persons should not be used as means at all or in any way. And the maxim does only apply to Persons; its application presupposes 'Personhood' (which has fostered the bioethical discussion of a possible 'Zygotic Personhood').

7 The different nature of the argument based on status and the maxim of means–ends so frequent in the public debate on human embryonic stem cells, and the four 'canonic principles' of professional biomedical ethics: autonomy, non-maleficence, beneficence and justice (cf. Beauchamp and Childress, 2001), is as striking as it is often overlooked.

8 The National Institutes of Health has since changed the *Primer*, apparently in order to better reflect the possible potentials of adult stem cells. An update of 17 March 2002 has thus omitted the figure reprinted here and instead added: 'Until recently, there was little evidence that stem cells from adults could change course and provide the flexibility that researchers need in order to address all the medical diseases and disorders they would like to. New findings in animals, however, suggest that even after a stem cell has begun to specialize, it may be more flexible than previously thought'.

9 Shortly before he joined ACT's Ethical Advisory Board, Ronald Green published the retrospective and self-reflexive *The Human Embryo Research Debate*, which can be read as the cleaning up of concepts necessary for the new, open position. A key insight is thus that 'biological occurrences are processes rather than events' and 'because biological realities involve processes, the determination of significant points within these processes inevitably involves choice and decision on our part' (Green, 2001, p26).

10 The emerging new profession is organized around the American Society of Bioethics and Humanities and *The American Journal of Bioethics*, www.bioethics.net. Donaldson (2001) and Elliott (2001) are critical reviews of this development.

11 Baroness Warnock, now a member of the House of Lords, returned during the debate to the 1990 report. She restated the legitimacy of the decision taken by Parliament 'that the early embryo did not have the right to the protection that presumably belongs to persons', but she regretted that 'in the original report that led up to the 1990 legislation we used words such as "respect for the embryo". That seems to me to lead to certain absurdities. You cannot respectfully pour something down the sink – which is the fate of the embryo after it has been used for research or if it is not to be used for research or anything else' (Warnock, 2002).

References

Advanced Cell Technology *InformationPacket*, www.advancedcell.com (various versions)

Alexander, B. (2003) *Rapture: How Biotech Became the New Religion*, Basic Books, New York

American Association for the Advancement of Science (1999) *Stem Cell Research and Applications: Monitoring the Frontiers of Biomedical Research*

Beauchamp, T. L. and Childress, J. F. (2001) *Principles of Biomedical Ethics*, 5th edition, Oxford University Press, Oxford

Benford, R. D. and Snow, D. A. (2000) 'Framing processes and social movements: An overview and assessment', *Annual Review of Sociology*, vol 26, pp611–639

Bush, G. W. (2001) *Remarks by the President on Stem Cell Research*, www.whitehouse.gov/news/releases/2001/08

Bush, G. W. (2002) *Remarks by the President in Meeting with Bioethics Committee*, The White House, Office of the Press Secretary, 17 January 2002 www.bioethics.gov/presjan

Cibelli, J. B. et al (2001) 'Somatic cell nuclear transfer in humans: Pronuclear and early embryonic development', *E-biomed: The Journal of Regenerative Medicine*, 26 November, www.livertpub.com/ebl

Clarke, D. et al (2000) 'Generalized potential of adult neural stem cells', *Science*, vol 2888, 2 June, pp1660–1663

Coghlan, A. and Young, E. (2001) 'Adult skin cells are turned into heart cells without creating embryos, claim scientists', *New Scientist*, 23 February

Colter, C. C. et al (2001) 'Identification of a subpopulation of rapidly self-renewing and multipotential adult stem cells in colonies of human marrow stromal cells', *Proc. Natl. Acad. Sci*, US, 26 June

Donaldson, T. (2001) 'The business ethics of bioethics consulting', *Hastings Center Report*, vol 31, no 2, pp12–19

Dwayne, A. B. and Fossel, M. (1989) 'Telomeres, cancer and aging: Altering the human life span', *Journal of the American Medical Association*, 278, pp1345–48

Elliott, C. (2001) 'Throwing a bone to the watchdog. Bioethics in business', *Hastings Center Report*, vol 31, no 2, pp9–12

Evans, J. H. (2002) *Playing God? Human Genetic Engineering and the Rationalization of Public Bioethical Debate*, University of Chicago Press, Chicago

Evans, M. J. and Kaufman, M. H. (1981) 'Establishment in culture of pluripotential cells from mouse embryo', *Nature*, vol 292, 9 July, pp154–156

Foucault, M. (1971) *L'Ordre du discours*, Gallimard, Paris

Fuchs, E. and Segre, J. A. (2000) 'Stem cells: A new lease on life', *Cell*, vol 100, pp143–155

Fukuyama, F. (2002) *Our Posthuman Future: Consequences of the Biotechnology Revolution*, Farrar, Straus and Giroux, New York

Garr, D. (2001) 'The human body shop', *Technology Review*, April, pp73–79

Geron Corporation http://www.geron.com (various versions)

Geron Corparation United States Securities and Exchange Commission, Form 10-K, For the Fiscal Year Ended 31 December 2002

Gould, S. J. (2001) 'What only the embryo knows', *The New York Times*, 27 August

Green, R. M. (2001) *The Human Embryo Research Debates: Bioethics in the Vortex of Controversy*, Oxford University Press, Oxford

Habermas, J. (2002a) *Die Zukunft der menschlichen Natur: Auf dem Weg in einer liberalen Eugenik?* Suhrkamp, Frankfurt am Main, Expanded edition

Habermas, J. (2002b) 'Auf schiefer Ebene' Interview, *Die Zeit*, 24 January

Hall, S. S. (2003) *Merchants of Immortality: Chasing the Dream of Human Life Extension*, Houghton Mifflin, Boston, MA

Holden, C. and Vogel, G. (2002) 'Plasticity: Time for reappraisal?', *Science*, vol 296, 21 June, pp2126–2129

Jasanoff, S. (1995) 'Product, process, or programme: Three cultures and the regulation of biotechnology', in Bauer, M. (ed) *Resistance to New Technology: Nuclear Power, Information Technology and Biotechnology*, Cambridge University Press, Cambridge

Kant, I. (1965 (1785)) *Grundlegung zur Metaphysik der Sitten*, Verlag von Felix Meiner, Hamburg

Kass, L. (2001) 'Why we should ban cloning now: Preventing a Brave New World', *New Republic*, 21 May, pp30–39

Kerry, J. and Edwards, J. (2002) *Supporting Stem Cell Research to Find Cures for Millions of Americans Suffering from Debilitating Diseases*, Press Release www.johnkerry.com/issues/health_care/stemcell.html

Kuhn, T. S. (1962) *The Structure of Scientific Revolutions*, Chicago University Press, Chicago

Lebacqz, K. et al (1999) 'Research with human embryonic stem cells: Ethical considerations', *Hastings Center Report*, March–April

Martin, G. R. (1981) 'Isolation of pluripotent cell line from early mouse embryos cultivated in medium conditioned by teratocarcioma stem cells', *Proceedings of the National Academy of Sciences*, vol 78, no 12, pp7634–7638

Mulkay, M. (1997) *The Embryo Research Debate: Science and the Politics of Reproduction*, Cambridge University Press, Cambridge

National Institutes of Health (2000) *Stem Cells: A Primer*, http://www.nih.gov/news/stemcell/primer.htm

National Research Council (2001) *Stem Cells and the Future of Regenerative Medicine*, National Academy Press

Nationaler Ethikrat (2002) *Stellungnahme zum Import menschlicher embryonaler Stammzellen* (Position on Import of Human Embryonic Stem Cells)

The New York Times (1988) 'Scientists Cultivate Cells at Root of Human Life', 6 November, pp1–2

Okarma, T. B. (2001) 'Human embryonic stem cells: A primer on the technology and its medical applications', in Hollander, S. et al (eds) *The Human Embryonic Stem Cell Debate: Science, Ethics, and Public Policy*, MIT Press, Cambridge, MA, pp3–13

Perry, D. (2000) 'Patient's voices: The powerful sound in the stem cell debate', *Science*, vol 287, p1423

President's Council on Bioethics (2002) *Human Cloning and Human Dignity: An Ethical Inquiry*

Regalado, A. (1998) 'The troubled hunt for the ultimate cell', *Technology Review*, July–August, pp34–41

Schröder, G. (2001) 'Rede des Bundeskanzler zur konstituierenden Sitzung', *Bulletin der Bundesregierung*, vol 8, no 39–3, June, www.ethikrat.org/publikationen/reden/bundeskanzler

Scientific American (2002) 'The first human clone: The clone makers tell their story', January, front page and pp43–51

Scolding, N. (2001) 'New cells from old', *The Lancet*, vol 357, 3 February

Shamblott, M. J. et al (1998) 'Derivation of pluripotent stem cells from cultured human primordial germ cells', *Proceedings of the National Academy of Sciences*, vol 95, pp13726–13731

Thompson, T. G. (2001) *Embryonic Stem Cell Research: Testimony by Tommy G. Thompson, Secretary of Health and Human Services*, www.hhs.gov/news/speech/2001/010905

Thomson, J. A. (2001) 'Human embryonic stem cells', in Hollander, S. et al (eds) *The Human Embryonic Stem Cell Debate: Science, Ethics, and Public Policy*, MIT Press, Cambridge, MA, pp15–26

Thomson, J. A. et al (1995) 'Isolation of a primate embryonic stem cell line', *Proceedings of the National Academy of Sciences*, vol 92, August, pp7844–7848

Thomson, J. A. et al (1998) 'Embryonic stem cell lines derived from human blastocysts', *Science*, vol 282, 6 November, pp1145–1147

United States Patent 6,245,566, *Human embryonic germ cell line and methods of use*

United States Patent 6,200,806, *Primate embryonic stem cells*

Vogel, G. (1999) 'Capturing the promise of youth', *Science*, vol 286, 17 December, pp2238–2239

Warnock, Baroness (2002) 'Stem Cell Research: Select Committee Report', Lords Hansard text for 5 December, www.publications.parliament.uk

Weismann, I. L. (2000) 'Stem cells: Unit of development, unit of regeneration, and unit in evolution', *Cell*, vol 100, pp157–168

West, M. D. (2003) *The Immortal Cell: One Scientist's Quest to Solve the Mystery of Human Aging*, Doubleday, New York

Wilmut, I. et al (1997) 'Viable offspring derived from fetal and adult mammalian cells', *Nature*, vol 385, 27 February, pp810–813

Winner, L. (1986) 'Do artifacts have politics?', *The Whale and the Reactor*, University of Chicago Press, Chicago, pp19–39

Wolpe, P. R. and McGee, G. (2001) '"Expert bioethics" as professional discourse: The case of stem cells', in Holland, S. et al (eds) *The Human Embryonic Stem Cell Debate: Science, Ethics, and Public Policy*, MIT Press, Cambridge, MA, pp185–207

10

The Monster in the Public Imagination[1]

Wolfgang Wagner, Nicole Kronberger, Siv Froydis Berg and Helge Torgersen

As modern biotechnology intervenes in existential matters such as reproduction, food, life, death and destiny, it not only challenges our everyday life, but also touches and interferes with our deep-seated cultural ideas about how the world is put together and why it should be so. Both in the form of technological innovation and in the form of more or less fantastic future scenarios, modern biotechnology brings the cultural categories of yesterday into question while challenging our ability to imagine order in the world of tomorrow.

For contemporary society, biotechnology provides new answers to old questions such as what is a human being, what is nature and what is culture. In particular, modern biotechnology challenges our ideas about what is the natural and what is the unnatural order. It proposes new ways of categorizing the world. It is, therefore, no wonder that both fascination and fear characterize the European public's attitudes towards biotechnology (Gaskell and Bauer, 2001).

This chapter is about one of the cultural sources that guide our thinking as we enter the era of genetic engineering. As we will show, it has as much to do with cultural categories and their boundaries as it has to do with monsters. In other words, there is a particular way of thinking about violated natural kind boundaries in general and the widely unfamiliar products of genetic engineering in particular.

Matters out of place, monsters and monstrosity

In the Bible, as in most creation myths, the first activity is to bring about order, to put chaotic material into categories. Humankind continues to do that. But when we categorize to create order, deciding whether something is socially and morally acceptable or unacceptable, proper or improper, clean or unclean, there will always be something that falls between categories. Be it a hair in the soup or pork meat on a Muslim's plate; it is a matter out of place. It is disturbing – and we experience it as unclean. It disturbs us because the contradiction between the clean and unclean articulates deep-seated ontological contradictions between order and disorder, cosmos and chaos. The hair in the soup is one of those things that oppose categorical division (Douglas, 1966).

Such matters out of place provide privileged access to investigating both order and the cultural premises of order. They are outside the categories and thereby define the culturally set boundaries themselves. In transcending the boundaries of order, these things also signal danger and are perceived with ambiguity (Douglas, 1966).

In cultural history, the idea of monsters is a point in case. Monsters fall between categories. They are usually regarded as dangerous but with an ambiguous fascination. In European history, monsters were familiar to both scholars and lay people. Monsters existed both in folk stories and in the classical books of writers like Aristotle, Augustine and Pliny. All three writers paid much attention to monsters. For the pre-modern researcher of nature, these three were the main sources concerning monstrosity.

Etymologically, the word *monster*, or *monstrum*, comes from Latin *monstrare*, meaning both 'that which reveals' and 'that which warns'. It is about demonstrating, to present something, to show something off (Friedman, 2000).

There is an important difference between the terms *monster* and *monstrosity*. The monster is a specific expression belonging to and reflecting a particular time and place, a particular culture. Of necessity, it is always changing. Monstrosity is about the very 'essence' of the monsters, about what makes the monster a monster: the change. Over the centuries, monsters have had different expressions, functions and explanations. But monstrosity never changes. Where there are people, there are monsters.

The ever-changing monster

In pre-modern times, a monster was a common description for what was not part of God or Nature's order, and as such it did not have a single or specific name. It was a common description given to what could not be described, an explanation for what could not be explained. The monsters themselves could never be fully explained or properly categorized. The reason for this was that the monster was treated as a message. It could be a warning about hubris or catastrophes, but it could also be a reminder of the greatness of God or the divine order imposed by natural law. It could be a powerful political, religious and social tool for those who knew how to interpret it, had the power to tell and a public to listen.

As late as the 16th and 17th centuries, the monsters and prodigies represented a specific category about the knowledge of the world (Park and Daston, 1981). To Ambroise Pare and Francis Bacon, both surgeons, the unnatural was still a part of nature. The discovery of unknown worlds also provided evidence of earlier ideas about monsters, and gave new life both to imaginations and to moral and religious power struggles about how to interpret these messages.

In the age of modernity, when God and Nature disappeared as the reference point for explaining the world, so did the monster. Essentially, monsters were reduced to images. Their function became aesthetic; something for people to gaze at or to be scared about (like the ape woman Julia Pastrana or the Elephant Man). They were no longer understood as messages or warnings. This brought about a change in how monsters were to be understood.

During the period of enlightenment, monsters became the shadow following the light of reason and science and took their place in novels. Horace Walpole's *The Castle of Otranto* from 1756, often considered to be the first horror novel in history, was soon accompanied by the English Gothic novel and a little later by the German *Schauerroman* and the French *roman noir*. These novels and the numerous films about horror in later times opened up a new tradition and interpretation of the shape and expression of the monster. Monsters disappeared as parts and categories of the visible nature, and were increasingly connected to the hidden and dark sides of the human mind. Consequently, the monsters were given new looks – like Janus, the doubling of the human being, addressed in *Dr. Jekyll and Mr. Hyde,* there is Nosferatu, the overwhelming sexual desire, depicted in Bram Stoker's *Dracula* (Skårderud, 2000).

What about today? Our claim is that the monsters are still here, posing questions and carrying messages. As in older times, monsters and monstrosity can be found wherever categories and the boundaries of natural kinds are challenged. One place to look is in modern science and technology. The monster pops up in representations of biotechnology, such as in cartoons and newspaper photographs, and in the popular imagination of possible 'new species' resulting from genetic engineering. These representations are empirically illustrated in the next two sections. First, we present results from a study analysing pictorial material collected from Austrian newspapers and magazines over a period of four years. We show that the monstrous can be depicted directly or indirectly, for example through its absence in a suggestive context. Second, experimental studies show how respondents imagine genetic hybrids relative to natural animals. Here it is shown that, besides considering genetic hybrids as having mixed essences, people seem to endow hybrids with certain 'monstrous' attributes that are absent in natural animals. Finally, we place and discuss the findings within the wider context of western cultural history.

Monsters in newspaper photographs and cartoons about biotechnology

The following description of pictorial material concerned with the issue of modern biotechnology is based on a sample of cartoons, photographs and other pictorial material published in Austrian daily newspapers between 1997 and 2000. The material was categorized according to common themes. In this section, different ways of depicting the danger emanating from monsters and from the monstrous are illustrated. Generally speaking, danger emerges in two forms: as the visible or the invisible monster.

The visible monster

The monster as a hybrid

Just as in the imaginations of earlier eras such as the ubiquitous gargoyles on ancient cathedrals, as well as in children's drawings, depictions of visible monsters in newspapers (cartoons and drawings) blend one or more natural kinds. The resulting monster then possesses organs from different species where some body parts are exaggerated and others absent. Like those well-known monsters in cultural history, such hybrid beings are the enigmatic visible expression of what the products of biotechnology can be in terms of blurring the boundaries between natural kinds in Douglas's (1966) sense (Figure 10.1).

Source: Der Standard, 15 September 1997, online version

Figure 10.1 *Cartoon – 'Even the ancient Greeks . . . Of course we have to keep them in a hidden place, otherwise this uproar about ethics and genetic engineering will start again!' by Dieter Zehentmaier*

Frankenstein or 'the monster hitting back'

A subtheme of the visibly monstrous is articulating the monster with its creator, mostly mad scientists happily crossing the borders. Sometimes the monsters are depicted as deformed, representing only a mountain of flesh bereft of shape. Such shapeless monsters reduced to pure function are inactive and passive patients of the scientist's doings. More frequent, however, are monsters getting out of control and turning on their creators, just as the young Frankenstein became a victim of his creation. Such monsters do not cross the boundaries of natural kinds but are characterized by excessive size. They are monstrous not only in appearance but also because they turn the moral order upside down: it is no longer humans who control animals, but enormous mice, rats or other creatures with humanlike intentions and gestures, who control humans. The cartoons symbolize hubris and failed experiments that threaten life *per se* and turn against the taken-for-granted social order (see Figure 10.2). Frequently it is not clear which is more monstrous:

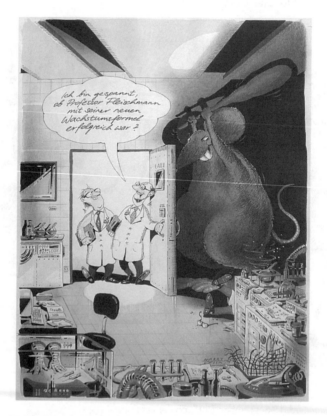

Source: Neue Kronen Zeitung, 12 April 1997, p1

Figure 10.2 *Cartoon – 'News from the (gene-)lab: I'm curious whether Professor Fleischmann was successful with his new growth formula' by Harry O'Feem*

the creator or the created. The overconfident and naive attitude of scientists who have lost their sense of reality appears to be more dangerous than the monster itself.

Invisible monsters

What is striking in the pictorial material on biotechnology in these two Austrian newspapers is how difficult it is for writers and cartoonists to capture the message of biotechnology. The new 'monster' of genetic engineering is actually invisible. The material conveys a strong sense that there is something dangerous about biotechnology, but what is the danger and how can it be addressed? In Figure 10.3, the reasonable or unreasonable fear of fiddling with genes is anchored in the standard joke of arachnophobia or fear of mice. Unfortunately, however, genes are not as visible as spiders and mice ('Genes? Where?' screams the woman on the chair).

Source: *Der Standard*, 15 September 1997, p21

Figure 10.3 *Cartoon – 'Genes? Where?' by Jean Veenenbos*

Highlighting the monster through its absence

The most frequent way of illustrating the monstrous aspect of biotechnology is to depict examples where danger is *absent*: salespersons happily smiling in front of piles of organic food (see Figure 10.4), innocent children enjoying explicitly 'natural' food or policemen safeguarding crop fields.

By labelling Figure 10.4 as 'Retailers react to the consumer's request, which is: genetechnology-free food', allusion is made to the risks of biotechnology or at least to something undesirable. Similarly, the heading of a picture showing Prince Charles, a declared opponent of genetic manipulation, wandering across his land reads 'Enjoying the True, the Beautiful and the Honest: Great Britain's Prince Charles does not allow GM plants on his property' (*Der Standard*, 12–13 June 1999, p8). The tension between picture and labelling refers to the false, the ugly and the dishonest in the new technology. The more trusting, happy and easygoing the actors depicted in the pictorial material, the more we become aware of a diffuse danger of the unknown.

Especially with food, there is also the idea of infection or contagion; incorporating the monstrous leads to monstrosity from within. This is well depicted in a cartoon showing a maize-eating woman giving birth to a maize cob with human feet. The manifestation of the monster is delayed.

Source: Neue Kronen Zeitung, 11 January 1998, p9

Figure 10.4 *Picture – 'Retailers react to the consumer's request, which is: genetechnology-free food'*

Constructing the monster by emphasizing the 'normal'

Another way of capturing the invisible monster is to describe the 'normal'. By paying attention to the taken-for-granted in the pictorial 'text', the abnormal is sensed in the 'subtext' of the picture. Under normal circumstances, we would not find half-page photographs of common maize cobs in newspapers and magazines. Generally, sheep and calves are not depicted in a portrait format. We rarely read and hear about such animals being born or giving birth, about their kinship relations and about their name, such as Dolly the sheep, or George and Charlie the clone-calves, for example.

In reports about biotechnology, the seemingly normal takes on a different meaning. Take, for example, the well-known pictures of Dolly the sheep. When we see that Dolly's wool has been used for knitting a pullover, when we are informed about Dolly's pregnancy and giving birth, when we hear about Dolly's well-being (even poor Dolly has problems with getting fat and suffers from psychological problems) and about other genetically manipulated sheep (like Polly, Molly, Holly, Olly and all the others), the message lies in the subtext. The photographs of ordinary-looking animals and plants are described in an anthropomorphic way akin to that used for celebrities. There is something fascinating and at the same time alarming about this news. By describing the normal in unexpected detail some anomaly is implied (e.g. *Der Standard*, 19 August 1998, p20; *Der Standard*, 5 December 1998, p35).

The conspicuous difference between the normal and the imagined threat residing in its shadow is perhaps a better illustration of monstrosity than any explicit cartoon and, above all, is politically very potent. The 'monster in absence' figures in the invisible difference of its creation.

Similar in their message but more explicit are pictures where two readily identifiable exemplars of a natural object such as mice or plants are presented side by side: cob beside cob, mouse beside mouse (see Figure 10.5). Usually the GM version is the larger one, but in a photograph, size can only be conveyed in contrast to the 'normal'. Without a point of reference, the monster escapes.

The 'living dead': the monster as multiplication

When humans are the objects of biotechnology, an image of 'the living dead' (*Der Standard*, 13 June 1997) is often used. Humans become monsters when they apparently are artefacts (e.g. *Profil*, 3 March 1997, front page). Although these beings have human shape, they lack essence, identity and uniqueness. The 'copy-humans', though living and with movement, are bereaved of 'real' life.

The monstrous is captured either in the idea of mass production or in their reduction to pure function (being human is just being a body). Crowds of copied baby faces or multitudes of superstars, bad guys or geniuses (like Claudia Schiffer, Adolf Hitler or Albert Einstein) allude to the horror of the faceless masses (e.g. *Der Standard*, 15–16 March 1997, p25). The original disappears among its copies. In the copy-shop theme, the monster therefore enters as *a lack of difference*. A living being's identity as a unique entity is violated in his or her multiplicity.

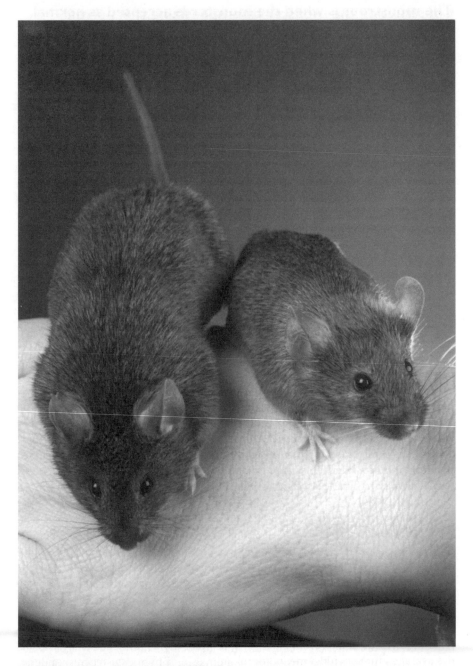

Source: Neue Kronen Zeitung, 4 May 1997, p5

Figure 10.5 *Picture – 'A normal mouse beside the two to three times stronger genetically manipulated one'*

The monstrous is when the monster is accepted as normal

In the sections above, it has been pointed out that the invisible monster is frequently depicted by presenting the 'normal' in an attractive way. One message of such pictures is the horrifying idea that people could *get used* to the science fiction scenarios of biotechnology and that they could finally accept this unfortunate development. If, in a copy-shop cartoon, Frankenstein orders '100 clones 1:1' and the employee in the copy shop asks: 'black and white or colour?' (*Der Standard*, 4 March 1997), the monstrous is in the normal reaction of the employee to the order. With a changing technological reality, it could follow that we might also lose our capacity to judge what is good and what is not, what is desirable and what is to be avoided. If future developments lead us to conclude that such conditions are good, then our sense of a moral order is lost. At that point, humans will be reduced to stupid, self-satisfied creatures that can be modelled to whatever standard anybody desires.

Imagining genetic hybrids: Blended essence and emergent monstrosity

In the previous section, diverse ways of depicting the monstrous were shown to be used in newspaper and magazines' reporting of biotechnology. Is it this media reporting alone that gives us the idea that biotechnology results in monstrous acts, or do people see biotechnology in this way when they think of genetically modified organisms? To address this question, we investigated what is going on in people's imaginations when thinking about genetically manipulated animals in two experimental studies. A total of about 400 respondents were asked how they rate natural animals and hybrids resulting from genetic manipulation on attribute scales. The same scales were used for natural and hybrid animals. They included pairs of opposite attributes such as dangerous–gentle, small–big, ugly–pretty, weak–strong, passive–active, slow–fast, simple–complicated, ordinary–noble, tame–wild.

When people are asked to imagine an animal that has been implanted with the gene of another animal, at least two effects can be observed in the judgement they make. The first is the mixing of animal essences, making the hybrid's characteristics a mix of the gene recipient's and the gene donor's attributes. The second is the emergence of a set of attributes that the hybrid does not share with the gene recipient and the gene donor. The detailed findings are shown in the following figures.

As an example, Figure 10.6 shows the positions of a dog, a goldfish and the resulting hybrids in a two-dimensional space of a correspondence analysis using the average attribute judgements for all animals and hybrids as correspondence measures. Each animal is depicted twice, once judged as a gene donor (triangles, small letters) and once judged as a gene recipient (squares, capital letters). There are two hybrids in this example, a dog having received a goldfish gene and a goldfish having received a dog gene. Additionally we show the points of some

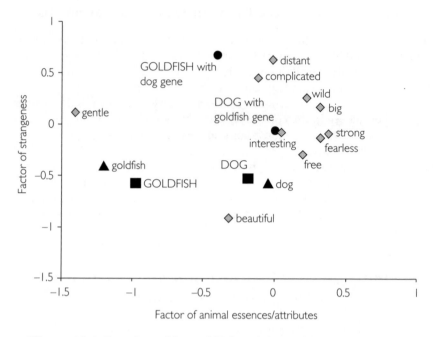

Figure 10.6 *Locations of dog, goldfish and the resulting genetic hybrid in the two-dimensional space of a correspondence analysis (Experiment 1)*

characteristic attributes. Among others, goldfish are perceived as gentler than dogs while dogs are perceived to be more fearless and stronger than goldfish.

The horizontal dimension (*x*-axis) contrasts the different attributes of the natural goldfish and dog. As seen on this axis, a goldfish gene transplanted to a dog does not change the characteristics of the resulting hybrid very much. The dog's essence seems to be perceived as more or less inert with regard to the goldfish's gene. A goldfish with a dog gene is perceived to be more of a mix of essences, as shown by its intermediate position between dog and goldfish on the *x*-axis.

The vertical dimension (*y*-axis) contrasts the natural animals against the two hybrids. The higher up on this dimension and the further to the right on the *x*-axis, the more an object is being judged as distant, complicated, wild, big and not beautiful. This set of characteristics captures an idea of monstrosity that is unrelated to the natural animals. This point can be seen even more clearly from the scatter plot of all animals and hybrids in the correspondence space (see Figure 10.7).

Figure 10.7 shows all six natural animals receiving genes and their 30 hybrids located in the same correspondence space. The cloud of hybrid points is located higher up on the vertical dimension than the natural animals, showing that monstrosity is a feature that emerges from the mixing of the natural animals' genes.

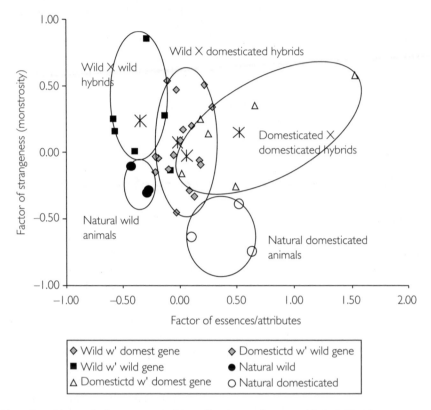

Note: Asterisks mark the average position of each set of comparable hybrid points

Figure 10.7 *Locations of three wild and three domesticated natural animals as gene recipients or gene donors and their genetic hybrids in the two-dimensional space of a correspondence analysis (Experiment 1)*

The same point is illustrated by a second experiment where respondents imagined the genetic manipulation of humans, chimpanzees and a set of three domesticated animals (not reported here). As in the first experiment, the monstrosity dimension emerging from a correspondence analysis is clearly independent of the blending dimension and determined by attributes such as strangeness, particularity, complexity, wildness and, to a lesser extent, large size. Above all, hybrids are definitely not beautiful.

The findings provided by correspondence analyses were replicated by path models showing that hybrids are seen to possess an attribute dimension that is not determined by the natural animals' attributes (not reported here).

Both the path model and the correspondence analyses of the two independent experimental data sets corroborate the proposition that monstrosity is an emergent property of genetic hybrids. Our respondents perceive genetically manipulated animals as possessing both a mixture of the natural gene donors' and recipients' essences and an independent essence of monstrosity. While the mixed attributes of the hybrids may be the result of essentialist thinking or of a semantic transfer of attributes from the natural to the hybrid animals, such thinking does not explain the strangeness or monstrosity factor. While the idea of mixed attributes illustrates the betwixt and between characteristic of genetic hybrids, monstrosity emerges as a set of attributes that is quite independent of the original animals and a proper essence of the genetic 'monster' itself. As such, it can be taken to express the creation of a new kind of animal that transcends hitherto known categories that structure our familiar world of living beings.

The contemporary message of monsters

These empirical studies have three main results. First, monsters can be visible or hidden, and it is often the hidden aspects in the seemingly 'normal' that convey the strongest sense of the monstrous and the threat emanating from it. Second, and as outlined in the Introduction, the idea of the monstrous is strongly linked to a sense of violated natural boundaries between kinds. Third, the terms of monstrosity that emerge autonomously when imagining the new cannot be accommodated within the taken-for-granted order of the familiar world.

There are several dimensions along which we can attempt to compare and contrast traditional with modern representations of monstrosity in the context of biotechnology.

They are *comparable*, first, because both representational systems are cultural products; second, because both challenge our traditional way of seeing the world; third, because both elicit fear, repugnance and curiosity; and fourth, because, at least during the late Middle Ages *and* today, they are taken as *portents* of future harm.

They are *contrasting* conceptions; fifth, because traditional and modern representations differ with regard to the agents involved in creating monstrous organisms; sixth, because monstrosity in the traditional understanding is visible whereas genetic monstrosity is invisible in many cases; and seventh, because traditional monsters were rarely encountered in everyday life, whereas biotechnological 'monstrosity' may eventually be ubiquitous in the post-biotechnology world. Each of these points will be discussed in turn.

Cultural products

First, there is no doubt that monsters and monstrosity are part of mentality and cultural convention. They are a received cultural topic that is present even in our scientifically enlightened times and even if monstrosity is no longer labelled as such. This cultural convention is a way of collective symbolic coping with the unfamiliar and, as such, a response to perceived threat (Wagner et al, 2002). It allows people to bundle judgements about causes and reasons as well as the consequences of natural or social events into one representation that is as emotionally charged as it is cognitively rational and that allows a collective value judgement about a phenomenon.

A challenge to our traditional way of seeing the world

Second, monstrosity is called upon when the common categories of cognition collapse. The idea of monstrosity, whatever its particular make-up may be, is evoked when the 'ordinary' categories about *what is and what is not* are challenged by innovations in the technological or cultural realm. When traditional ways of understanding the world in terms of familiar categories are challenged, so are their boundaries or the field in between order and disorder (Carroll, 1990). The monstrous signals an epistemological problem and is a harbinger of Category Crisis (Cohen, 1996). During the past centuries, malformed babies or creatures from faraway regions were such deviations from the received structure of the world. In biotechnology, it is the idea of mixing unfitting natural species that entails monstrosity, as was shown in the earlier reported experiments. The monstrous 'mixing' of neighbouring species in works of art such as paintings was, for Jean François Marmontel, in his *Encyclopédie* article, just indicating a deranged artistic imagination (Daston and Park, 2001, p212). Today it is the scientifically planned design of living beings. No surprise, hence, that in cartoons the 'emblem' of mixed species is used to characterize biotechnology, just as the experimental respondents imagined genetic hybrids to be a mix of the natural animals.

The idea of monstrosity 'dwells at the gates of difference' (Cohen, 1996). It pops up where the boundaries between taken-for-granted natural kinds break open and the difference between species, such as in our experiments, is being blurred. There, our respondents were not content to characterize genetic hybrids as beings with mixed essences, but, and perhaps unwittingly, added a factor of monstrosity to the hybrids that sets them radically apart from the natural animals. It is not simply a 'form suspended between forms' (Cohen, 1996, p6). To imagine this, genetic hybrids would only need to be imagined as animals with blended essences. It is the additional and autonomously emerging property of monstrosity that signifies the cultural fact of 'monsters'.

This fact has a parallel in risk debates of the 1980s and early 1990s about whether genetic engineering would produce additive or synergistic effects. The concept of additive effects would predict that the outcome of introducing a foreign gene, for example a *Bacillus thuringiensis* (BT) gene, into a recipient organism, for example conventional corn, would only result in a BT-producing corn without any other properties. The concept of synergistic effects would predict that the resulting BT-producing corn could be expected to also possess hitherto unknown properties that transcend the known attributes of the original species and the property conveyed by the gene. Synergistic effects would by definition be unknown and therefore unpredictable (Idel and Katzek, 1991); they were often depicted as potentially catastrophic. Many advocates of genetic engineering discard the synergistic concept, while opponents tend to support it. Interestingly, the respondents in our experiments are clearly more inclined towards the synergistic view, as shown by the emergence of the strangeness or monstrosity factor.

Traditional and modern representations evoke fear, repugnance and curiosity

Third, the affective side of the representation of monstrosity is horror, repugnance and avoidance. Across the many shades of dealing with monsters that are recounted at the beginning of this chapter, the emotional charge of monsters always implied avoidance, even when they served as attractive exhibits for the curious. They could be enjoyed because they were on a stage or in an exhibition that was markedly offset from everyday life. Had the contemporaries of the 14th and 15th centuries encountered these 'sources of pleasure' in everyday life, their reaction would most probably also have been avoidance. Until today, the contemporaries of the age of biotechnology have also encountered their monsters only in newspaper and electronic mass media reports. However, the political and economic reality is such that regulatory activity requires opinions and decisions from everybody. This need to act makes the idea of monstrosity and its associated fear more real (Wagner et al, 2002).

However, there is ambivalence present in the emotions. Take the pictures of Dolly, the cloned sheep. She is a sheep and, as such, not more attractive than any other. If the picture deserves a place in the prime pages of newspapers, this is only because of Dolly's embodying some monstrosity due to the way she was created. This is what makes her more attractive than other sheep. To a certain extent, monstrosity is attractive and repelling at the same time (Einsiedel et al, 2002).

Portents of future harm

Fourth, the times when priests interpreted monsters as signs of God's wrath and impending punishment are long past. Alive and well, however, is the belief that tinkering with nature in producing genetic monstrosity will eventually bring us disaster (Kronberger et al, 2001). Nowadays, people believe in the scientists' sin of hubris and the ensuing revenge of an animistically interpreted nature in the long term (Wagner et al, 2001). The monstrosity in genetically engineered organisms is taken as a sign of future harm in the form of long-term ecological disaster.

Being positioned at the very limits of our knowledge, 'the monster polices the borders of the possible' (Cohen, 1996). In former times, monsters were positioned at the borders of the geographical world, such as Africa and the Far East. In myths, monsters are often used as guardians (the giants of Patagonia, the dragons of the Orient, the Sirens and the Cyclops in Odysseus) and warn that curiosity will be punished, or that specific knowledge is required to pass (the Sphinx). The monsters in these cases prevent unrestricted mobility and secure stability and order. To step outside this 'official' geography of the accepted epistemology was to risk attack by some monstrous border patrol or, even worse, to become a monster oneself. The role of monsters is to guard the limits of knowledge beyond which the land of hubris and therefore existential *danger* begins (Douglas, 1966). Today it is positioned at the borders of the thinkable and used as a warning of an uncertain future that biotechnological products might harbour for us. In contemporary debates about biotechnology, projecting monstrosity onto this technology serves a similar purpose in political propaganda of the technology's opponents.

Differences resulting from traditional and modern means of creation

Fifth, here ends the plain analogy between traditional and modern representations of monstrosity. The greatest difference between present-day genetic monstrosity and its traditional idea is their very *raison d'être*. They are no longer seen as accidents of nature or God's will as an answer to sinful doings, but as monstrosity by design. It would not have made sense for medieval people to reject or to 'vote' against God's will. This makes sense only today, when the creators of uncategoriz-able organisms are human themselves, as the often forceful rejection of certain biotechnological applications shows (Gaskell et al, 2000).

Another and, at first sight, paradoxical difference is the lack of a possibility to sustainably instrumentalize the monster. Modern monsters come to life inten-tionally, and only for the purpose of serving their human creator. But unlike their medieval brethren that could be tamed for eternity and taken to service the higher glory of God by giving them a subordinate position, nowadays monsters are unlikely to be enslaved for good. Modern myths, from *Frankenstein* to *Star Wars*, again and again invoke the fear that artificial creatures will eventually reverse the relationship between themselves and their human creator who had wanted to make use of them. Hence, benefit can be expected only for the few and for a short period, and the relation is bound to end in catastrophe or the enslavement of humankind.

This marks a rupture within society that juxtaposes, on the one hand, science and the biotechnology industry profiting in the short term and, on the other hand, the common people, who would have to bear the risk. Monstrosity, as it is vividly depicted in the media pictures, is a signal of a potential social problem as well as a cultural problem.

Genetic monstrosity is often invisible

Sixth, contrary to traditional monsters, genetic engineering and biotechnology present us with a new world of monstrosity, where the causes of monstrosity – the manipulated genes – are invisible to the eye of the average person. The phenotype, that is, the everyday appearance of a genetically altered organism, rarely carries a visible mark of the genetic changes. Examples whose phenotypes are nearly unchanged with regard to the normal organisms are Roundup Ready soya, BT-corn and lactoferrin-producing cows. Visibility that made 'traditional' mon-sters frightening is no longer a criterion in everyday cognition. The danger lurks in the dark and is therefore the more frightening (Wagner and Kronberger, 2002). Instead of understanding the monster through its appearance, people are required to understand monstrosity in the invisible realm of the organisms' genetic make-up. While the genesis itself is horrible, it gives rise to a seemingly normal creature; the monster is not easily detected as such and even with the most familiar beings you can never be sure who is who. Just as with those elegant vampires, beyond the shiny surface horror may prevail.

The ubiquity of biotechnological monstrosity

Seventh, and this needs only brief mention, biotechnologically tailored organisms are likely to become ubiquitous. Once genetically modified cows and sheep are procreated through cloning, are producing pharmaceuticals on a widespread level, and once the majority of humankind's crops are resistant to pests and pesticides due to genetic modifications, there will be no need to see these organisms as monstrous. The loss of monstrosity of some biotechnological organisms will mirror a similar process in the past, when congenital malformations ceased to pose a threat as a prodigy. As common sense dictates: habituation makes monsters familiar. From today's perspective, however, the prospect of our becoming accustomed to such facts is perceived as a moral threat.

By searching for the cultural bearings of monsters and monstrosity in the image of modern biotechnology, we hope to shed some light on our contemporary culture and how we deal with technological innovation. What the monstrosity that emerges in people's imagination of genetic hybrids as well as in pictorial material of mass media shows is that our category system of what is and of what is thinkable is deeply challenged by the new technology. This is the real message of imagining the monstrous in biotechnology, filling us with ambiguity, with fascination and fear. Thus, our culturally constructed ideas of monsters and monstrosity link us to a cultural past long bygone and make us human in the deepest sense.

Notes

1   The authors gratefully acknowledge the help of Margareta Benka, Sofia Daimonakou, Caroline Egger, Petra Pichler and Judit Toth in collecting the media material and experimental data. Thanks are also due to Trond Haug, Milena Marinova, Torben Hviid Nielsen and Henrik Treimo for helpful comments on an earlier draft. The data used in Experiment 1 are part of Petra Pichler's Master's thesis, Universität Linz, 1999.

References

Carroll, N. (1990) *The Philosophy of Horror or Paradoxes of the Heart*, Routledge, London
Cohen, J. J. (1996) 'Monster culture (seven theses)', in Cohen, J. J. (ed) *Monster Theory: Reading Culture*, University of Minnesota Press, London
Daston, L. and Park, K. (2001) *Wonders and the Order of Nature 1150–1750*, Zone Books, New York
Douglas, M. (1966) *Purity and Danger: An Analysis of the Concepts of Pollution and Taboo*, Routledge and Kegan Paul, London
Einsiedel, E., Allansdottir, A., Allum, N., Bauer, M., Berthomier, A., Chatjouli, A., De

Cheiveigné, S., Downey, R., Gutteling, J. Kohring, M. et al (2002) 'Brave new sheep – The clone named Dolly', in Bauer, M. and Gaskell, G. (eds) *Biotechnology: The Making of a Global Controversy*, Cambridge University Press, Cambridge

Friedman, J. B. (2000) *The Monstrous Races in Medieval Art and Thought*, Syracuse University Press, New York

Gaskell, G., Allum, N., Bauer, M., Durant, J., Allansdottir, A., Bonfadelli, H., Boy, D., de Cheveigné, S., Fjaestad, B., Gutteling, J. M. et al (2000) 'Biotechnology and the European public', *Nature Biotechnology*, vol 18, pp935–938

Gaskell, G. and Bauer, M. (eds) (2001) *Biotechnology 1996–2000: The Years of Controversy*, Science Museum, London

Idel, A. and Katzek, J. (1991) 'Gentechnik und gentechnisch hergestellte Produkte im Bereich der Landwirtschaft' (Gene technology and gene technological products in agriculture, German), in Umweltbundesamt (ed) *Gen- und Biotechnologie, Nutzungsmöglichkeiten und Gefahrenpotentiale, Handlungsbedarf für Österreich zum Schutz von Mensch und Umwelt* (Gene- and biotechnology, uses and dangers, action requirements for Austria for the protection of man and environment, German). Monographien des Umweltbundesamts, vol 28, Vienna

Kronberger, N., Dahinden, U., Allansdottir, A., Seger, N., Pfenning, U., Gaskell, G., Allum, N., Rusanen, T., Montali, L., Wagner, W. et al (2001) 'The train departed without us – Public perceptions of biotechnology in ten European countries', *Notizie di Politeia*, vol 17, no 63, pp26–36

Park, K. and Daston, L. (1981) 'Unnatural conceptions: The study of monsters in sixteenth and seventeenth century France and England', *Past and Present*, vol 92, The Society of Past and Present, Oxford

Pliny, D. E. (1942) *Historia Naturalis*, Penguin Classics, London

Skårderud, F (2000) 'Beven' (Trembling, Norwegian), in Hoff, A. (ed) *Mitt liv som film* (My life as a dog, Norwegian), Tiden, Oslo

Wagner, W. and Kronberger, N. (2002) 'Discours et appropriation symbolique de la biotechnologie' (Discourse and symbolic coping with biotechnology, French), in Garnier, C. and Rouquette, M.-L. (eds) *Les Formes de la pensée sociale*, Presses Universitaires de France, Paris

Wagner, W., Kronberger, N., Gaskell, G., Allum, N., Allansdottir, A., Cheveigné, S., Dahinden, U., Diego, C., Montali, L., Mortensen, A. et al (2001) 'Nature in disorder: The troubled public of biotechnology', in Gaskell, G. and Bauer, M. (eds) *Biotechnology 1996–2000: The Years of Controversy*, Science Museum, London

Wagner, W., Kronberger, N. and Seifert, F. (2002) 'Collective symbolic coping with new technology: Knowledge, images and public discourse', *British Journal of Social Psychology*, vol 41, pp323–343

References (newspaper material)

Cartoon – 'Schon die alten Griechen . . .' (Even the ancient Greeks . . ., German) by Dieter Zehentmaier (15 September 1997), *Der Standard*, online version

Cartoon – 'Neues aus dem (Gen-)Labor' (News from the (Gene-)Lab, German) by Harry O'Feem (12 April 1997), *Neue Kronen Zeitung*, p1

Cartoon – 'Gene? Wo?' (Genes? Where?, German) by Jean Veenenbos (15 September 1997), *Der Standard*, p21

Der Standard, 12–13 June 1999, article – 'Charles forbids the release of manipulated plants', p8

Der Standard, 19 August 1998, article – 'When it is about biotech, the Scots are not stingy', p20

Der Standard, 5 December 1998, article – 'Dolly is physically healthy, but psychically abnormal', p35

Der Standard, 15–16 March 1997, article – 'Gene euphoria and new designability', p25

Picture – 'Der Handel reagiert auf den Wunsch der Konsumenten. Und der heißt: Gentechnik-freie Lebensmittel' (Retailers react to the consumer's request, which is: genetechnology-free food, German) (11 January 1998), *Neue Kronen Zeitung*, p9

Picture – 'Eine normale Maus neben der zwei- bis dreimal so starken genmanipulierten' (A normal mouse beside the two to three times stronger genetically manipulated one, German) (4 May 1997), *Neue Kronen Zeitung*, p5

Part 3

Global Perspectives

11

Towards a Global Pop Culture of Genes?

Toby Ten Eyck[1]

Media audiences are increasingly faced with images that show the 'wonders' of genetic engineering: living dinosaurs, half-human/half-animal creatures, glowing fish, to name but a few. At the same time, they may read of the current, mainly illegal, practice of using anabolic steroids and other genetic treatments to enhance athletic performance. Given that standard news coverage of biotechnology and genetics highlights controversial issues (Gaskell and Bauer, 2001; Ten Eyck and Williment, 2003), it is not surprising that for audiences faced with the world of genetics what is real and what is make-believe becomes less and less clear. These images and stories, which have passed through various genres of popular culture, are not confined to the privileged audiences of developed countries. Hollywood films, sporting events and even the reporting of such events play out in many different regions for various audiences around the world. In every case, there are individuals and organizations that benefit from such presentations, while others suffer. In Burkina Faso, for example, one of the poorest nations in Africa, the policy-making elite who read French newspapers are likely to rank snow skiing as riskier than childbirth (Kone and Mullet, 1994), an opinion which could lead to less concern with developing policies that aim to improve infant mortality.

Popular culture is too often overlooked by social scientists who view it as an opiate of the masses, turning them into one-dimensional cultural dupes (Marcuse, 1964). Following certain interpretations of Marx, culture, and in particular, popular culture, is thought of as merely reflections of the economic infrastructure of a given society (The *Tabloid* Collective, 1997). Popular culture, as with all enterprises, is a source of power (Agger, 1992), and has become much more than a reflection of class values. When powerful institutions such as science and politics are threatened by popular culture, it can no longer be taken for granted.

This chapter aims to present a critical perspective of the gene in popular culture as it appeared in four different contexts: the book and subsequent movie *Jurassic*

Park, genetically modified (GM) aquarium fish, the use of anabolic steroids in sports, and general news accounts of popular culture. Our approach seeks to identify those who benefit from such an account, and those who are challenged. The main focus will be on scientists, although the roles of other actors are also examined.

The value of popular culture

Any event which takes place within a cultural sphere, such as ballet, sculpture or the cinema, must be thought of as an act of a collective (Becker, 1974), with the worth of the event derived from its use or exchange value within that collective. If the collective is wealthy, the event can net a good profit. However, not all collectives are interested in consuming events in all cultural spheres. Peterson and Kern (1996) argue that the consumption of culture is a signifier of class status, while Bourdieu (1984) contends that one's habitus is derived in part from the cultural habits in which one engages. To put it simply, some individuals will feel that certain cultural events are either beneath them or beyond their abilities or interests. In the world of fine arts, one masterpiece may be worth thousands (if not millions) of dollars, and only a small collective will be able to engage in such an event, that is, the purchasing of fine art. Popular culture, on the other hand, relies on the economic strength of the masses (Fiske, 1992). So, while a sculpture created by one person may be worth millions of dollars, a blockbuster movie which employed hundreds of people will gross millions of dollars even though each viewer is only paying a small amount of money to purchase an opportunity to view it. In short, there is nothing intrinsic in any piece of art which gives it its value; instead, its value is derived from the social networks in which it moves.

According to Agger (1992), this aspect of cultural spheres offers an opportunity for a critical approach to its study. Such an approach seeks to identify those individuals and/or organizations that benefit from the value of the cultural sphere. Often the beneficiary may be obvious: movie production studios, book publishers or news outlets where the measure of success is based on economic strength. The actions of activist groups against television networks highlight the importance of these channels of communication in terms of the norms, values and beliefs of society (Montgomery, 1989). A history of the banning and burning of books emphasizes the political aspect of cultural spheres and the values placed on these items among groups outside the production studios and audiences who are interested in consuming them (e.g. Neurath, 1995; Thomas, 1983). Popular culture is often more than just mere entertainment for audiences and potentially lucrative undertakings for producers.

This approach is well suited to science fiction and other mass presentations of science. Writers and producers of science fiction novels, movies, television series and so forth may primarily seek monetary profits and acclaim, while audience members seek gratification through fantasy experiences.[2] Scientists and politicians have both applauded and scorned popular treatments of science principles, at times because of profit concerns, and at others due to a concern with the values attached to the scientific endeavour (Dunwoody and Ryan, 1985; Nelkin, 1995).[3] Science and technology enjoy a deep resonance within many developed countries (Galison et al, 2001), and science fiction has a long history of depicting both the benefits and the horrors of science. For example, science fiction writers portrayed characters landing on the moon long before Neil Armstrong did land. Orson Welles caused a large-scale panic in the US when he broadcast *War of the Worlds*, in which he described aliens landing on Earth and devouring its human inhabitants (Lazarsfeld and Kendall, 1948).

The horrific in science fiction can be detrimental to scientists, as scientists are considered legitimate spokespersons with regard to risk in modern society (Beck, 1999; Habermas, 1973). Rewards to this group are often based on their abilities to solve problems in fields such as medicine, physics and economics which are meant to minimize the uncertainty of everyday life (Leiss, 1974). When this ability is questioned, such as in the 'mad cow' crisis, scientists can lose the trust of the public, their ability to be taken seriously is called into question, and their status, and possibly rewards, decline (Powell and Leiss, 1997). It is in their best interests, as with most groups, to have their work taken seriously, and not to be challenged by outsiders.

The imagination of humans goes beyond what can possibly be achieved with current science. Welles's *War of the Worlds* was a fantastic story of aliens landing on Earth, but the radio broadcast of this story coincided with Germany's invasion of other European countries in 1938, the beginning of World War II. At the same time, science was heading into the nuclear and space age. The notion that space travel would mean alien encounters was reflected in the cartoon characters of the period: Flash Gordon and Buck Rogers as well as in the science fiction film *The Strange Invaders*. An alien invasion may have seemed far-fetched for most listeners, but at the time some took it seriously. The same could be said for genetics. The double helix and its manipulation have been fodder for science fiction writers such as Bruce Sterling in *Distraction*. In addition, the occurrences of genetic mutations, whether natural or engineered by humans, make the catastrophes of science fiction seem all too real. It is only the philanthropic nature of real-world scientists that keeps the world of Dr Moreau's island (1977) at bay.

The question then becomes: are scientists being challenged in popular cultural accounts which concern genetics, and if so, who is gaining by taking such a stance? While there are many science fiction accounts of genetics, we focus on only four: *Jurassic Park*, because so many people have knowledge of the book and film; genetically modified aquarium fish, which entered the US market at the end of 2003; the use of anabolic steroids in sports; and news accounts of popular culture from Europe, Canada and the United States.

Jurassic Park

According to the *Internet Movie Database* (www.imdb.com), in 2004, *Jurassic Park – The Movie* ranked fourth in all-time worldwide box office sales (reported at $919,700,000). Based on a bestselling novel by Michael Crichton, the film portrayed scientists developing dinosaurs through the use of genetic engineering on an island off the coast of Central America. Following a Frankenstein-esque plot,[4] a few of the more dangerous dinosaurs break loose and begin eating people, including some of the scientists who were working on the project. Problems begin when one of the characters tries to smuggle dinosaur eggs off the island reserve (this character meets his doom thanks to some poison-spitting dinosaurs). These two factors, losing control of a creation, and greed, are concerns that Crichton has with regard to genetic engineering in general, and he begins his book with this warning:

> The late twentieth century has witnessed a scientific gold rush of astonishing proportions: the headlong and furious haste to commercialize genetic engineering. This enterprise has proceeded so rapidly – with so little outside commentary – that its dimensions and implications are hardly understood at all. (Crichton, 1990 pix)

Such warnings led to scientists contending they were being unduly targeted. The *Boston Globe* ran a story about how some genetic engineers were concerned with the film's portrayal of genetic research (5 April 1992, p76). However, fear of genetic engineering quickly turned into dinophilia after the film was released. Stories about amber containing dinosaur DNA (*The Record*, 26 August 1993, pC1), editorials about the realities of cloning dinosaurs (*The New York Times*, 18 July 1993, pp4, 18) and the science of cloning dinosaurs (*Boston Globe*, 12 July 1993, p9) could be found in 'news' sections of newspapers in the US and in other parts of the world. The focus of these reports was often a fascination with dinosaurs and the notion that it would be a good thing if they could be resurrected.

There seem to be two factors that triggered this crossover in the public from a fear of genetic engineering to a desire for the reappearance of dinosaurs: first, the scientific discussions about cloning that were taking place; and second, the movie's lifelike portrayal of science. It was shown at a time when audience members were hearing about new advances in cloning and other genetic technologies, and it used sufficiently plausible portrayals of scientific laboratories and endeavours to drive the human imagination. Much like alien movies from which we believe we are learning more about space, audience members may not have thought of the movie as completely fictional, at least in terms of the not-so-distant future. However, given the greed and lack of foresight demonstrated by some of the research and staff member characters in the movie and the problems with free range, meat-eating dinosaurs, it would not have been surprising if some audience members may have decided that genetic engineering was nothing but trouble.

Polan (1997) asserts that horror films emphasize aspects of otherness, typically embodied by the monster and slasher characters in early horror films, although recent films embody otherness within the human characters. The scientists of *Jurassic Park* are portrayed as something other than human who not only create the human-eating dinosaurs, but then rationalize their actions as well as those of their creations. These scientists are not willing (or even able) to destroy their work, as doing so would symbolize failure. The underlying message is that while any 'rational' thinking person would destroy the dinosaurs, scientists are so concerned with their status and the economic possibilities of their work that they are blind to the human and social costs of their research. Given that the scientists of *Jurassic Park* are incompetent in legitimate business endeavours, their capitalist motives are pursued through fantastical and ultimately fatal research.

It should also be noted that two of the heroes of the story were a mathematician and a palaeontologist. Neither of these individuals, who were both males, worked on the island; they had been brought in as 'experts' to witness and add legitimacy to the experiments. The fact that mathematics and palaeontology are both disciplines based on scientific principles does not seem to fly in the face of Crichton's warning against big science. Instead, the underlying message seems to be that neither mathematicians nor palaeontologists could be motivated by profits, as these are both established disciplines and filled by eccentric people more concerned with pure knowledge.

Genetic realities: Fish and sports

In December 2003, the US Food and Drug Administration (FDA) concluded that a genetically modified small, freshwater aquarium fish named zebra danio was neither edible nor posed a threat to the environment, thus opening the door for marketing these fish in pet stores. According to a news account of the fish (Rook, 2004), the initial genetic modifications involved inserting a sea coral gene into the fish to indicate water pollution when exposed to it, making the fish an environmental monitoring tool. Once it was realized that aquarium hobbyists might be interested in adding a colourful fish to their tanks, researchers began seeking approval for sale, which was granted in the US. The FDA were satisfied that it was unlikely that drunken fraternity brothers would be swallowing these fish during rush week.

The opening paragraphs in the *Lansing State Journal* article in which Rook described the fish are reminiscent of the media discourse with regard to genetically modified foods:

> They're more high tech than a Tamagotchi, more freaky-sci-fi than a virtual dog. They're GloFish – a cross between man's best friend and Lite-Brite.
>
> The science and marketing that brought us genetically engineered Franken-food has now given us a Franken-pet by combining the genes of standard aquarium-tank fish – the white and black zebra danio – with the genes of fluorescing sea coral. (Rook, 2004, D1.

While the monster theme is present, much as it is in *Jurassic Park*, the news is not all doom and gloom; Frankenstein and his bride are not completely out of their aquatic cage. Rook goes on to say:

> *Don't get freaked by the idea of people in lab coats messing around with DNA. Breeders have actively engineered pets for centuries – think cats with curled ears and Lhasa apsos. (Rook, 2004)*

In addition, Rook cites the FDA as a legitimate source in defining risk, and since the FDA said the fish poses no risk, it must be minimal if non-existent. The only other actors to be quoted in the story were two pet shop owners and a marketing consultant, all of whom were interested in the fish but were less than enthusiastic about its money-making potential in the long run.

An editorial in *The Los Angeles Times*, on the other hand, contended that it was lucky that California officials had banned the sale of the fish because it was considered 'frivolous', but science would have to be consulted

> *when a scarier biotech fish comes up for approval in 2004: a salmon that grows at five times the normal rate. Since these salmon would be farmed in ocean pens, scientific panels already are raising alarms about their ability to escape and compete for food with wild salmon. (Editorial 2004:Part 2, p10)*

The *St Louis Post-Dispatch* in a front-page story quoted a scientist from Purdue University on 2 January 2004 saying that while the Glofish posed little threat to the environment (because it is from tropical waters, it would quickly die in cooler US waters), other genetically modified fish could be harmful. It was also mentioned that sales of the fish had not caused much of a stir at local pet shops (Kintisch, 2004).

Scientists and pet shop owners were not the only sources quoted in the press, nor was the story always about fish. In a report about the Californian ban that appeared in an Australian newspaper, the Commissioner of the California Fish and Game Commission was quoted as saying that his vote against the selling of the Glofish was based on a value judgement, not scientific evidence (Associated Press, 2003), while another report of the story that appeared in Canada asked the question about whether or not similar techniques could be used to engineer glowing people. According to a molecular biologist at the University of Toronto, the ability to create glow-in-the-dark people was not out of the question (Gonda, 2003).

This combination of risk and money highlights the tensions of popular culture. Scientists sought a way to develop a fish as an environmental monitoring tool, yet the potential to sell it at a mass consumption level caused some concern for environmentalists, even if only as a harbinger of worse things to come. Discourses of Frankenfish and glowing people (as well as other animals) were associated with scientists and business owners who may be able to benefit financially from selling the Glofish, in a way suggesting these groups were concerned mainly with profit, although other scientists were urging caution. Such a rush to make money would only open the door to more novel, if not more horrific, scientific and marketing endeavours.

While five-dollar fish that glow even after lights have been turned off may seem non-threatening to many readers, the use of some genetic products has been linked to illegal activities and even fatalities in the world of sports. One of the more recent drugs began innocently enough. In 1987, Amgen was awarded a patent for the process of making recombinant erythropoietin (EPO), which was to be used for treating anaemia in dialysis patients by generating red blood cells. In an article published by *The New York Times* on 2 November 1987, no mention was made of possible abuses of the drug by athletes who could gain an advantage by having more red blood cells in their system, which would lead to being able to handle more oxygen in the blood (Adelson, 1987). By 1990, two articles appeared in the US press warning of possible use of the drug in athletic competitions. *The Washington Post* ran a story on the use of EPO in an experiment on athletes, referring to those using the drug as 'supermen' (Specter, 1990) while *The Washington Times* mentioned that the International Olympic Committee would be banning EPO as rumours that abuses were already taking place were forcing them to take action (Mackall, 1990).

It is interesting to note that the use of steroids in some sports is referred to as 'doping' (e.g. *Agence France Presse*, 2003; Fotheringham, 2003), conjuring up images of hippies and intravenous drug users; marginal people involved in marginal activities. At the same time, the use of steroids has been linked to such prestigious sporting events as the Tour de France and the Olympics. Mark McGuire became an American baseball icon after breaking the single-season home run record, and his image was little tarnished after it became known that he was using androstenedione, a steroid that is banned in many other sports. This juxtaposition of images – doping and heroes – seems to be unproblematic for the press and its readers. In fact, well-known athletes often cultivate cult-like status by playing on deviant themes to bolster their fan base (e.g. Dennis Rodman, Allen Iverson). Someone who is unfamiliar with the world of sports may find it unsurprising that these athletes would use drugs to enhance their performances. It is not, however, only the athlete that is involved in many of these controversies. Doctors have been involved and even taken to court for supplying athletes with banned substances (e.g. Whittle, 2003), as have coaches and businesses within the pharmaceutical industry (Barron, 2003). Linking of these illegal activities to such individuals and institutions may cause the general public's trust in them to falter.

The reverberations of such actions touch more than just the athletes and their trainers. Given the amount of fame and money which accompanies triumphs in such events as the Tour de France, it is not impossible to imagine other athletes trying these techniques as they seek to gain an advantage over their opponents and share in the accolades of appreciative fans and potential sponsors. Public accounts of illegal activities in the world of sports have never been a deterrent for those who measure themselves by their athletic prowess. Making an impression on the right person or audience seems often to take precedence over the chances of getting caught.

Popular culture in the news

The above examples of specific issues related to both genetics and popular culture were meant to show that these portrayals are not all science fiction, and that the monetary and status rewards for successfully navigating popular culture can be considerable. We now turn to a wider treatment of this topic by focusing on the mainstream press and how reporters have covered a number of these issues. The objective of many media research projects is to find a linkage between encoders and potential decoders. Third-person effects research, for example, argues that viewers are subject to media messages, but typically think that other audience members are more inclined to act on that information (e.g. Atwood, 1994; Gunther, 1991; Ten Eyck, 2000). The cultivation hypothesis states that people who watch a lot of television tend to think that portrayals on television are real (e.g. Gerbner et al, 1980; Heath, 1984). Phillips (1982) found that suicides presented on television, including fictitious portrayals such as a soap opera suicide, led to an increase in the suicide rates among the general public. Reviews of such studies have varied from complete endorsement such as that by the National Institutes of Health (1982) to stinging critiques by Doob and Macdonald (1979) and Kessler and Stipp (1984). This is all part of the debate about whether viewers are active or passive in relation to mass media messages (Biocca, 1988). The complexity of this debate is due largely to the multivalent characteristic of the media (Gamson et al, 1992), as well as to the heterogeneity of most mass audiences (Hoijer, 1992; Morley and Brunsdon, 1999).

The level of knowledge concerning genetics and biotechnology among the lay public is, for the most part, unknown. While stories of genetics have been around for a few decades if not longer (some argue that the beginning of biotechnology, including genetic engineering, was marked by the Asilomar Conference in 1975, though popular science fiction scenarios of cloning have been available since at least 1956 with the release of the movie *Invasion of the Body Snatchers*), these are not necessarily issues with deep cultural resonance. Public opinion polls on biotechnology issues have been available since the 1980s (Hamstra, 1998). However, some polls show that up to a third of the population do not know how genetic engineering will affect their lives in the future (Gaskell and Bauer, 2001).

Given that these are not issues which most people deal with on a daily basis, the media become important sources of information from which opinions are formed. While opinions can develop in seconds as well as years, we felt an 11-year period of reporting would encompass a great deal of potential opinion-forming stories, as well as highlight any trends in reporting practices. Using Lexis-Nexis's group of Arts and Sports News, we searched on the term biotech(!)[5] in the period 1990 to 2001 for all three categories within this grouping: Reviews of books, movies, etc., Entertainment news and Sports news. This approach generated 551 articles from 77 newspapers and other types of publications such as news wires and public relations services, from four countries: the US, Canada, the UK and France. The latter two are collapsed into a European category, as there were only three articles from *Agence France Presse*. This is a very wide net with many holes; nevertheless, it was felt that this would offer a general view of how the mass media have covered this topic.

Table 11.1 shows that of the 551 articles, 460, or 83.5 per cent, appeared in the US. This can be partially explained by the fact that this was a US-based search. While the number of articles appearing each year started to climb in 1993, the difference between the number in 1993 (48) and 2001 (60) is not enormous. Table 11.1 also shows that the 'progress' frame, meaning biotechnology will improve our way of life, was most often used by reporters, followed by the 'Pandora's box' frame where the implication is that if we let this happen, it will only cause problems, and the economic frame, where the story is reported in the

Table 11.1 *Description of reporting, 1990–2001*

Characteristics	*N = 551*	*(%)*
Country		
US	460	(83.5)
Canada	41	(7.4)
Europe	50	(9.1)
Year		
1990	36	(6.5)
1991	29	(5.3)
1992	34	(6.2)
1993	48	(8.7)
1994	47	(8.5)
1995	40	(7.3)
1996	42	(7.6)
1997	48	(8.7)
1998	59	(10.7)
1999	48	(8.7)
2000	60	(10.9)
2001	60	(10.9)
Frame		
Progress	229	(41.6)
Pandora's box	161	(29.2)
Economics	130	(23.6)
Ethics	22	(4.0)
Deal with the devil	9	(1.6)
Type		
Non-fiction	423	(76.8)
Fiction	128	(23.2)

Source: Lexis Nexis Arts and Sports News 1990–2001 on the term 'biotech(!)'

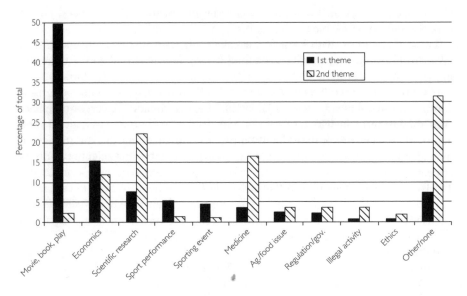

Figure 11.1 *Content of articles*

context of stock prices and financial statements. This is different from the overall coverage in the US, in which economics was second to the progress frame (Ten Eyck and Williment 2003). Finally, just over three-quarters (76.8 per cent) of the articles were non-fictional.

The content of the articles is also very diverse. Figure 11.1 highlights some of the more qualitative aspects of the coverage. Over half of the articles (286) focused on a movie, book, play or some other kind of popular cultural presentation. The second most popular theme was scientific research (165 articles), followed by economics (150 articles). The most used source in the coverage was public and media opinion (e.g. polls, reporters making statements about a situation, etc.) (220), followed by industry representatives (112) and scientists (98).

The final two categories in Figure 11.1 are based on Schonbach's (1990) work on account episodes. According to this research, a norm breach is often followed by three stages of an account episode – a question phase, an account phase and an evaluation phase. Depending on the severity of each phase, including the breach, Schonbach argued that his model could predict the likelihood of conflict escalation or management among the involved actors. Applying this to press coverage of genetic issues, we assumed that reporters would question the use of genetic engineering (for example, using anabolic steroids to improve athletic performance), and the account given by sources would lead to readers deciding whether or not the situation was under control. If the accused actor either refused to give an account or justified the action, this would probably lead to an escalation of conflict (readers becoming more upset about the situation). However, if the accused actor gave an excuse or concession, conflict was more likely to be managed. Of the 551 articles coded, 229 carried some part of an account episode.

Of the accounts given, 11 were refusals, 160 justifications, 44 excuses, and 14 concessions. Applying Schonbach's theory to newspaper accounts, readers who question the actions of the sources are likely see the sources as shrinking from taking responsibility for their actions, leading to poor evaluations and an escalation in the conflict.

If sources are most likely to justify their actions leading to a higher degree of conflict, this would lead readers to question their legitimacy. In a cross-tabulation (not shown here) in which scientists and doctors were compared to all other actors, they were much more likely to use accounts leading to escalations than management ($p = 0.026$). In fact, of the 70 articles in which a scientist or doctor appeared and an account was given, excuses and concessions were only used in 11 (16 per cent), while in the 159 articles in which someone other than a scientist or doctor was used as a source and an account was given, 47 (30 per cent) carried excuses or concessions. If this is a general trend among scientists and doctors, it could easily lead to a decline in trust in these institutions.

If scientists are more likely to escalate conflict when their actions are questioned, we might expect reporters to use this to link them to a frame that is unflattering such as Pandora's box or deal with the devil. We tested this proposition on our data. In a logistic regression in which frames were dichotomized into progress (1) and all other frames (0), and the independent variables consisted of the motivations used in an account, the size of the article, whether or not the story was fictional or non-fictional, whether a metaphor was used, and whether the main source was a scientist or doctor, this last variable is negatively related to progress frames ($b = -0.35$, $se = 0.11$, $p = 0.002$), a finding contrary to that reported by Ten Eyck and Williment (2003), who studied all types of coverage in *The New York Times* and *Washington Post* between 1971 and 2000. In other words, in hard news, scientists are linked to reporting on progress, while in soft news they are more likely to be tied to other types of frames.

There is, however, a caveat to all of this. In the same regression model, reports dealing with fictional events were more likely to be tied to a progressive frame than those relating to non-fictional accounts ($b = 0.56$, $se = 0.12$, sig. $= 0.000$). While not directly related to scientists, it does show that fictional accounts of biotechnology are not necessarily negative; science fiction is not necessarily all about naysaying, and audience members who read only the light sections of the newspapers are not necessarily going to be exposed only to negative portrayals.

Such a finding – that in soft news sections scientists are linked not to progress but to science fiction – seems to support the argument that the media are multivalent, and therefore objective in the sense that all things are available to all people.

No clear winners or losers

There are rewards and punishments attached to genetic engineering and biotechnology, some quite significant. Supporters and proponents of these technologies have vested interests in how they are portrayed to the general public, as the success of many applications will be decided in the marketplace (Nottingham, 1998). Some within popular culture genres, such as science fiction writers, movie producers, athletes and pet store owners, have also found that genetics can bring rewards. This intersection of science, economics and popular culture is a site of intense struggle, as the legitimacy of each actor is called into question. Since libel and slander are less of an issue in fictional portrayals, challenges to authority can become quite direct and sensational.

Many of the challenges to authority described in this chapter focus on scientists and the scientific enterprise, although other actors have been considered as well. According to the account, the monster theme has been a frequent anchor within popular culture. For example, human-eating dinosaurs and Frankenfish appear regularly and scientists are portrayed as the main designers of these creatures, even if they are unaware that they lack the ability to control them once created. Given the history of scientific progress where disasters ensued – nuclear power as a clean and cheap source of energy and thalidomide as a cure for morning sickness during pregnancy – this anchor has some resonance. At the same time, societies that support capitalistic markets may feel that it is the marketplace that should determine if genetic engineering is acceptable or not. As DiMaggio (1990, 1994) has argued, the causal link between economics and culture is often blurred, as the marketplace is driven by ideas, while ideas are often shaped by economic possibilities. If monsters – real and fictional – sell well, others are likely to follow.[6]

This is not to say that popular culture has been only detrimental to science. In fact, the only clear winners in this account are the movie producers who have grossed over a billion dollars with *Jurassic Park* and its sequels. While it is without doubt that Michael Crichton and other writers have benefited from people buying their products, if the purpose for writing these stories was to frighten people, it may have backfired. As mentioned, some of the reporting after *Jurassic Park* was released focused on the ability of scientists to resurrect dinosaurs through genetic engineering, and much of this reporting was framed as progressive or interesting in the sense that having dinosaurs in zoos and other animal parks would be a great thing. The substantial monetary rewards have been countered by cultural defeats.

In the end, it is difficult to define clear winners and losers from both an economic and cultural point of view. Specific stories may question the legitimacy of a scientific stance or the appropriateness of an athlete using performance-enhancing drugs, yet other news reports, novels or movies and the reactions of audience members highlight the fact that any number of portrayals are available, and that the interpretations of these accounts are highly varied. In an age when mass media are becoming more and more ubiquitous and playing a larger part in the development of ideology (Thompson, 1990), it is extremely important that we do not forget the role of popular culture in the shaping of science and technology.

Notes

1   The author wishes to thank Giorgos Sakellaris and Rebecca Sullivan for their contributions to this chapter.

2　There is even a cable television channel in the US devoted to showing science fiction shows and movies (*The Sci-Fi Channel*).
3　At a recent meeting on nanotechnology, scientists and industry personnel interested in marketing nanotechnology were concerned that the public would be led astray by science fiction writers such as Michael Crichton. His novel *Prey* (2002) is a thriller about biogenetics, nanotechnology and distributed processing.
4　The Frankenstein label has been used in much of the anti-GM literature.
5　The exclamation mark (!) is used as a wild card character by LexisNexis, so words such as biotechnology, biotechnological, biotech, etc. are included in the search.
6　This is evidence of the fact that *Jurassic Park – The Movie* spawned two sequels, with a third planned for release in 2008 (http://www.the-numbers.com/movies/series/JurassicPark.php).

References

Agger, B. (1992) *Cultural Studies as Critical Theory*, Falmer Press, Washington, DC

Atwood, E. L. (1994) 'Illusions of media power: The third-person effect', *Journalism Quarterly*, 71, pp269–281

Beck, U. (1999) *World Risk Society*, Polity, Malden, MA

Becker, H. S. (1974) 'Art as collective action', *American Sociological Review*, 39, pp767–776

Biocca, F. A. (1988) 'Opposing conceptions of the audience: The active and passive hemispheres of mass communication theory', *Communication Yearbook 11*, pp51–80

Bourdieu, P. (1984) *Distinction* (translated by Richard Nice), Harvard University Press, Cambridge, MA

Crichton, M. (1990) *Jurassic Park*, Ballantine, New York

DiMaggio, P. (1990) 'Cultural aspects of economic action and organization', in Friedland, R. and Robertson, A. F. (eds) *Beyond the Marketplace*, Hawthorne, NY, pp113–136

DiMaggio, P. (1994) 'Culture and economy', in Smelser, N. J. and Swedeberg, R. (eds) *The Handbook of Economic Sociology*, Princeton University Press, Princeton, NJ, pp27–57

Doob, A. N. and Macdonald, G. E. (1979) 'Television viewing and fear of victimization: Is the relationship causal?', *Journal of Personality and Social Psychology*, vol 37, pp170–179

Dunwoody, S. and Ryan, M. (1985) 'Scientific barriers to the popularization of science in the mass media', *Journal of Communication*, vol 35, pp26–42

Fiske, J. (1992) 'Audiencing: A cultural studies approach to watching television', *Poetics*, vol 21, pp345–359

Galison, P., Graubard, S. R. and Mendelsohn E. (eds) (2001) *Science in Culture*, Transaction, New Brunswick, NJ

Gamson, W. A., Croteau, D., Hoynes, W. and Sasson, T. (1992) 'Media images and the social construction of reality', *Annual Review of Sociology*, vol 18, pp373–393

Gaskell, G. and Bauer, M. W. (eds) (2001) *Biotechnology 1996–2000: The Years of Controversy*, Science Museum, London

Gerbner, G., Gross, L., Morgan, M. and Signorielli, N. (1980) 'The "mainstreaming" of America: Violence profile no 11', *Journal of Communication*, vol 30, pp10–29

Gunther, A. (1991) 'What we think others think: Causes and consequences in the third-person effect', *Communication Research*, vol 18, pp355–372

Habermas, J. (1973) *Legitimation Crisis* (translated by Thomas McCarthy), Beacon, Boston

Hamstra, A. (1998) *Public opinion about biotechnology: A survey of surveys*, European Federation of Biotechnology, Task Group on Public Perceptions of Biotechnology, The Hague

Heath, L. (1984) 'Impact of newspaper crime reports on fear of crime: Multi-methodological investigation', *Journal of Personality and Social Psychology*, vol 47, pp263–276

Hoijer, B. (1992) 'Reception of television narration as a socio-cognitive process: A schema-theoretical outline', *Poetics*, vol 21, pp283–304

Kessler, R. C. and Stipp, H. (1984) 'The impact of fictional television suicide stories on US fatalities: A replication', *American Journal of Sociology*, vol 90, pp151–167

Kone, D. and Mullet, E. (1994) 'A societal risk perception and media coverage', *Risk Analysis*, vol 14, pp21–24

Lazarsfeld, P. F. and Kendall, P. (1948) *Radio Listening in America*, Prentice Hall, New York

Leiss, W. (1974) *The Domination of Nature*, Beacon, Boston, MA

Marcuse, H. (1964) *One-Dimensional Man*, Beacon, Boston, MA

Montgomery, K. C. (1989) *Target: Prime Time*, Oxford University Press, New York

Morley, D. and Brunsdon, C. (1999) *The Nationwide Television Studies*, Routledge, New York

National Institutes of Health (1982) *Television and Behavior*, US Department of Health and Human Services, Rockville, MD

Nelkin, D. (1995) *Selling Science*, W. H. Freeman, New York

Neurath, P. (1995) 'Sixty years since Marienthal', *Canadian Journal of Sociology*, vol 20, pp91–105

Nottingham, S. (1998) *Eat your Genes*, Zed, New York

Peterson, R. A. and Kern, R. (1996) 'Changing highbrow taste: From snob to omnivore', *American Sociological Review*, vol 61, pp900–907

Phillips, D. P. (1982) 'The impact of fictional television stories on US adult fatalities: New evidence on the effect of the mass media on violence', *American Journal of Sociology*, vol 87, pp1340–1359

Polan, D. (1997) 'Eros and syphilization', in Gibian, P. (ed) *Mass Culture and Everyday Life*, Routledge, New York, pp119–127

Powell, D. and Leiss, W. (1997) *Mad Cows and Mother's Milk*, McGill-Queens University Press, Montreal

Rook, C. (2004) 'Glowing debut: Genetically engineered freshwater fish shimmer due to coral gene', *Lansing State Journal*, 2 January, D1, D6

Schonbach, P. (1990) *Account Episodes*, Cambridge University Press, New York

The *Tabloid* Collective (1997) 'On/against mass culture theories', in Gibian, P. (ed) *Mass Culture and Everyday Life*, Routledge, New York, pp14–25

Ten Eyck, T. A. (2000) 'Interpersonal and mass communication: Matters of trust and control', *Current Research in Social Psychology*, vol 5, pp206–224

Ten Eyck, T. A. and Williment, M. (2003) 'The national media and things genetic: Coverage in *The New York Times* (1971–2000) and *Washington Post* (1977–2000)', *Science Communication*, pp129–152

Thomas, C. (1983) *Book Burning*, Crossway, Westchester, IL

Thompson, J. B. (1990) *Ideology and Modern Culture*, Stanford University Press, Stanford, CA

References (newspaper material)

Adelson, A. (1987) 'Business people: Amgen chief confident on biotechnology gains', *The New York Times*, 2 November, D2

Agence France Presse (2003) 'Experts cast doubt on drug-free tour', 5 July

Associated Press (2003) 'Science watch', *The Australian World*, 8 December, p15

Barron, D. (2003) 'A growing conspiracy? The discovery of designer steroids might create an unprecedented scandal involving prominent athletes in every sport', *The Houston Chronicle*, 27 October, Sports 1

Editorial (2004) 'Bigger Frankenfish to fry', *Los Angeles Times*, Part 2, 5 January, p10

Fotheringham, W. (2003) 'Sport in brief: Cycling', *Guardian*, London, 13 January, p27

Gonda, G. (2003) 'New pet enjoys glowing reputation', *The Toronto Star*, 4 December, A13

Kintisch, E. (2004) 'Biotech fish that glow draw little fanfare in local debut, but lack of regulation makes some uneasy', *St. Louis Post-Dispatch*, 2 January, A1

Mackall, D. (1990) 'Sports roundup', *The Washington Times*, 13 April, D2

Specter, M. (1990) 'Supermen on new blood drug endanger sports and themselves', *The Washington Post*, 2 April, A3

Whittle, J. (2003) 'Armstrong stands accused in latest drug furore', *The Times*, London, 8 July, Sport, p35

12

Competing Voices, Contrasting Frames in North America[1]

Susanna Hornig Priest[2]

Attentive and engaged publics

Modest differences in support for various gene technologies exist between the United States and Canada. In general, recent data suggest that in the aggregate, Canadians seem to stand somewhere between US and European populations on many issues (see, for example, Pollara/Earnscliffe, 2003). But this observation in itself provides little guidance for those attempting to understand or communicate with North American audiences or to develop public policy that takes public opinion fully into account. This chapter is an attempt to suggest alternative ways of conceptualizing audiences and publics vis-à-vis these technologies, using US and Canadian populations as cases in point.

A variety of ways of thinking about the audiences for information related to science and technology have been developed. Arguably one of the best known is Jon Miller's concept of the 'attentive audience' for science (Miller, 1983, 1998), which draws in turn on earlier comparative work in political theory (Almond, 1950; Amond and Verba, 1963). According to Miller's analyses, only a small percentage of the population is scientifically literate; only this group tends to be regularly and predictably interested in news accounts covering this area. However, the focus on a small, consistently attentive audience that is scientifically literate has been challenged on several grounds. For example, an emphasis on formal scientific literacy can ignore important forms of knowledge that exist in the repertoire of everyday people (Wynne, 1989, 1991) and also tends to cast all public criticism of science in a pejorative light (Ziman, 1992).

These differences of perspective cannot be understood as involving only methodological issues or debates over measurement schemes but are actually part of a broader academic discussion of the nature of democracy and contemporary society. If ordinary people are not scientifically literate or even interested in science, then to engage them in science policy debates and decisions is clearly pointless. If, however, differences of perspective between ordinary people acting as citizens of democracies, on the one hand, and scientifically trained experts, on the other, result from other differences (such as differences in cultural values, position in the social structure, and so on), then the prospect of excluding non-scientists from the discussion of science policy takes on a different and much more problematic significance. In other words, the relationship between knowledge or literacy and one's point of view on science policy questions has implications for the disenfranchisement (or, conversely, the empowerment) of ordinary citizens with respect to the participation in democratic debates involving science.

As illustrated for the US by Figure 12.1, while those of higher educational levels have higher levels of knowledge of genetics, attitudes towards gene technologies do not follow the same pattern. It appears that knowledge of genetics is only a weak predictor of attitudes towards these technologies (Priest, 2001; Priest et al, 2003). Although some researchers argue persuasively that knowledge does make a statistically independent contribution (Sturgis and Allum, 2004), as a practical matter it is very difficult to untangle the possession of particular forms of knowledge from other variables such as educational level, social class membership or occupation (e.g. scientist) that are also likely to be connected to various types of attitudes towards science and technology.

Public opinion is not necessarily fickle but it may appear so in a rapidly evolving opinion climate, especially when complex science is involved. As knowledge gap

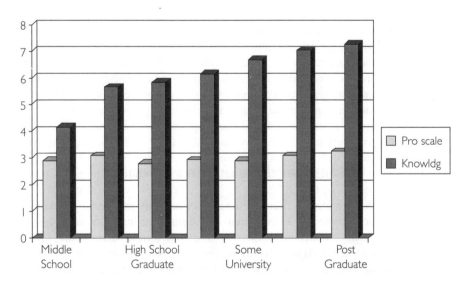

Note: Bar chart showing the relationship between education level, knowledge of genetics and attitudes towards a variety of gene technologies. Based on year 2000 survey data for the US collected by the author in cooperation with the International Research Group on Biotechnology and the Public

Figure 12.1 *Education, knowledge and attitudes: US 2000*

theory (Tichenor et al, 1970) has proposed, people of different educational levels can acquire different information at different rates and in different ways. But when people become interested – for whatever reason – in a complex development, it is possible they may 'close the gap' by acquiring needed knowledge from media accounts and other sources. While research continues on whether and when active information seeking can overcome knowledge gaps, on a conceptual level it should not be surprising that knowledge may not directly predict attitudes; rather, attitudes, interests and concerns can also influence the acquisition of knowledge. Sometimes in the case of novel ideas this process may be associated with a flurry of critical media attention while people struggle to come to terms with unanticipated scientific and technological developments (Wagner et al, 2002). The result may be opinion that evolves and changes, even polarizes, as people see a need to seek information and make up their minds. This suggests some early-stage volatility but is not the same thing as being fickle (i.e. capricious or arbitrary).

While Miller may be perfectly correct in asserting that prior knowledge will predict attentiveness in the normal course of events, other conditions (such as perceived potential benefits, perceived risk of social, health, economic or environmental disruption, or perceived ethical or moral imperatives) can arise that focus public attention on particular developments, largely independent of people's ambient levels of interest in science or technology. In political terms, the concept of an 'engaged public' (Gaskell and Bauer, 2001) may be more directly relevant than the 'attentive public' concept for understanding public responses to new technologies and their regulation. However useful the 'attentive public' concept may be in characterizing the small audience that is interested in routine developments in science and technology in the absence of especially compelling circumstances, the situation in which people outside this group, often in circumstances outside the normal course of events, assume an actively political role is quite different. And in modern democracies that purport to develop policy in a transparent communication environment, the interests and concerns of this larger group should not be ignored.

Understanding other audiences

Who are the other audiences, then, for science or technology that has come to be perceived as controversial? Given that demographics such as age, gender, religiosity and political affiliation do not go much further than knowledge in predicting attitudes towards gene technologies, that survey summaries do not generally capture factors that seem to explain broad national and cultural differences in this context, and that data from small numbers of focus groups and public consultation experiments do a poor job of representing public sentiment in entire national populations, this is a more complex question than it might appear. Using a dataset provided by the Canadian Biotechnology Secretariat and including recent (2003) survey data from both the US and Canada, cluster analysis procedures suggest these populations may be meaningfully divided into five groups (see Priest, 2006 for further details). These groups, with interpretive comments that in most cases augment what the statistical information can directly establish, are summarized below. The results are based on analysis of answers to a broad variety of general attitudinal questions and opinions about specific technologies (medical, agricultural and environmental).

True believers think that biotechnology is generally progressive, that its regulation is generally to be avoided, and that decisions in this area should be made by experts. Anyone who has been involved with biotechnology policy debates in the past decade has encountered the attitude, perhaps most predominant within the community of biotech researchers but certainly not limited to them, that opposition to any form of gene technology is necessarily due to ignorance. This perspective is very consistent with 'true believer' thinking. 'True believers' are unlikely to put much stock in public opinion as meaningful input to public policy and seem more likely to view public engagement as interference. This group is over twice as common in the US as in Canada; however, even in the US it is less than one-quarter of the population (Figure 12.2).

Utilitarians[3] also prefer that experts should decide but believe that both risks and benefits should be weighed in making the decision, rather than making the assumption that gene technologies are inherently positive. While 'utilitarians' are not necessarily anti-technology, they want decisions based on data regarding both negative and positive dimensions. It is easy to imagine utilitarian attitudes prevailing among regulators and other technocrats specifically charged with making rational and unbiased policy decisions on behalf of entire populations; however, this group is certainly not limited to regulators but is actually the most common group in *both* the US and Canada.

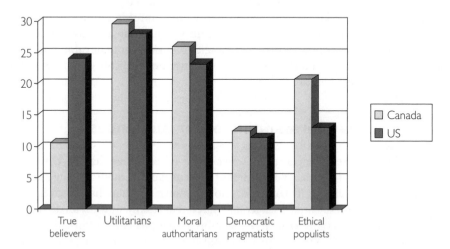

Note: Bar chart showing proportional distributions of the five attitude groups in Canada and the US. Based on year 2003 data for simultaneous surveys done in each country by Pollara/ Earnscliffe Research with funding from the Canadian Biotechnology Secretariat

Figure 12.2 *Canadian and US distributions (per cent)*

Moral authoritarians, also common in both countries but slightly more so in Canada, believe that experts should decide these matters but that ethical norms should be more important than risks and benefits in the decision. 'Moral authoritarians' might be conceptualized as those who would be more likely to turn to religious leaders for guidance rather than scientific, medical or environmental experts, though the data do not directly indicate what kind of 'experts' are envisioned.

Finally, two smaller groups believe that ordinary people, not experts, should decide policy in these areas: the *democratic pragmatists*, who believe ordinary people should decide on the basis of risks and benefits; and the *ethical populists*, who believe ordinary people should decide on the basis of ethical considerations. If combined, this group would rival the 'true believers' in the US and outnumber the utilitarians in Canada. 'Ethical populists', while a small group, are much more common in Canada than in the US.

The biggest observable differences between the two countries, then, are the greater proportion of 'true believers' in the US and the greater number of 'ethical populists' in Canada. It seems likely – although the data available do not directly prove this – that the differences between these two countries can be accounted for by a larger number of people in the US who are convinced that biotechnology is good and that 'top down' decision making should proceed on this basis, combined with a larger number of people in Canada who believe ordinary individuals should be empowered to make these decisions personally and on ethical grounds. However, most people in the two countries are members of the other, larger groups.

These five positions are not easily reconcilable. The two larger groups in each country both believe experts should decide, but one believes the basis should be risks and benefits and the other believes the basis should be ethics. The former conjures up images of laboratory scientists and government administrators poring over the results of experimental data. The latter suggests religious leaders counselling their flocks about the right thing to do. These are not simply different audiences, publics and paths but widely disparate perspectives – represented by images with few elements in common. It seems reasonable to suggest that each of these perspectives should have a voice in a democratic policy debate. However, neither 'true believers' nor 'moral authoritarians' may cede very much authority to public opinion – nor to one another.

An additional context for thinking about the meaning and dynamics of these seemingly disparate perspectives comes from a separate study of US public opinion in which spiral of silence theory was applied to biotechnology-related issues (Priest et al, 2004). Traditionally, spiral of silence studies have concentrated on fear of social ostracism as a motivator in reducing people's willingness to voice certain opinions (in particular, those seen as being in a minority or descending in popularity). However, for biotechnology, an additional factor appears to be the extent to which morality is actually framed in scientific terms. In this study, an open-ended question about the type of moral issue that was associated with biotechnology produced a variety of responses. Those who answered this question in a way that stressed the element of science as progress (for example, hypothetically, 'science is beneficial') were more willing to speak out than those who responded with environmental or religious/moral associations (for example, hypothetically, 'changing nature is wrong').

Because these were separate studies, it is not possible to go further without speculating. But there appears to be an interesting resonance between the 'true believer' audience category and the higher willingness to speak of those who see morality from a scientific frame of reference. While relatively small in numbers even in the US (and even smaller in Canada), it is possible that the 'true believers' are disproportionately more visible and/or influential because of this dynamic. A climate of public opinion is not influenced only by the number of persons having different ideas but by the relative strength of their voices.

Regional differences in distribution exist as well. In Canada, the 'utilitarians' are the modal category in the East, the 'ethical populists' most common in the prairie provinces, and the 'moral authoritarians' in the West. In the US, the 'utilitarians' are the most common category in the North-East (New England) and the Western region (including the Pacific states), the 'moral authoritarians' are modal in the South, and the 'true believers' are most common in the remaining areas (Midwest and South-West).

Taken together, these various analyses suggest the substantiveness of the challenge that gene technologies represent for communicators, policy makers and researchers who want to move beyond thinking only in terms of 'science literacy' to understanding and engaging additional audiences.

Media messages and gene technologies

Finally, given the suggested existence of these distinct groups or 'publics' for gene technologies, the evidence of regional variations in their distribution that seemed responsive to cultural variations existing in each country, and an active interest in understanding the implications for communication research and practice of these observations, a selection of news media messages were analysed for their degree of resonance with these disparate perspectives, using stem cell coverage in Canada and the US during February 2004. All news articles included in the commercial LexisNexis database under the keyword 'stem cells' were analysed beginning the first of that month and continuing through a 'constructed week' of coverage.[4] This was the month of the American Association for the Advancement of Science (AAAS) 2004 meeting in Seattle in which Korean scientists reported advances in human embryonic cloning in connection with stem cell research, so the opportunity was available to see how this announcement was received differently across different parts of the North American continent.

Each article was classified by the researcher as to its dominance by a particular 'frame' or way of defining issues corresponding to an attitude group's way of thinking: emphasis on the progressive nature of science, emphasis on identifying risks and benefits, emphasis on moral leadership, or emphasis on popular thinking (combining groups four and five; Figure 12.3). Across four regions of the US,[5] 'true believer' frames dominated most articles. In Canada, this was not the case; 'moral authoritarian' frames dominated.

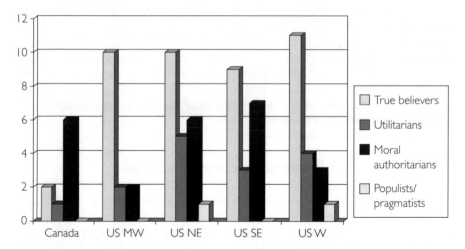

Note: *Bar chart showing number of sampled February 2004 stem cell articles in the LexisNexis database dominated by frames corresponding to the perspective of identified audience groups in Canada and four US regions*

Figure 12.3 *Stem cell 'frames'*

Further, in the Midwestern US, where 'true believers' dominate, no other news frame competes, while in the South-East the 'moral leadership' frame is a relatively close second. (There is no separate LexisNexis category for the South as a region.) A 'utilitarian' news frame is more likely in the North-East, where members of this group dominate, than in the other regions – though it is dwarfed by the 'true believer' perspective. (As the AAAS meeting took place on the West coast, it is possible that the Canadian coverage was influenced by the higher proportions of 'moral authoritarians' in western Canada; however, there were not enough articles to justify a region-by-region analysis of the Canadian news.)

While this analysis is based on relatively subjective and in other ways imperfect data categorizations, it is highly suggestive of two things: first, the dominance across the US (but not Canada) of a 'true believer' news frame, probably stemming from the intense public information and public relations activities typically accompanying major scientific announcements at AAAS meetings, which are always held simultaneously with National Association of Science Writer meetings; and, second, the resonance in both the US and at least potentially Canada of news frames of secondary importance that seem in several cases to reflect definite regional differences in modes of thinking.

Characterizing the relationship between media content and public opinion or other aspects of popular thinking has always been difficult. Media content both reflects and to some indeterminate extent shapes popular frames of reference. The research continues because this subtle chicken-and-egg relationship is difficult to tease out, even with more sophisticated statistical analyses. It seems this brief case study of stem cell coverage captures the simultaneous effects of both the 'top down' information subsidies created by key institutions and spokespeople, in this case creating 'true believer'-shaded news, and the 'bottom up' effects of cultural values and local political activity, creating secondary news frames that vary in ways that appear to resonate with regional values. Nothing in this analysis is presented as 'proof' of such relationships, but the results appear intriguingly consistent with an understanding of news frames as products of *both* organized public relations activity (information subsidies) and cultural values and modes of thinking (which in this case vary by nation and region).

Rethinking audiences

The purpose of this chapter was to take a data-based (but interpretive) approach to understanding the important North American 'publics' on the issue of news about gene technologies in a way that would facilitate understanding of how 'science literacy' is not the only socially relevant variable important for understanding related audiences, opinions and messages. Slightly different distributions of these publics are apparent in Canada and the US, and these differences may well help to explain opinion differences between the two countries that can be observed despite broad general similarities in attitude. These distributional differences help conceptualize how subtle differences in public sphere dynamics may characterize two countries that share a single language and whose cultural histories have much in common. What are the implications of these observations for researchers, communication practitioners and policy makers?

From a research perspective, this chapter suggests – of course – the need for further research. This would include research concerned with a broader interpretation of spiral of silence theory to accommodate issues of which perspectives on science are privileged within a certain cultural space and how this in turn affects the development of particular news accounts and opinion climates; continued research on the interactions among cultural values, information subsidies and news frames; and research contributing to a reconceptualization of audiences as composed of disparate publics with distinctive (and in this case to some extent irreconcilable) ways of analysing issues and responding to events. Considerable theoretical work is also needed to rethink what it means for a pluralistic society to engage in collective decision making about science and technology policy.

From a communication practitioner perspective, this chapter's most important message may involve the third research point primarily – the reconceptualization of audiences. Audiences for news and information about gene (or other) technologies, even in the more developed societies of North America, should not be thought of as composed only of a relatively small number of scientifically literate, science-attentive individuals. If all reasoned points of view should have a place at the table in democratic debate, the practitioner (whether journalist, bureaucrat or advocate) who wants to reach and engage multiple perspectives must think more broadly. Not all of the potential audiences for these discussions will view science or technologically as inherently interesting or inherently benign, and they will differ in the extent of their educational and knowledge base. This may complicate the work of communicators, but it has the potential to create stronger democracies.

And audiences are to publics, perhaps, as consumers are to citizens. Not only must information efforts reach these disparate audiences – the varied consumers of both news about technologies and technologies themselves – but also as groups of citizens these audiences need information that will empower them to participate in informed debate. However, the key implication of this analysis for civic life is that various forms of public debate – however valuable as democratic processes that often clarify the nature of opinion differences – are unlikely to resolve or eliminate these differences; in fact, they may only serve to highlight and define them. Some publics, and some citizens, believe that science is inherently progressive and must be embraced; others believe its place in society should be determined on moral or utilitarian grounds. It is not clear how public debate, however constructively intended or well informed, will ever reconcile these perspectives. Society must learn how to proceed despite them, while remaining democratic.

This analysis has used survey data developed for other purposes and cannot claim to have developed ideal categories or exhausted the universe of relevant subgroups. Where do environmentalists fit in, for example? Many will be among the utilitarians who want to take risks as well as benefits into account. Others may be moral authoritarians or ethical populists whose environmental ethos is based on a firm belief that the natural world should be left alone. In other words, it is important not to reify this particular set of five categories, which are in some ways artefacts of the dataset and its limitations. However, these groupings are never-theless suggestive of the general range of perspectives that might be found in at least some 21st-century pluralistic societies, and they do suggest the difficulty of the task ahead, which may lie less in reducing differences of opinion in order to generate consensus and more in finding ways to proceed without it.

Finally, the media analysis – while no more than a preliminary illustration – reminds us how the news media simultaneously reflect both elite influence and popular thinking. Themes and voices prominent in the news about stem cell research in early 2004 undoubtedly reflect the activities of pro-research advocates working at the national level, and also the influence of regional voices and cultural themes that are less universal. Those regional voices (also likely to be those of leaders rather than ordinary citizens) may be heard most loudly where they most strongly resonate with the values of local communities, as politicians and journal-ists alike try to appeal to those local communities (of which they are also members). The media often do help set both national and local agendas, they define what are considered legitimate and what are considered marginal positions, and they frame news stories in ways that very often reflect a variety of advocacy positions. But they do their work of creating opinion climates in an atmosphere already coloured by the perspectives of both advocates and audiences, and this is not a one-way influence.

Notes

1   Based on previous research supported by the Canadian Biotechnology Secretariat, the US National Science Foundation Program in Ethics and Values Studies, and the Office of the Vice President for Research at Texas A&M University. An earlier version of this material was presented at a workshop sponsored by the Canadian Biotechnology Secretariat in Ottawa, March 2004.
2   Associate Professor and Director of Research, College of Mass Communication and Information Studies, University of South Carolina, Columbia.
3   In early discussions of these findings, the 'utilitarian' group was referred to as 'precautionary' to distinguish them from 'true believers' who may see only the positive sides of technological developments. However, 'utilitarian' is a more appropriate term, because this group may include – but is certainly not limited to – individuals who subscribe to the so-called 'precautionary principle' for environmental and science policy.
4   That is, articles on Sunday of week one, Monday of week two, Tuesday of week three, Wednesday of week four, and then Thursday of week one and so on were included to create a sample distributed evenly across the days of the week as well as across the entire month.
5   LexisNexis defines four US regions only.

References

Almond, G. (1950) *The American People and Foreign Policy*, Harcourt, Brace and Company, New York

Amond, G. A. and Verba, S. (1963) *The Civic Culture: Political Attitudes and Democracy in Five Nations*, Princeton University Press, Princeton, NJ

Gaskell, G. and Bauer, M. W. (2001) 'Biotechnology in the years of controversy: A social scientific perspective', in Gaskell, G. and Bauer, M. (eds) *Biotechnology 1996–2000: The Years of Controversy*, Science Museum, London

Miller, J. (1983) *The American People and Science Policy*, Pergamon Press, New York

Miller, J. D. (1988) 'The measurement of civil scientific literacy', *Public Understanding of Science*, 7, pp202–223

Pollara Research and Earnscliffe Research and Communications (2003) *Public Opinion Research into Biotechnology Issues in the United States and Canada*, Eighth Wave Summary Report prepared for the Biotechnology Assistant Deputy Minister Coordinating Committee, Government of Canada (March)

Priest, S. (2001) 'Misplaced faith: Communication variables as predictors of encouragement for biotechnology development', *Science Communication*, vol 23, no 2, pp97–110

Priest, S. (2006) 'The public opinion climate for gene technologies in the Canada and the United States: Competing voices, contrasting frames', *Public Understanding of Science*, vol 15, pp55–71

Priest, S., Bonfadelli, H. and Rusanen, M. (2003) 'The "trust gap" hypothesis: Predicting support for biotechnology across national cultures as a function of trust in actors', *Risk Analysis*, vol 23, no 4, pp751–766

Priest, S., Lee, J. and Sivakumar, G. (2004) 'Public discourse and scientific controversy: A spiral of silence analysis of biotechnology opinion in the US', refereed paper presentation, Science Communication Interest Group, Association for Education in Journalism and Mass Communication, Toronto, Canada (August)

Sturgis, P. and Allum, N. (2004) 'Science in society: Re-evaluating the deficit model of public attitudes', *Public Understanding of Science*, vol 13, pp55–74

Tichenor, P. J., Olien, C. N. and Donohue, G. A. (1970) 'Mass media flow and differential growth in knowledge', *Public Opinion Quarterly*, vol 34, pp159–170

Wagner, W., Kronberger, N. and Seifert, N. (2002) 'Collective symbolic coping with new technology: Knowledge, images and public discourse', *British Journal of Social Psychology*, vol 41, no 3, pp323–343

Wynne, B. (1989) 'Sheep farming after Chernobyl: A case study in communicating scientific information', *Environment Magazine*, vol 31, no 2, pp10–15, 33–39

Wynne, B. (1991) 'Knowledges in context', *Science, Technology and Human Values*, vol 16, no 1, pp111–121

Ziman, J. (1992) 'Not knowing, needing to know, and wanting to know', in Lewenstein, B. V. (ed) *When Science Meets the Public*, American Association for the Advancement of Science, Washington, DC, pp13–20

13

Transatlantic Tensions over GM Crops and Food

Diverging perspectives

George Gaskell, Jonathan Jackson, Toby Ten Eyck,
Edna Einsiedel and Susanna Hornig Priest

Transatlantic differences on research policy and the adoption of particular applications of biotechnology have been a feature of the past decade. While federal funding for stem cell research is effectively banned in the US, with researchers limited to a few existing cell lines, in some European countries, for example the UK, it is progressing with Government support. However, it is with agricultural and food biotechnologies that the transatlantic differences have been most pronounced and most controversial. The US and Canada have millions of hectares cultivating various genetically modified (GM) commodity crops such as soya, canola and maize, and in the supermarkets half the products have GM ingredients. In Europe, by contrast, research on GM crops has been largely stalled and, with the exception of Spain, the continent is more or less a GM-free zone.

One of the roots of these different fortunes for agricultural biotechnologies on either side of the Atlantic was the early decisions on the choice of regulatory procedures. In the US and Canada, regulation was settled in the 1980s. It was based on the associated principle of substantial equivalence. A tomato is a tomato, whether it is of a conventional or GM kind. In this way, existing regulations were applied to the novel GM products, calls for the labelling of GM food rejected and environmental concerns sidelined. Europe, by contrast, struggled until 2001 to come to an agreement on the regulation of agricultural biotechnologies. The struggle started with a compromise to opt for process, rather than product, based regulation. Thus, GM, a novel process, did not fit into existing regulations for food and crops. From the 1980s to 2000, debates about risk assessment, potential short- and longer-term environmental and health impacts and the labelling of GM products exercised governments, regulators, pressure groups, the media and sections of the public. And unlike in the US and Canada, environmental ministers for the European Union (EU) member states were centrally involved in shaping policy decisions.

From the mid-1990s, the US was actively pursuing markets for its harvest of GM commodity crops. In the post-World War II decades, supported by considerable subsidies, US farmers had become highly efficient agricultural producers. Even before the GM revolution, the US was the world's major exporter of agricultural products. With the presumed benefits in yields from the new strains of GM seeds, the export and economic potential was obvious. Monsanto liked to characterize itself as the Microsoft of the new age of agriculture – bringing leading-edge science to farming. Europe's resistance was a double blow to this vision. It denied US farmers access to a large and wealthy market and, at the same time, was not a good advertisement for GM products to other parts of the world.

Through various channels, the US administration and the biotechnology companies tried to persuade European governments and consumers to open up to GM crops and foods. But through the second half of the 1990s, the debate and opposition to GM became so intense in many European countries that what was called a 'de facto moratorium' came into being in 1998. Effectively, this banned the commercial exploitation of GM agricultural products in the majority of Europe's member states.

After failed attempts to persuade Europe to lift its moratorium on the import and cultivation of GM crops, 2003 saw the US, with Canada and Argentina, call for the World Trade Organization (WTO) to overturn this ban. At the same time, the European Commission (EC) had been trying to lift the moratorium, introducing new rules for traceability of GM products and the labelling of food products containing more than 0.9 per cent of GM material.

But these new European rules did not have the desired effect. In December 2003, an EU regulatory committee considered an application to approve a GM maize – Syngenta's Bt-11 – on which a positive decision would have effectively ended the moratorium. The stage was set for a vote in favour as the European Food Safety Authority (EFSA) had announced that another GM maize was safe for human consumption. In the event, Syngenta's application was not approved as six countries – Austria, Denmark, Greece, France, Luxembourg and Portugal – voted against its introduction into Europe. Thus, the moratorium, widely seen in the US and Canada as little more than protectionism in disguise, continued – in part because, as an EC spokesperson said, 'it's a difficult situation for the member states, it's something that's difficult to explain to citizens and consumers'. That said, it was never a Europe-wide ban on GM crops. Spain, for example, had had tens of thousands of hectares planted with GM maize for a number of years.

But in April 2004, with the implementation of new regulations on labelling of GM food and the traceability of GM organisms, the moratorium was 'unofficially' lifted, and in 2005 a GM maize (Mon863) gained approval. In February 2006, in response to the complaint lodged by the US, Canada and Argentina, the World Trade Organization ruled against the EU, calling on the region to end its moratorium.

Does this signal the end of Europe's anti-GM saga? It is probably too early to tell. But the history is worth revisiting – how did the moratorium come about? And how did it come to be reversed? To cast some light on these changes in policy, we return to the events surrounding GM crops and foods and the accompanying climate of public opinion. And in trying to provide an account of the past, we may learn some lessons for the introduction of future technological innovations.

The climate of public opinion

The difficulties with GM crops and food in Europe go back to 1996–1999 – the 'watershed years' of agricultural biotechnology (Gaskell and Bauer, 2001). In addition to conflicts over the introduction of GM agriculture, these years saw the unfolding bovine spongiform encephalitis/Creutzfeldt-Jakob disease (BSE/CJD) crisis, other food scares and concerns about industrial farming. Worries about the environmental and health impacts of GM agriculture became amplified, leading to the disruption of experimental crop trials and supermarket boycotts of GM products.

While those countries appealing to the WTO to force Europe to lift the ban accused 'Old European' governments of erecting trade barriers purely to protect economic interests, it is arguable that the moratorium was motivated by concerns other than economic. It was a political response to a hostile climate of public opinion. The European public's precautionary approach to GM agriculture set the stage for the international dispute. To explore this claim, we look closely at the climate of public opinion on both sides of the Atlantic over the period 1996 to 2002.

Our analysis of public opinion in the US, Canada and the EU is through the lens of the Eurobarometer surveys on biotechnology of 1996, 1999 and 2002/2003. These representative sample surveys were fielded in each of the 15 member states of the EU as well as in the US and Canada, with around 1000 respondents for each country. With the survey data we build up a picture of some striking contrasts between Europe, Canada and the US.

As early as the 1970s, it was clear that the European public was uneasy and troubled by the idea of gene technology. As Cantley wrote:

> *[W]hat the sector ignored above all was public perception . . . the public were learning to see gene technology, genetic engineering, biotechnology and so on as a single, vague and disquieting phenomenon. (Cantley, 1992)*

A Eurobarometer survey in 1979 found that 35 per cent of the European public saw genetic research as an unacceptable risk and 49 per cent thought the same about 'synthetic food'. Further surveys up to the early 1990s showed a fairly consistent picture of concerns about biotechnology (Gaskell et al. 1997). Were such negative attitudes to biotechnology just one example of a wider questioning of – even disenchantment with – technology? Strumpel (1990), a theorist of the industrial society, argued that mass prosperity and welfare state provisions of the past 30 years undermined the dominant values of economies directed towards production and growth. Inglehart (1997) documents the emergence of post-materialist values as societies outgrow their drive for material possessions and look to quality of life, environmental protection and civil liberties to provide a more meaningful existence. Has such disengagement from the materialist world-view resulted in declining optimism about technology in Europe?

In the 2002 surveys, respondents were asked the following question about a number of technologies: 'Do you think it will improve our way of life in the next 20 years, it will have no effect, or it will make things worse?' Figure 13.1 shows the percentages of respondents (excluding 'don't knows') saying that each of four technologies will improve our way of life. For the internet, public opinion is equally optimistic in all three cases; for mobile phones, Europeans are more optimistic than those who live in Canada or the US. By contrast, Europe has the lowest percentage of optimists for nuclear power. On biotechnology, although the European figure for optimists is lower than for either Canada or the US, the fact that 65 per cent of the European public who express an opinion say they are optimistic is hardly evidence for a widespread anti-technology culture in Europe.

Since this particular question was used in earlier Eurobarometer surveys, we can assess changes in optimism and pessimism over the period 1996 to 2002 using a summary index that takes into account the proportion of optimistic, pessimistic and 'no effect' responses. For each case (the US, Canada and the EU) the percentage of pessimists was subtracted from the percentage of optimists and the result divided by the combined percentage of optimists, pessimists and those who say the technology will have no effect ('Don't know' responses are again excluded). A positive score reflects a majority of optimists over pessimists and a negative score a majority of pessimists over optimists.

Figure 13.2 shows positive scores in all three cases, and throughout the period 1996 to 2002 people in the US and Canada have been significantly more

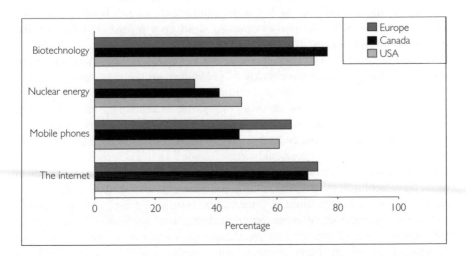

Figure 13.1 *Technological optimism, 2002*

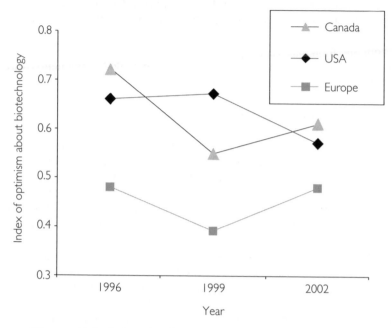

Figure 13.2 *Index of optimism about biotechnology, 1996–2002*

optimistic than Europeans ($p < 0.01$); but there are interesting differences. Canada and Europe follow a similar path: a decline in optimism from 1996 to 1999, followed by an increase in 2002. In the US, by contrast, optimism is stable from 1996 to 1999 and declines thereafter.

Are these patterns an indication of a convergence in opinion across the Atlantic? Are the Europeans and Canadians overcoming their concerns about biotechnology, while public concerns are beginning to surface in the US? Parallel shifts are also discernible in recent patterns of media coverage. In Europe, the fall in optimism from 1996 to 1999 corresponds to the 'watershed years', in which there was high-profile and critical coverage of GM foods in the news media (Bauer et al, 2001). The subsequent rise in optimism, seen in most European countries, is paralleled by a lowering of the heat of the media debate about agricultural biotechnology. Canada also witnessed an increase in critical media coverage from 1996 to 1999 (Einsiedel and Medlock, 2001). Since then, attention has shifted to the more positively viewed medical biotechnologies. In the US, media coverage is becoming more ambivalent; while scientists continue to be linked to a 'progressive' stance on biotechnology, the regulators are increasingly depicted as taking a more cautious stance (Ten Eyck and Williment, 2003).

Yet while the index of optimism about biotechnology in Europe has risen since 1999, Figure 13.2 still shows a significant gap between Europe and the US and Canada. Might this be the result of differing views about the benefits and risks associated with biotechnology?

Respondents were asked whether they thought GM crops and GM food are *useful to society* and *risky for society*. For each question, responses on a four-point scale are collapsed to agree and disagree.

We categorize individuals into one of four groups on the basis of their responses to the use *and* risk *questions, for GM crops and GM food separately. For readability we will adopt the term* benefit *in preference to* use.

- *The* relaxed group – GM crops/food – *beneficial with no risks.*
- *The* sceptical group – GM crops/food – *risky with no benefit.*
- *The* trade-off group – GM crops/food – *both beneficial and risky.*
- *The* uninterested group – GM crops/food – *neither beneficial nor risky (since this group is relatively small in number, it is not included in the following analyses).*

Table 13.1 shows the percentages of people in the sceptical, trade-off and relaxed groups for 2002, excluding those respondents who had not heard of the particular application.

Around 40 per cent of all respondents in each case are in the trade-off group. But it is in the size of the sceptical and relaxed groups that transatlantic differences are apparent. In the US, only 10 per cent are sceptical while 42 per cent are relaxed. In Europe, the sceptics reach 24 per cent while 28 per cent are relaxed. Canada comes somewhere between the US and Europe in this regard.

On GM food, almost 40 per cent of Europeans are sceptical (no benefit and risk), with Canada, at 32 per cent, not far short of the European figure. Even in the US, where people have been eating GM food for years, nearly one in five is sceptical. It is also notable that the trade-off group is, at 44 per cent, the most prevalent group in the US – an indication that a sizeable proportion of the US public do not see GM food as risk free.

Figure 13.3 shows the changes in the percentages of the relaxed, trade-off and sceptical groups for GM food over the years 1996, 1999 and 2002. For the US, two related trends are apparent: a fall in the size of the relaxed group and an increase in the trade-off group. The relaxed group declines 23 per cent while the trade-off group increases 14 per cent. Furthermore, combining the trade-off and sceptical groups (both of whom perceive risks), the percentage thinking that GM food is risky increases by 31 per cent.

Table 13.1 *Risk–benefit groups for GM crops and GM food*

	GM crops			GM food		
	US	Canada	Europe	US	Canada	Europe
Sceptical	10%	18%	24%	19%	32%	39%
Trade-off	44%	42%	42%	44%	27%	32%
Relaxed	42%	37%	28%	33%	32%	18%

Note: All comparisons between the EU and separately the US and Canada are statistically significant, *p* < 0.05

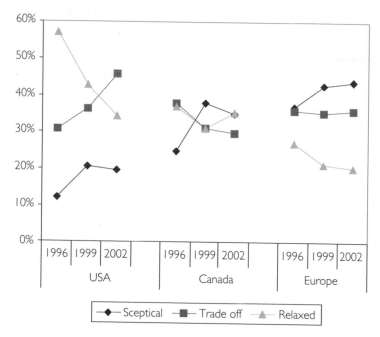

Figure 13.3 *Change in risk–benefit groups on GM food, 1996–2002*

In Canada, the largest change occurs between 1996 and 1999, with the sceptical group rising 13 per cent and the trade-off group declining by 6 per cent. This is the period when debate over GM food and crops attracts greater media coverage, primarily as a result of heightened NGO activity. Between 1999 and 2002, there is little change.

Europe follows a similar pattern with changes in the period 1996 to 1999 and relative stability post-1999. Between 1996 and 1999, the sceptical group increases 6 per cent, while the relaxed group declines 5 per cent. But whatever the changes from 1996 to 2002, the number of sceptics in the US remains a third less than in Canada and about half that in Europe.

Further evidence of differing risk and benefit perceptions is found in the responses to other questions in the survey. For example, when asked: 'Will GM foods be useful in the fight against hunger in the developing world?', the percentages agreeing are US 77, Canada 64 and Europe 44. And for the question: 'Do you think it is safe to eat GM foods?', the respective figures are 63, 45 and 22. With these questions about specific benefits and risks, the contrasts between Europe and the US and Canada are even sharper. The evidence is clear: Europeans are less convinced of the benefits and perceive greater risks associated with GM food than people in both Canada and the US.

What drives the perception of risks and benefits

We now explore three factors that may contribute to concentrating perceptions of risks and benefits of GM food: images or connotations of GM food, trust in the food chain, and social values.

To many people, genetic modification is still a new and unfamiliar technology. Some may understand it through formal or informal education, others through associations based on media stories, past experiences of technological innovations and popular cultural images. Such connotative meanings may lead people to see genetic modification as an advance on traditional plant or animal breeding, or as something akin to *Frankenstein* and *Jurassic Park*. From conversations with groups of the general public, we developed three survey questions addressing what we call 'menacing images'. The questions were: 'Ordinary tomatoes don't have genes but genetically modified ones do'; 'By eating a genetically modified fruit, a person's genes could also become modified'; and 'Genetically modified animals are always bigger than ordinary ones'. While agreement indicates an absence of knowledge about genetics, it also attests to the idea that food biotechnology is associated with primordial fears of, respectively, adulteration, infection and monstrosities. With these questions we had stumbled on the work of the various 19th-century anthropologists, including Sir James Frazer, on sympathetic magic, recently taken up by Rozin and colleagues (Rozin and Nemeroff, 1990). It may be two hundred years after the Enlightenment, but traditional ways of thinking inform the ways in which people make sense of some current events, particularly in relation to food and disease. Take a recent example: as the bird flu epidemic in Asia was featured in the European media, the household consumption of chicken declined. Here the scientific evidence is unequivocal – people cannot catch bird flu from the consumption of cooked chicken. This is an example of the law of contagion, the transfer of essences and summarized as 'once in contact, always in contact'. Genetic modification appears to invoke these 'primitive' ways of thinking; science may claim to have the rational answer, but magical thinking can sometimes trump rational argument.

Table 13.2 *Menacing images of GM food*

	Percentage in agreement		
	US	Canada	Europe
1 Ordinary tomatoes do not contain genes, while genetically modified tomatoes do	24	23	36
2 By eating a genetically modified fruit, a person's genes could also become modified	17	22	20
3 Genetically modified animals are always bigger than ordinary ones	15	22	26

The data show that these images are held, or at least taken to be plausible, by around 20 per cent of the publics in all three cases. But the first two are more prevalent in Europe than in Canada or the US. Interestingly, when we look at only those respondents with a graduate-level education, the percentages fall in the US and Canada, but much less so in Europe. We constructed a scale from the responses to the three items, where high scores indicate the holding of more menacing images. The mean score for Europe is 1.77, significantly higher than the US mean score 0.96 and Canada 1.10. For whatever reasons, and one is probably media labelling and cartoons, GM food is more stigmatized in Europe (Flynn et al, 2001).

Public trust in industry, scientists, regulators and government became a focus of attention in Europe following the BSE/CJD crisis and the controversies of GM agriculture. One response to apparent 'trust deficits' has been the establishment of a European Food Standards Authority, modelled along the lines of the US Food and Drug Administration.

We measured trust in the food chain by asking respondents: 'Now I'm going to ask you about some people and groups involved in the various applications of modern biotechnology and genetic engineering. Do you suppose they are doing a good job for society or not doing a good job for society?' The targets included government, industry, farmers and shops. A summary scale of trust in the food chain was calculated. In Europe, there is significantly less trust in the food chain than in either the US or Canada ($p < 0.01$). The mean score for Europe is 1.42, for the US 1.87 and for Canada 1.49.

For each of the target institutions we computed an index of trust by subtracting the percentage of respondents who say 'doing a bad job' from those saying 'doing a good job'. A positive score indicates a confidence surplus, while a negative score indicates a confidence deficit. Every institution, with the exception of the Canadian government, has a trust surplus,[1] a finding that does not support the idea of a crisis of confidence in the key organizations dealing with agricultural biotechnology. However, there is a striking contrast for industry, which has a confidence surplus of 56 points in the US compared to 31 in Canada and 20 in Europe. This may be an example of what Lane (1986) calls the 'harmony of interests' between industry and the public in the US, a cultural belief that what is

Table 13.3 *Trust in the food chain*

	Confidence surplus/ deficit		
	USA	Canada	Europe
Our government making regulations on biotechnology	32	−12	27
Industry developing new products with biotechnology	56	31	20
Farmers deciding which types of crops to grow	61	57	44
Shops making sure our food is safe	36	24	38

good for industry is also good for the public. Our data show that Europeans, with their history of industrial conflict, do not hold this belief as strongly. This raises the possibility that social values, relatively stable belief systems underlying attitudes to particular issues, may also be part of the explanation of the differences between the publics in the US, Canada and Europe.

Our questions tapped into two values that may have a bearing on people's views of biotechnology. Three questions, for example, 'Economic growth brings better quality of life', formed a scale of progress values; a further three questions, for example, 'Nature can withstand human actions', formed a scale of environmental values. A comparison of the three cases shows that Europeans are significantly more concerned about the environment than people in the US or Canada and more ambivalent about progress.

In our final analysis, we pull these strands together in a multivariate analysis, looking at the extent to which risk and benefit perceptions are related to progress and environmental values, technological optimism, menacing images and trust in the food chain. We use multinomial regression to predict membership of the 'relaxed', 'trade-off' and 'sceptical' groups. The contrasts are between the 'trade-off' group and the other two. The comparison of the 'trade-off' and 'relaxed' groups contrasts *benefit and risk* with *benefit and no risk*, thus showing the correlates of the perception of risk, while holding benefit constant. Similarly, the comparison of the 'trade-off' and 'sceptical' groups contrasts *benefit and risk* with *no benefit and risk*, showing the correlates of the perception of benefit, while holding risk constant. Given that the majority of the trade-off group are supporters of GM foods, we expect that the contrasts between the 'relaxed' and 'trade-off' groups will not be as large as the contrasts between the 'trade-off' and 'sceptical' groups. To illustrate the analysis, we will present the comparison between the 'sceptical' and 'trade-off' groups and then briefly describe the second contrast.

Table 13.5 shows the predictors and the results of two multinomial regression models in terms of the odds ratios and their confidence limits. All these predictors

Table 13.4 *Environmental and economic values*

	Percentage in agreement		
	USA	Canada	Europe
Modern technology has upset the balance of nature	68	70	82
Exploiting nature is unavoidable if humankind is to progress	50	48	45
Nature can withstand human actions	50	39	29
Economic growth brings better quality of life	85	74	68
What is good for business is good for the citizens	26	25	19
Private enterprise is the best way to solve [our country]'s problems	49	34	46

Table 13.5 *Contrasting the 'sceptical' and 'trade-off' groups*

Predictors of 'sceptical' group membership compared to 'trade-off'	Odds ratio	95% confidence limits
Model 1: Countries only		
Europe (reference category US)	2.80	± 0.59
Canada (reference category US)	2.69	± 0.73
Model 2: All predictors		
Europe (reference category US)	1.90	± 0.17
Canada (reference category US)	1.93	± 0.44
Male (reference category female)	0.69	± 0.09
Technological optimism (scale –7 to +7, positive score optimistic)	1.21	± 0.08
Menacing images (scale 0 to 3, high score more images)	0.83	± 0.06
Trust in the food chain (scale 0 to 3, high score more trust)	0.79	± 0.05
Green values (scale 0 to 3, high score equals green)	1.49	± 0.11
Materialist values (scale 0 to 3, high score more materialist)	0.87	± 0.07

are significant, $p < 0.01$. Age and educational level are included in the analysis but are not significant when the other predictors are included, so are not shown in the table.

First of all we fitted a model including only the country variables. The odds of being in the sceptical group compared to the trade-off group are far higher in Europe and Canada than in the US; on average more than two times greater for people in Europe compared to people in the US.

Table 13.5 shows that, compared to the US (the reference category) and controlling for the effects of all the other predictors, Canadians and Europeans are still more likely to be 'sceptical' rather than hold a 'trade-off' position. Introducing the various predictors makes a contribution to the explanation of the differences between Canada, Europe and the US, but clearly, as the odds ratios are still well above 1.0, and indeed around 1.9, there is much more to be explained.

In comparison to the 'trade-off' group, the sceptics are less optimistic about technology, entertain more menacing images, have less trust in the food chain, are greener, are less materialist and are less likely to be male. Given that the comparison between the sceptical and the trade-off groups contrasts the perception of benefits (both groups perceive risk), this analysis suggests that the absence of perceived benefits of GM foods is associated with a spectrum of views about technology, nature, economics and regulation.

A similar analysis contrasted the 'relaxed' and 'trade-off' groups. As expected, the model is less successful in identifying the differences between the two groups. In fact, what distinguishes the relaxed group (benefits and no risks) from the trade-off groups (benefits and risks) is more confidence in the food chain. In other words, confidence in the food chain is associated with lower risk perception.

Our research shows that, over time, Europeans are becoming less sceptical, perhaps as a consequence of the moratorium, while in the US there are signs of increasing ambivalence, as in Canada, to a lesser extent. Yet people in Europe are still twice as likely – and in Canada one and a half times as likely – as people in the US to think that GM foods have no benefits and constitute a risk for society.

Conclusions

So, what divides European, Canadian and US public opinion on GM food? The survey data point to differences in trust in the food chain, in environmental and progress values, the extent of negative stereotypical images of genetic modification and a general optimism about new technology. All these factors appear to be implicated in the perception of the extent of benefits of GM food. For risk perception the principal issue appears to be trust in the food chain. The fact that the perception of benefits, or for many Europeans the absence of benefits, is multiply determined shows why the de facto moratorium on GM products was such a convenient political response. It would, as the European Commission's representative said, have been 'difficult to explain to consumers and the public'.

What of North America? Survey data seldom tell the whole story and this is particularly true in relation to the US. Policy-makers' impressions of public opinion on both sides of the Atlantic are likely to be influenced by media coverage that is the product of subtly different news environments. In the US, the media paint a positive picture, relying largely on sources from within the pro-biotechnology scientific and industrial communities (Priest, 2001). And this is evident even in times of controversy. For example, in 2001, a GM agricultural product which had gained approval for animal feed was found in human food products. The item in question was StarLink corn, and the concern was that the corn might cause allergic reactions in people, which indeed some people reported. According to *The New York Times* on 14 June 2001,

'Government scientists said yesterday that they found no evidence that any people had had allergic reactions to the genetically modified StarLink corn.

'The findings could dispel public concern that the corn, which spread through the nation's food supply even though it was never approved for human consumption, represents a threat to public health.

'The results, however, announced by the Centers for Disease Control and Prevention, could also clear the way for the Environmental Protection Agency to permit small amounts of the corn to be present in food without leading to recalls, something that would greatly relieve the farmers, grain processors and food companies.'

This report is typical of much of the journalism around controversial science issues. First, there is the reiteration of a concern (StarLink and allergies), followed by a legitimation of the science by agencies with expertise in these areas (Centers for Disease Control and the Environmental Protection Agency). This legitimation leads the reporter to argue that this may offer an opening to the corn becoming part of the human food supply.

Yet from the 1980s, public dissent was present; in fact, opinion in North America has been quite polarized and continues to grow gradually more so. But this opposition has received relatively little public attention. By contrast, the European press coverage was more diverse, consistent with a professional tradition less wedded to the American 'objectivity' ethic and more inclined to take campaigning positions. Thus, some newspapers turned GM into a political issue and gave the impression that everyone in the EU was up in arms over GM foods.

In fact, as the data in this chapter show, opinion on both sides of the Atlantic was diverse, although somewhat differently distributed. It is difficult to say whether anti-GM forces in Europe were that much more highly motivated or whether they simply received more coverage, a factor that in itself can (in turn) help fuel a nascent social movement.

But it is important to remember that policy, arguably never directly driven by public opinion, may be as much influenced by news framing of the issues as by what ordinary people actually think. And that coverage certainly left the impression that popular dissent was a much more powerful factor in Europe than in North America, inviting North American policy makers to discount dissenting voices as belonging to a 'fringe' minority – and setting those policy makers up for a shock when Europeans' objections began to surface. Yet rather quietly, in 2004 the moratorium was 'unofficially' lifted and in 2005 a Monsanto-developed GM maize (Mon863) gained approval. Thus far, this policy volte-face does not appear to have reignited the controversies of the late 1990s. How could this be? Speculatively, we suggest that the wider climate of public debate has changed in Europe. By public debate we include media coverage, pressure group activities, regulatory debates and the perceptions of the public themselves. A key indicator of the public domain is the mass media, in which two related changes are apparent from around 2000 to 2001. First, the intensity or frequency of coverage of the GM issue saw a secular decline. Second, the campaigning and critical front-page narratives of the 1990s have given way to rather terse factual accounts. Evidently, for the media the GM issue no longer has 'news value'. But why did editorial judgement decide that GM no longer sells newspapers? The development of new European regulations may be a factor. This started with the regulation 2001/18/EC, which introduced more stringent regulatory criteria for GM agriculture concerning risk assessment, labelling, longer-term monitoring of impacts and public consultation, and set the basis for the more recent regulations on labelling and traceability. With these regulations, and in the context of EFSA's continued assertions that GM food posed no risk to human health, at least some consumer groups may have felt that the battle had been won. Consumer choice had been one of their major concerns.

A more prosaic explanation is that the introduction of the moratorium took the steam out of the debate and effectively closed the political battleground. National politicians, particularly environment ministers, were able to say that their territory was a GM-free zone and, if necessary, to blame Brussels for all the problems. Over the four years of the moratorium, passions cooled and, perhaps, for the public 'out of sight is out of mind'.

However, the question remains: is this a temporary lull in the GM food debate that may be re-ignited as the European Member States consider measures for the co-existence of genetically modified crops with conventional organic farming; or have agri-food biotechnologies in Europe moved beyond the political phase to become a 'normalized' technology?

Acknowledgements

This research was supported by grants from the EC Directorate General for Research for the project 'Life Sciences in European Society' (QLG7-CT-1999-00286), the US National Science Foundation, Ethics and Values Studies (0115380) and Genome Canada for the project 'Genomics, ethics, environmental, ethical, legal and social studies project within Genome Prairie'.

Note

1   The drop in confidence in government among Canadians may be partially explained by the fact that the survey was carried out immediately after the announcement by the Raelians, a Canadian-based organization, that they had cloned a baby. This was followed by considerable media discussions about the Government's failure to pass a bill regulating reproductive technologies and banning cloning.

References

Bauer, M. W., Kohring, M., Allansdottir, A. and Gutteling, J. (2001) 'The dramatisation of biotechnology in the elite media', in Gaskell, G. and Bauer, M. W. (eds) *Biotechnology 1996–2000: The Years of Controversy*, Science Museum, London

Cantley, M. (1992) 'Public perception, public policy, the public interest and public information: The evolution of policy for biotechnology in the European Community, 1982–92', in Durant, J. (ed) *Biotechnology in Public*, Science Museum, London

Einsiedel, E. and Medlock, J. (2001) 'Canada on the gene trail', in Gaskell, G. and Bauer, M. W. (eds) *Biotechnology 1996–2000: The Years of Controversy*, Science Museum, London

Flynn, J., Slovic, P. and Kunreuther, H. (eds) (2001) *Risk, Media and Stigma*, Earthscan, London

Gaskell, G. and Bauer, M. W. (eds) (2001) *Biotechnology 1996–2000: The Years of Controversy*, Science Museum, London

Gaskell, G., Torgerson, H., Einsiedel, E., Jelsøe, E. and Frederickson (1997) 'Europe ambivalent on biotechnology', *Nature*, 387, pp845–847

Inglehart, R. (1997) *Modernization and Postmodernization: Cultural, Economic and Political Change in 43 Societies*, Princeton University Press, Princeton, NJ

Lane, R. (1986) 'Market justice, political justice', *American Political Science Review*, 80, no 2, pp383–402

Priest, S. (2001) *A grain of truth: the media, the public and biotechnology*, Rowman & Littlefield Publishers, Lanham Maryland, USA

Rozin, P. and Nemeroff, C. (1990) 'The laws of sympathetic magic', in Stigler, J., Sweder, R. and Herdt, G. (eds) *Cultural Psychology: Essays on Comparative Human Development*, Cambridge University Press, Cambridge, pp205–232

Strumpel, B (1990) 'Macroeconomic processes and societal psychology', in Himmelweit, H. and Gaskell, G. (eds) *Societal Psychology*, Sage, Newbury Park

Ten Eyck, T. A. and Williment, M. (2003) 'The national media and things genetic: Coverage in the *New York Times* (1971–2001) and the *Washington Post* (1977–2001)', *Science Communication*, 25, pp129–154

14

The Japanese Experience

*Motohiko Nagata, Aiko Hibino, Toshio Sugiman and
Wolfgang Wagner*

This chapter examines Japanese perceptions of biotechnology, specifically using genetic engineering, during recent years. In Japan, modern biotechnology has been growing rapidly, and is often said to bring various benefits. The application of biotechnology is expected to be a great boon in such areas as medicine, agriculture and industry. With this in mind, the Japanese government has drawn up plans to promote domestic biotechnological research and development (Biotechnology Strategy Council, 2002; Kayukawa, 2001). At the same time, public debate on biotechnology seems to be mute in Japan except for two issues: genetically modified organisms (GMOs) and cloning humans. With regard to GMOs, a large-scale citizen movement is claiming that GMOs might bring serious risks to human health and the environment. There is also a strong rejection of cloning humans among ordinary citizens in Japan. Other applications, such as medical ones, raise few concerns among the public.

Around the world, biotechnology engenders a remarkable discourse about risks and benefits, moral and regulatory issues; Japan is no different. In Japan, as elsewhere, many parties and stakeholders participate in and shape this debate. This chapter focuses on three arenas of public discourse in Japan: discourse in the mass media, discourse in governmental policy making and discourse in the everyday conversations of ordinary people.

The development of mass mediated discourse

To understand the development of the mass media discourse we analysed articles from a Japanese daily newspaper. We selected the *Asahi* newspaper and searched for articles on biotechnology between 1985 and 2000; a total of 850 randomly sampled articles were then content-analysed. *Asahi* is a major nationwide newspaper with a daily circulation of 12 million (World Press Trends, 2002), and is considered to be the opinion-leading press in Japan. Two-thirds of Japanese regularly read a newspaper. An electronic database is available for all articles published after 1985.

The intensity of media coverage (i.e. the number of articles referring to biotechnology) increased sharply in the year 1997 and thereafter, as shown in Figure 14.1. The same tendency was found in other Japanese nationwide newspapers. Public attention towards biotechnology has risen significantly since 1997, mainly due to issues related to genetically modified (GM) soya and the unveiling of the cloned sheep Dolly. Here Japan follows, or even exceeds, the global trend.

While some European governments were promoting biotechnology and instigating public debates during the 1980s, and consumer groups and environmental organizations were campaigning on biotechnological issues, the Japanese government did not take an active role until the late 1990s (Kuniya and Oyama, 1999). There was little or no reaction from Japanese consumer and environmental groups at this time. In 1996 and 1997, genetically modified foods and cloned animals were reported somewhat sensationally by the Japanese mass media, which may have triggered certain public concerns in Japan.

Table 14.1 summarizes the results of content analysis of themes, predominant actors, general framing and frequency of risk/benefit discourse in biotechnology-related articles. Among these coding items, frame refers to the patterns of interpretation, presentation, selection and emphasis (or exclusion), which are all aspects of developing a general storyline. As shown in Table 14.1, media coverage of biotechnology has been consistently positive. Specifically, both the frame of progress and the benefit-only stories were consistently dominant. On average, half

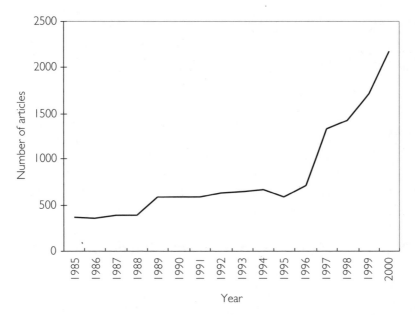

Figure 14.1 *Number of newspaper articles on modern biotechnology in Japan, 1985–2000*

Table 14.1 *Media profile of Japan and Europe*

	Phase I (1986–89)	Phase 2 (1992–96)	EU (1992–96)	Phase 3 (1997–2000)	EU (1997–99)
Frame (%)	–	–		–	
Progress	55	53	50	47	42
Economic prospects	24	12	17	11	14
Ethical	7	10	12	11	10
Pandora's box	3	6	4	5	6
Runaway	0	1	2	1	3
Nature/nurture	0	2	4	1	8
Public accountability	4	13	10	16	16
Globalization	8	5	2	3	2
Psych. attachment	–	–	–	5	–
*Theme (%)**	–	–		–	
Biomedical (red)	19	29	28	20	23
Agrifood (green)	7	13	15	14	20
Generic research	24	10	14	8	9
Economics	14	5	14	5	8
Moral issues	2	3	2	2	2
Public opinion/ policy	10	12	4	11	7
Regulation	10	12	6	15	6
Genetic identity	2	8	15	6	12
Cloning	1	1	0	15	9
Other	11	7	6	4	4
Actor (%)	–	–		–	
Independent science	45	59	45	47	39
Interest groups, NGOs	1	4	4	8	5
Politics	16	15	16	18	15
Moral authorities	0	1	2	1	2
Media/public opinion	0	2	6	3	7
Business	21	10	21	8	20
International	2	1	1	1	2
EU	0	0	2	1	4
Other	15	10	4	14	6

Table 14.1 *continued*

Benefit/risk (%)	–	–	23	–	25
Both	7	12	23	11	25
Risk only	4	7	9	10	15
Benefit only	61	45	44	53	39
Neither	28	36	25	26	21
N	150	200	3871	500	5580

Note: * = Multiple coding

of all articles framed biotechnology in terms of progress and about the same percentage discussed biotechnology exclusively in terms of its benefits, while a mere 8 per cent of the articles referred to potential risks.

We can distinguish three periods of changing media coverage of biotechnology that are defined by certain characteristics of reporting. The characteristics of each phase are described below.

Biotechnology as a promising field of research and development (1985–1989)

There were few articles mentioning biotechnology in this phase, but those few describe it as a promising field. More than three-quarters of articles report biotechnology within a frame of progress or economic prospects. A total of 61 per cent of articles portray the new technology as bringing benefit only, while only 11 per cent refer to potential risks. Their dominant themes are generic research and medical applications. The dominant actors are scientists and the business sector.

Diversification of discourse (1990–1996)

The intensity in this phase increases slightly and is paralleled by a diversification of themes. Medical themes dominate and the issues of GMO and genetic identity appear more frequently. Frames of concern, particularly public accountability and ethics, increase, while the frame of economic prospects is reduced by half, although more than half of the articles frame biotechnology as progress. Nevertheless, the number of articles that mention the risks of biotechnology increases even though benefits still dominate.

Intensification and diversification of concern (1997–2000)

This period brings an almost exponential increase in reporting intensity and a much more diverse attitude towards biotechnology than the previous phases. The number of articles mentioning risks and concerns, especially about public accountability, increases while the progress frame declines slightly. As for actors, the role of non-governmental organizations (NGOs) and the media increases.

In this phase, we found a particular aspect of Japanese media coverage of biotechnology. Many articles reflected psychological endearment towards cloned animals. As shown in Table 14.1, 5 per cent of articles expressed this comparatively peculiar attitude to cloned animals. Psychological endearment means an emotional attachment similar to the one a mother might feel towards her baby or infant, exceeding the kindness or respect for animals that one would normally expect. A typical example is the following citation:

> *Mr Nakaoki, Governor of Ishikawa Prefecture, named the cloned calf Chie, a name derived both from the name of the location of the laboratory and from its implication of 'prospering in the future'. On that day, the calf walked timidly when she was taken out of the pen. A keeper said, 'she is so amiable, and seems to fancy herself to be a human, because she was detached from her mother soon after her birth'. Governor Nakaoki, who named her, said, 'because she is the only cloned calf now surviving in Japan, we should take all possible measures to raise her successfully. I would like you to love Chie-chan'.*

Here Chie is a popular girl's name. 'Chan' in 'Chie-chan' is a diminutive suffix for a name that typically indicates relational closeness to a child or an infant.

This particular frame of psychological endearment in Japan suggests that the representation of biotechnology might be different in Japan. Underlying this might be the Japanese traditional animistic perception of animals which emphasizes equality of all living beings, including any animals and human beings (Mito, 1995), as well as the recent pet boom where an increasing number of Japanese people regard a pet animal as a member of their family. They feel a strong attachment not only to natural animals but also to pet robots like 'Aibo'.

Finally, we examine the association between themes, frames and risk or benefit discourses and their change during the last two phases. Figure 14.2 shows the results of a correspondence analysis for the last two phases between the framing of three biotechnology applications in agrifood (green), biomedical (red) and cloning. As the figure shows, each application is closely associated with particular frames: red applications are often framed in progress discourse throughout the two phases; green applications are more strongly related to concern frames such as public accountability and globalization in the third phase than in the second phase; cloning is framed more frequently as a discourse of nature/nurture and of psychological attachment in the third phase than in the second phase. Note, however, that these two latter frames are rather infrequent overall.[1]

Figure 14.3 shows the results of the correspondence analysis for the last two phases between green and red applications cross-tabulated by risk and benefit themes. The figure clearly indicates that red applications were strongly and uniquely associated with the benefit-only discourses. In other words, the Japanese media coverage perceives biomedical applications as promising throughout the last two phases. By contrast, green applications of biotechnology to food and

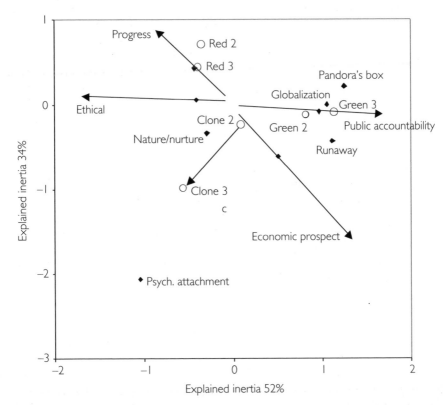

Figure 14.2 *Graph of the correspondence analysis of cross-tabulation of red, green and cloning applications in Phases 2 and 3 by frames*

Note: Applications are shown by circles, frames by diamonds. For increased intelligibility of the graph the vectors (see Note 1) of only the most important frames are shown as arrows and labelled at the end of the arrows. All other frames are less frequent and indicated only as diamonds. The bold arrow indicates a relevant change of framing between Phases 2 and 3 for cloning

agriculture were perceived ambivalently in terms of risks and benefits in the second phase, while in the third phase they become much more closely associated with risk-only discourses than earlier. In other words, the Japanese press came to portray agrifood applications as posing risks and threats, similar to the media coverage in European countries (see Bauer et al, 2001). It is interesting to note that reports about cloning applications, while still benefit related in the second phase, were significantly covered in other terms than risk or benefit in the third.

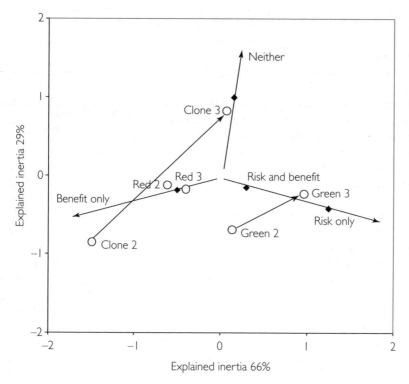

Note: Applications are shown by circles, frames by diamonds. Vectors (see Note 1) are shown for themes. The bold arrows indicate a relevant change of themes between Phases 2 and 3 for cloning and green applications. The framing of the red applications does not change significantly from Phase 2 to Phase 3

Figure 14.3 *Graph of the correspondence analysis of cross-tabulation of red, green and cloning applications in Phases 2 and 3 by themes*

The law on cloning 2001: The regulatory discourse

The Japanese government adopted a policy of promoting the development of biotechnology relatively late. In August 1999, the Millennium Project was announced, a joint effort involving government, industry and Japan's universities. It aimed at bringing about major technological innovation and is focused on analysis of the human genome, the rice genome and on regenerative medicine. It was claimed that there was very strong support for this project from the industry sector.

The policy-making process is characterized by the following major features: first, these policies aim at developing the biotechnology industry in Japan. Second, policy decisions are made in strongly hierarchical systems and the communication between ministries and government organizations involved is limited. Third, much of the discussion focuses on problems that might occur, and there is little discussion over the principles of past and future policies.

We will focus on 'The Law Concerning Regulation Relating to Human Cloning Techniques and Similar Techniques', and the process that led to the establishment of this law will be analysed. For this we examined formal documents related to its establishment.

Before cloning technology began to attract mass media attention in 1997, there was little discussion of cloning technology and related areas. For example, for the issue of biotechnology applied to reproductive medicine, concerning the manipulation of the 'beginning of life', public attention was low. This is in striking contrast to the debate about the 'end of life' and the definition of 'brain death' (Nudeshima, 2001). There were no legal regulations related to the handling of human embryos, except that the Japan Society of Obstetrics formulated some guidelines of its own. With regard to recombinant deoxyribonucleic acid (DNA) experiments and cloning of livestock, debate was limited to expert circles and rarely entered the public sphere.

The situation changed after February 1997, when Dolly, a cloned sheep, was presented to the world press. The cloning of body cells and bringing the sheep to birth meant that the subject of cloning humans took on a realistic aspect and debate broke out. In September 1997, a new, permanent government Bioethics Committee was given the task of deliberating the related ethical issues. Under this committee, Cloning Subcommittees were set up. The prevailing view was that only human cloning had to be prohibited by law and the regulation of other types of cloning could be regulated by official guidance. Concerning other types of cloning, key guidelines were generated that were to be used for regulating cloning, as was to be specified in the Cloning Regulation Law.

The second factor that stimulated active debates on the cloning issue occurred in November 1998 when a group from Wisconsin University succeeded in producing embryonic stem (ES) cells. Based on this, the possibilities for developing regenerative medical technology using human embryos rose dramatically. A new Human Embryo Subcommittee was established to study guidelines for regulating ES cell experimentation. ES cell research in Japan was to be pursued under official guidance and the process of formulating guidelines was carried out.

In April 2000, the Science and Technology Agency, as it existed at that time, received a report from the Cloning Subcommittee and the Human Embryo Subcommittee and submitted this report, entitled 'Recommendation for a law concerning regulation of the use of cloning technology as related to cloning of human beings', to the Diet. This proposal for legislation did not pass in the Diet and was resubmitted to an Extraordinary Session of the 150th Diet Session in October, when it was passed by the Upper House of the Diet on 30 November 2000. The law finally came into effect in June 2001.

This law regulating the cloning of human beings had two special features (Ogoshi, 2001; Kayukawa, 2003; Nudeshima, 2001). First, if the clone was not allowed to develop to birth, the law did not limit the cloning and manipulation of embryos. Second, the law did not regulate the use of fertilized eggs or human embryos. Concerning the positioning of the regulation of experimentation using human embryos, the law stated that guidelines were to be established. The law was criticized on the grounds that by nominally prohibiting human cloning, it may actually permit and advance the wide use of cloning technology, especially that connected with the use of human embryos.

Within the debate surrounding the Cloning Regulation Law, what types of discourses emerged? What were the basic issues and arguments publicly expressed and what were the hidden issues?

We analysed the deliberative proceedings that took place in the three bodies that had the most direct role in the generation of the content of the law:

1   The Cloning Subcommittee (12 sessions from February 1998 to November 1999). The composition of this 16-member subcommittee consisted of four basic science researchers, four doctors, one member from the livestock industry, three law scholars, two ethics experts and two scientific research policy specialists. It should be noted that all members were males.

2   The Human Embryos Subcommittee (14 sessions from February 1999 to March 2000). This 12-member subcommittee consisted of three basic science researchers, three doctors, three law scholars, two science theory and history researchers, and one member connected with mass media. Eight of the members, including this subcommittee chairperson, were also members of the Cloning Subcommittee. There were two female Subcommittee members.

3   The 150th Diet Session Science and Technology Council (this group met five times in November 1999).

We also interviewed some of the persons who had participated in the deliberations directly or indirectly as well as some specialists of cloning technology to determine the unspoken assumptions that underlay this law. Many of these assumptions remained unspoken, but clearly influenced the proceedings. The persons who were interviewed were as follows: a representative of a citizen's group that held critical views concerning biotechnology; critical life ethics scholars who were against the manipulation of living creatures; a Government ES Cell Study Experts Committee member who was also playing the role of life ethics scholar; a journalist who was especially negative on cloning technology; a journalist who was against the Government-sponsored biotechnology promotion programme; a member of both of the two subcommittees who is a science and technology policy scholar; a member of the Human Embryo Subcommittee who is also a journalist; a doctor who specializes in mouse ES cell research; and a university researcher specializing in ES cell research.

The written records and the interviews allow us to characterize key positions underlying the deliberations of the Cloning Law. The basic underlying positions referred to here are not necessarily the discourses that emerged most frequently during the course of the deliberations. Rather, these key arguments, both positive and negative, underlie the perceived logic. They can be roughly divided into four major categories: discourses on cloning technology, on the beginning of life, on regulation and on personal responsibilities and rights. In all four of these categories, there were arguments brought to bear in encouragement of and in opposition to biotechnology that resulted in the Cloning Regulation Law, according to which cloning in research is legal as long as it is not carried out on humans.

The basic features of the discourse in favour of cloning technology were general appeals to scientific, medical and economic development in order for 'people to enjoy healthy lives'. Case-by-case regulation was suggested as a means to soften a too-strict approach to the cloning of human beings. The favourite example of genetic diseases used in the human cloning promotion discourse concerned mitochondrial abnormalities: 'Patients with abnormal mitochondria cannot have children and they are, in fact, suffering because of this. There is a need to help these patients as quickly as possible'. Likewise, there was the 'help the patient' argument, such as: 'If the number of persons that can be helped from such research is great, then the use of fertilized eggs should be permitted'. In addition there were appeals in favour of medical uses of reproductive and genetic treatment and cloning of human cells that were hard to reject.

In opposition to these kinds of arguments, discourses rejecting or cautioning against enthusiasm for human cloning invoked arguments about 'natural ethics' (manipulation of life by humans is not permissible), 'human ethics' (it is not permissible to use human beings as a means to an end or to make a product out of them) and beliefs that 'fertilized eggs constitute a form of human life'. This line of general arguments, however, was not part of the final decisions and was not incorporated in the resulting law.

Particularly in the discourses of the committee meetings and of the Diet, individual self-determination and the private ownership of the body were perceived to be truisms that supported the legitimacy of promoting the development of cloning technology. For example, the natural ethics type of argument that 'the manipulation of human embryos cannot be permitted' was flatly rejected by the self-determination argument that would give a patient the right to refuse treatment as well as the right to choose and receive such treatment. Promoters of medical cloning technology, hence, strongly focused on individual human rights issues guaranteeing access to health and rejected arguments bearing on an ethics of nature and life in general.

In addition, the anti-cloning faction made use of the personal decision rights and of the individual's ownership of the body concepts. For example, one argument brought forward was that the rights of patients receiving sterility treatment would not be properly protected if the patient had no say in the scientific and/or medical use or non-use of spare embryos. This would squarely contradict the human right to self-determination and the right of control over one's body. Finally, the contradicting interpretations of human rights issues were resolved in the Diet sessions by emphasizing an informed consent procedure:

> There is need to require reports of all uses of human embryos for research purposes . . . in such cases, the government plans to make full use of the process of the system of 'informed consent'. (Proceedings of the 150th Diet session)

However, although it is true that such concepts as the right to personal decision and 'the individual's body belongs to the individual' have strong persuasiveness in modern society, this does not mean such arguments will prevail in every situation. Values that counter such concepts also exist in Japanese society, where suicide and prostitution, two extreme forms of exercising the right of self-control over one's body, are judged much more liberally than in western countries (Tateiwa, 1997). If one considers the matter in a more profound way, it is evident that cloning technology contains the possibilities of forcing us to consider drastic changes in our perceptions of such concepts as life and self.

Given the present analysis of political discourse, it seems that the scale of the potential deliberation of a Cloning Regulation Law was limited in two ways. First, discussion of such basic principles as how to perceive the meaning of the embryo was stifled. Part of the meaning behind this is that there was a pre-existing underlying assumption to the effect that 'only cloning of humans should be prohibited and all other forms of cloning technology should be promoted', and the deliberation process proceeded in a manner that followed this concept. Second, no concepts were introduced that could put the main promotion concept into a larger framework of fundamental values that would allow doubt to be cast on the 'everything but human cloning' approach.

The discourse of everyday conversations

A series of focus group discussions were carried out to determine the level of acceptance that biotechnology has among the general public as well as the representations shared about this issue. The public's views ultimately influence policy decisions and also affect the biotechnology industry, as was shown by the industry's withdrawal from some European markets.

Four focus groups were carried out following the outline indicated in Table 14.2. The discussion topics were similar to those used by the European team (Wagner et al, 2001). In summary, the focus group participants were asked to give their opinions about such topics as the image of biotechnology, food products made by using recombinant DNA technology, and cloning. Participants also discussed such questions as regulation and other issues of social importance. Focus groups lasted about two hours, and each participant received 2,000 yen (about 15 euros) as compensation.

Japanese people express a range of fears that biotechnology evokes, which all have to do with an image of nature being disturbed and provoked by humankind's doings. Nature and its laws were perceived as being 'violated', 'slashed to pieces' and 'mocked'. Human egotism was seen as the driving force behind this meddling with nature, which 'will take revenge in due time'. Besides, focus-group participants expressed fears that creating GMOs and clones will ultimately disturb the natural order and dissolve the boundaries delimiting animals, plants, humans and oneself as a person. This was a recurrent worry with regard to almost every specific topic such as genetic testing, xenotransplantation and GMOs, where cloning was discussed most fervently.

Table 14.2 *Outline of the four focus groups*

	Date	Location	Composition	Ages	Occupations
Group 1	Sept. 2001	Nara	2 males, 2 females	32–55	Public servant, housewife
Group 2	Oct. 2001	Kyoto	4 females	47–53	Housewife
Group 3	Oct. 2001	Osaka	1 male, 3 females	42–45	Teacher, housewife
Group 4	Nov. 2001	Kyoto	1 male, 3 females	22–33	Public servant, office worker

Nature is seen as something more powerful than humankind, dwarfing man's attempts at changing natural givens, as can be seen in ecological problems. This should be warning enough not to attempt further meddling, because 'these things are not in the hands of man'. Ambivalence only emerged when humankind's progress in putting nature to good use was mentioned, because 'if humans make improvements on nature, isn't this a part of nature?'

GM food was seen as a long-term hazard because 'there is no way of predicting what will happen'. Nevertheless, the mere anticipation of danger was counterbalanced by acknowledging that 'in a modern society, if one starts worrying about risk, there's no end to it' and by attributing to GM food some usefulness in the case of serious food shortages. Some participants in the focus groups also perceived a problem with the speed with which this technology develops, and expressed doubts about ever being able to slow the development. This mix of doubts, perceived hazards and potential utility brought up the issue of societal control of risks, which, however, was not matched by a corresponding trust in such controlling institutions.

Given the prominence that cloning of animals has in Japan, it comes as no surprise that this was a hotly debated issue in focus groups that also expanded on the question of cloning humans. In this context, participants identified a series of problems that have to do with human rights of clones: 'If a human clone were produced in order to obtain a human heart, what about the human rights of the clone in such a case?'; and the question of identity and difference: 'In the case of cloning technology, wouldn't there be a danger of all human beings coming to resemble each other?' Both these aspects refer to the question of whether a clone is a 'perfect copy' or whether it can be regarded as an original, that is, an 'irreplaceable creation'. Hence, the focus of interest in some focus groups revolved around the definition of a human being, because the existence of cloned humans challenges the conventional definition. Besides this more philosophical interest in the question of cloning, focus group participants flatly rejected any usefulness of human cloning.

A particularly interesting line of argument emerged in the context of genetic testing. Because genetic testing paves the way to potentially control one's future illnesses and conditions, it was seen as utterly violating the 'real meaning of human life' that lies in 'the act of accepting one's fate', and hence going against human nature. Accepting one's fate and therefore human nature was a strong reason for rejecting this medical application of biotechnology for some participants. It must be mentioned here that the meaning of the Japanese terms 'fate' and 'laws of nature' coincides to a high degree and hence carries this line of argument over to the initial concerns about violating nature's laws in general, especially the fear of jeopardizing the natural order.

The usefulness of genetic testing would lie in knowing one's fate and thus being able to control it. Some participants also want to know about themselves in order to be able to enjoy a better life. At the end, the contradicting opinions came to be framed in the individual's right to choose and to decide for themselves: 'Whether one accepts the use of gene diagnosis or not is a decision for the specific individual'. Although even a self-chosen fate control was seen as potentially implying discrimination against those involved, the idea of individual choice allowed the discussion to find a compromise.

At this point, the topics of xenotransplantation, cloning animals and the use of recombinant DNA technology converged on the ethics of altering animals in the service of humans. Leaving nature – and natural animals, for that matter – as it is and accepting one's human fate versus controlling and changing nature, perceiving humans as equivalent to animals versus declaring human life as more important than animal life, divided the groups to a considerable degree. All this played an important role in the highly varied discussions, which ultimately could not be resolved.

Cross-cultural similarities

In the Japanese media coverage of biotechnology, the diversity of themes and actors increases with rising intensity of coverage, although the general outlook on biotechnology remains more positive than in Europe. As in Europe, medical applications are reported as more promising and beneficial, agrifood applications as harbouring more risks and threats; animal cloning receives a peculiarly different treatment in Japan: psychological endearment.

In short, the Japanese media coverage of biotechnology has increased in diversity of themes and actors mentioned, while overall coverage of biotechnology was persistently positive during the years. The discourse on risk/benefit of biotechnology in Japan and Europe differs. In Europe, benefit-only stories decline in the latter part of the 1990s, while in Japan they continue to grow. This suggests that media discourse on biotechnology was more positive in Japan than in European countries during the 1990s. A peculiarity of Japan is the reportage of cloned animals. While the initial coverage of cloning in Europe and Canada oscillated between the frames of progress and doom (Einsiedel et al, 2002), Japanese coverage showed an element of psychological endearment towards the cloned animals. This might reflect a difference in the underlying cultural segmentation of the world and the relationship between humans and animals; that is, a difference between the Japanese animistic world-view, accentuating unity of, and equality between, humans and animals, and the Christian world-view, which emphasizes a natural hierarchy with humans at the top.

The Japanese mass media, at least the opinion-leading press analysed here, show a higher intensity of reporting since 1997 – Dolly's appearance – than the European average, both in relative terms compared to the earlier years and in absolute terms. This pattern resembles the pattern in a few European countries such as Austria in 1996 and Greece 1998–1999, where, due to local developments, a sudden increase in media intensity signalled a corresponding increase in public interests and sentiments after a 'pre-history' of virtual disinterest in biotechnology. In these European countries, the explosive interest was accompanied by a significant increase of beliefs indicative of a popular representation of what biotechnology might be. This representational knowledge plays the same role as technical or scientifically valid knowledge in replacing ignorance (for example, 'Don't know' responses on knowledge items in surveys), which is usually high in countries with an uninterested public. The development of such representational knowledge can be seen as an emergency response in a situation of conflict and debate where people are required to take positions (Wagner et al, 2002). One may speculate that such a phase of collective symbolic coping might have taken place in Japan during the years 1997–1998 as indicated by the media data (Hibino and Nagata, 2006).

The policy and regulation discourse about cloning in Japan appears to differ from the cases of Europe. Many European countries enacted comprehensive laws specifying in detail the handling of embryos. In the case of these countries and against a background of a general feeling that the research of human embryos must be comprehensively regulated, there exists a conviction that human life must be respected from the embryonic stage onward (Grabner et al, 2001). Some authors argue that, compared to Japan, the European deliberations concerning fertility cures were more mature (e.g. Nudeshima, 2001).

In the European case, the personal right to choose is conditional. Many institutions utter a 'demand for public order that includes protecting the individual from the defects in his own personality'. In other words, concerning decisions that pertain to a human life and the body, the decisions of society supersede personal decisions. Biotechnology is a technology that manipulates life and it is certain that the time is nearing when it will be necessary to re-examine basic assumptions about such things as the concept of life and the human self. Therefore, it seems important that the public debate examines issues such as personal choice by using a wide frame of reference to have an influence on the policy-making process.

The everyday discourse about biotechnology as reflected in the Japanese focus groups exhibits a strong rejection of 'the rampant alteration of animals and nature' in the service of human egoism. This position was confronted by some supporters who embraced the potential usefulness of some biotechnological applications for which certain standards would need to be developed. As in Europe, Japanese focus group participants uttered deep-seated anxieties about violating the laws of nature, expressed doubt about the unconditional need for certain applications, and considered the right to personal choice in medical applications, particularly genetic testing, as crucial.

It seems that the Japanese differ from Europeans with regard to their emphasis on the role of one's personal fate in determining each person's individual meaning of life. Despite the persuasive power of genetic medical diagnosis and treatment for some, it did not dominate the discussions. Instead, importance was given to 'being natural, that is, naturalness', and medical treatment can sometimes be excessive and go too far, hence destroying human life's innate naturalness. Europeans, in contrast, perceive medical applications as almost unconditionally positive and frame them in terms of personal utility. Underlying this is the widely held view that human beings have a right to lead a 'normal life', and to make this possible, medical treatment is necessary. The topic of 'living one's fate' is far from prominent in the majority of European focus groups.

In conclusion, the present data create the impression that, despite some divergent topics, the general public in Japan and in Europe share rather similar views and related fears with regard to biotechnology. Given the different historical and cultural background of these two regions, this is a noticeable fact and a strong indicator of the homogenizing forces of global science and economy, irrespective of whether personally we like it or not.

Note

1   Figures 14.2 and 14.3 depict the two-dimensional solution of a correspondence analysis of a cross-tabulation. The way to interpret them is as follows: Suppose we want to know whether the frame 'public accountability' was relatively more frequent for green biotechnology applications in phase 3 than in phase 2. We draw a vector from the centre point (0/0) through the point 'public accountability'. Then we draw the orthogonal projections of the points 'green 2' and 'green 3' onto this vector. We can see that the projection of 'green 3' is farther out on the vector than the projection of 'green 2'. This is interpreted as meaning that green applications were mentioned relatively more often in the context of public accountability in the third phase than in the second phase. We proceed likewise for all other points. Note that it is not legitimate to interprete the Euclidian proximity of frame and application/phase points.

References

Bauer, M., Kohring, M., Allansdottir, A. and Gutteling, J. (2001) 'The dramatization of biotechnology in elite mass media', in Gaskell, G. and Bauer, M. (eds) *Biotechnology 1996–2000: The Years of Controversy*, Science Museum, London

Biotechnology Strategy Council (2002) 'Biotechnology Strategy Guidelines'

Einsiedel, E., Allansdottir, A., Bauer, M., Berthomier, A., Chatjouli, A., De Cheveigné, S., Downey, R., Gutteling, J., Kohring, M., Leonarz, M., Manzoli, F., Olofsson, A., Prztestalski, A., Rusanen, T., Seifert, F., Stathopoulou, A. and Wagner, W. (2002) 'Brave new sheep: A clone named Dolly', in Bauer, M. and Gaskell, G. (eds) *Biotechnology: The Making of a Global Controversy*, Cambridge University Press, Cambridge

Grabner, P., Hampel, J., Lindsey, N., and Torgersen, H. (2001) 'Biopolitical diversity: The challenge of multilevel policy making', in Gaskell, G. and Bauer, M. (eds) *Biotechnology 1996–2000: The Years of Controversy*, Science Museum, London

Hibino, A. and Nagata, M. (2006) 'Biotechnology in the Japanese media: A comparative analysis of newspaper articles on genetic engineering in Japan and Europe', *Asian Journal of Social Psychology* 9, 1, pp12–33

Kayukawa, J. (2001) *Human Biotechnology* (jintai baiotekunorojii), Takarajimasya, Tokyo (in Japanese)

Kayukawa, J. (2003) *Cloned Human* (kuroon ningen), Koubunsya, Tokyo (in Japanese)

Kuniya, M. and Oyama, M. (1999) 'Regulations on life science', in Kuniya, M., Oyama, M., Ito, K. and Kiba, T. (eds) *Legal Regulations on Advanced Science and Technology: Regulations on Life Science*, National Institute of Science and Technology Policy (NISTEP), Science and Technology Agency, Tokyo (in Japanese)

Mito, Y. (1995) 'The changes of the Japanese perception of animals examined by distribution change of Japanese macaque' (nihonzaru no bunpuhensen ni miru nihonjin no doubutsukan no hensen), in Kawai, M. and Hanihara, K. (eds) *Animals and Civilization* (doubutsu to bunmei), Asakurashoten, Tokyo (in Japanese)

Nudeshima, J. (2001) *The Rules of High Medicine* (sentan-iryou no ruru), Kodansya, Tokyo (in Japanese)

Ogoshi, K. (2001) *Is Human Cloning Technology Acceptable?* (hitokuroongijutu wa yurusareruka), Ryokufu Syuppan, Tokyo (in Japanese)

Tateiwa, S. (1997) *On Private Property* (shitekisyoyuuron), Keisou-Shobo, Tokyo (in Japanese)

Wagner, W., Kronberger, N., Gaskell, G., Allandottir, A., Allum, N., de Cheveigné, S., Dahinden, U., Diego, C., Montali, L., Mortensen, A., Pfenning, U., Rusanen, T. and Seger, N. (2001) 'Nature in disorder: The troubled public of biotechnology', in Gaskell, G. and Bauer, M. (eds) *Biotechnology 1996–2000: The Years of Controversy*, Science Museum, London

Wagner, W., Kronberger, N. and Seifert, F. (2002) 'Collective symbolic coping with new technology: Knowledge, images and public discourse', *British Journal of Social Psychology*, 41, pp323–343

World Press Trends (2002) http://www.wan-press.org/

15

Paradoxes of Resistance in Brazil

Martin W. Bauer

Between 1998 and 2004, the European Union saw a de facto moratorium on genetically modified (GM) crops and food. Many European food retailers are committed to either avoiding or labelling products with GM ingredients and thus to accommodating consumer sentiment. This policy and practice is only feasible for as long as Brazil and other crop exporters do not follow the US and Argentina in adopting GM crops. This chapter describes how Brazil followed a cautious practice over GM crops and reaped the benefits.

In 2003, Brazil was the second largest producer of soya, producing 26 per cent of the world's soya. Since the mid-1990s, exports to Europe and Asia have increased dramatically. Between 1998 and 2005, Brazilian producers were under a *judicial moratorium* for the planting and processing of GM crops. In this period, the tussles between courts, government and parliament were initiated and shadowed by civil society. The Consumer Protection Institute (IDEC) and Greenpeace were supported in the fight against GM crops by rural social movements, regional personalities and, if not in ideology then in deeds, by industrial farmers from the main producing regions of the North. Political parties had no consistent policy on '*transgênicos*'.

Rio Grande do Sul, the most southerly Brazilian region, was the initial arena for the public controversy over this modern biotechnology between 1998 and 2003. Declaring itself a 'zona livre dos transgênicos', paradoxically it became the main GM-producing region and incurred heavy export losses, whereas northern and central regions massively expanded traditional soya production, and their exports multiplied sixfold from 1996 to 2004.

The slow arrival of GM crops in Brazil demonstrates some paradoxical consequences of resistance (Bauer, 1995): first, an official GM-free policy created the contrary of what was intended: a GM crop region. Second, regions without anti-GM policy remained de facto GM-free and profited from international markets. Third, farmers who adopted GM technology lost out, while resistance to the 'New Green Revolution' paid off. I will trace the politics, mentalities and the currents of public opinion that sustained these Brazilian paradoxes between 1996 and 2004, and thus explore some explanatory factors.

Climates of opinion and the public debate

The heated debate over GM crops in Europe and North America is amply documented (e.g. Gaskell and Bauer, 2001). Key events occurred in late 1996. The freighter *Ideal Progress* arrived in Europe containing Monsanto's Roundup Ready GM soya. This delivery was legal according to EC regulations of 1990/91. But a loophole in labelling rules provided anti-GM activists with an opportunity for public action and a debate arose (Lassen et al, 2002). Europe saw a de facto moratorium on GM crops and food from October 1998 to 2004, supported by major food retailers. These events created a context for action with its own dynamics in Brazil.

Figure 15.1 charts the monthly frequency of political events related to GM crops in Brazil between May 1998 and January 2001, and shows the leading role of Rio Grande do Sul in the national debate. The dark bar shows biotechnology events in Rio Grande do Sul, the light bar events in the rest of the country. Events in the South reached a peak in late 1999, while the rest of Brazil saw the peak of activity in mid-2000 or later.

Public opinion does not fall from the sky, but is mobilized in and through civil society and variously impacts policy making or corporate strategy. Mobilization in the South was the result of a tit-for-tat between two networks of actors. On the one hand were many state municipalities, various research institutes, the big farmers' unions of Federação de Agricultura do Rio Grande do Sul (FARSUL), the processing industry and international corporations including Monsanto. On the other hand were the local government, IDEC, Greenpeace, Movimento dos Trabalhadores Rurais Sem Terra (MST) and small farmers, some state municipalities, the World Social Forum and various scientific organizations. In Brazil, environmentalism has become mainstream policy, while consumer protection remains a marginal issue with a very weak base among the middle classes (see Guivant, 2001). Public mobilization over GM crops through public events and pronouncements culminated in the 'Farroupilha of the municipalities' (Leite, 2000) where, one by one, regions declared themselves for or against GM crops, sometimes retracting earlier decisions.[1]

Changing media coverage

Figure 15.2 shows the number of articles about GM crops and food between 1998 and 2002 in the dominant daily newspaper of the South, *Zero Hora*. Over these 48 months, *Zero Hora* carried 296 major articles on the issue. Rio Grande do Sul, where *transgênicos* became a daily news issue, led the national debate. In the rest of Brazil, it was a bi-weekly topic at the best of times (Massarani et al, 2003). The editorship of *Zero Hora* prides itself on having set the agenda on this issue throughout 1999.

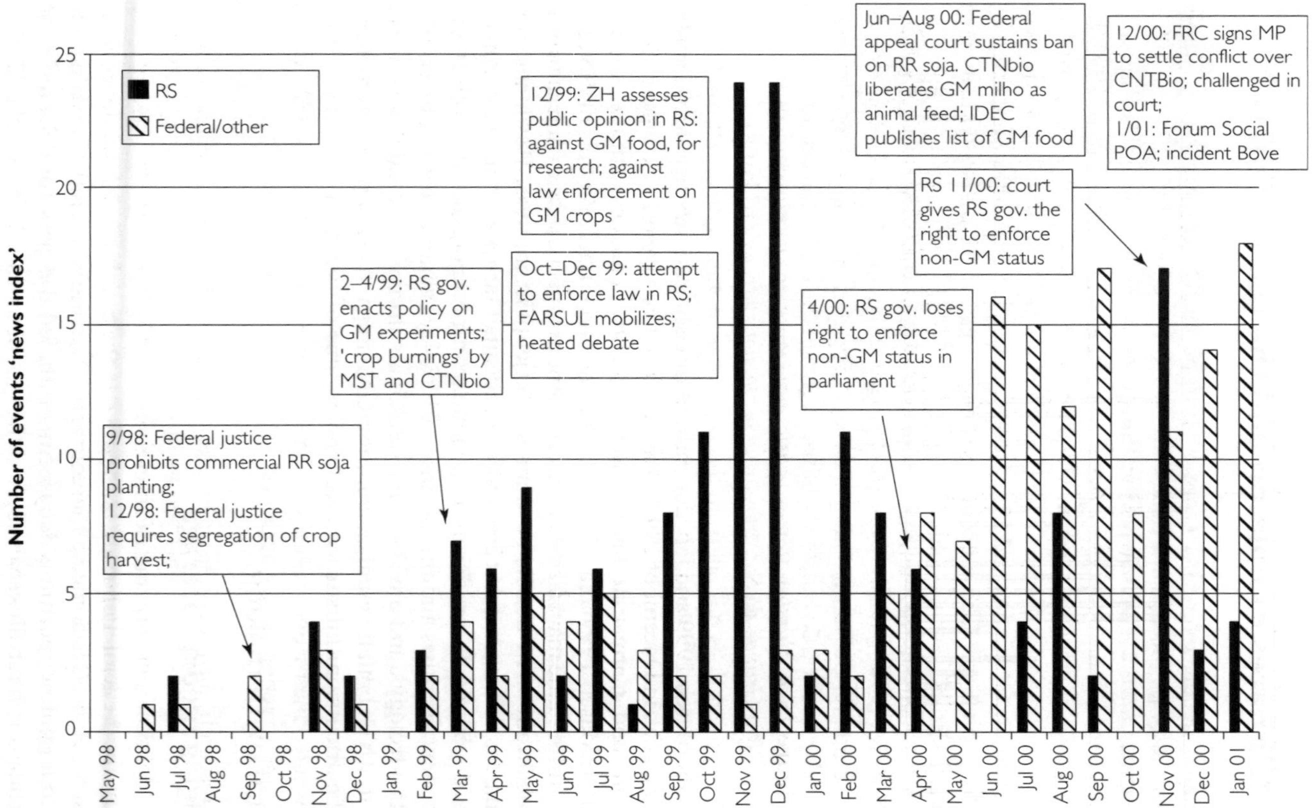
RS
Federal/other
Number of events 'news index'
25
20
15
10
5
0
9/98: Federal justice prohibits commercial RR soja planting;
12/98: Federal justice requires segregation of crop harvest;
2–4/99: RS gov. enacts policy on GM experiments; 'crop burnings' by MST and CTNbio
Oct–Dec 99: attempt to enforce law in RS; FARSUL mobilizes; heated debate
12/99: ZH assesses public opinion in RS: against GM food, for research; against law enforcement on GM crops
4/00: RS gov. loses right to enforce non-GM status in parliament
Jun–Aug 00: Federal appeal court sustains ban on RR soja. CTNbio liberates GM milho as animal feed; IDEC publishes list of GM food
RS 11/00: court gives RS gov. the right to enforce non-GM status
12/00: FRC signs MP to settle conflict over CNTBio; challenged in court;
1/01: Forum Social POA; incident Bove
May 98
Jun 98
Jul 98
Aug 98
Sep 98
Oct 98
Nov 98
Dec 98
Jan 99
Feb 99
Mar 99
Apr 99
May 99
Jun 99
Jul 99
Aug 99
Sep 99
Oct 99
Nov 99
Dec 99
Jan 00
Feb 00
Mar 00
Apr 00
May 00
Jun 00
Jul 00
Aug 00
Sep 00
Oct 00
Nov 00
Dec 00
Jan 01

Source: Various chronologies, e.g. Menasche, (2000a)

Figure 15.1 *Density of GM-related public and political events in Rio Grande do Sul, 1998–2001*

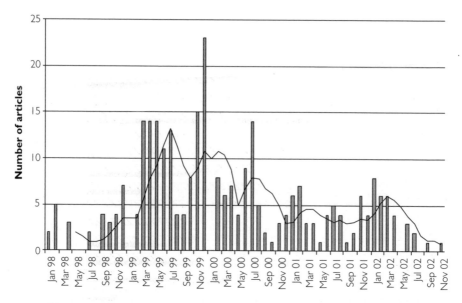

Figure 15.2 *Number of press articles per month about* transgênicos *in Rio Grande do Sul, appearing in the newspaper* Zero Hora

Between March 1999 and July 2000, there was a heated debate in Rio Grande, reaching a peak in December 1999. Our analysis of two papers (see Figure 15.3), *Zero Hora* and *Correio do Povo* (another quality newspaper of the South), comparing March 1999 and March 2000 shows a shifting discourse of biotechnology. In 1999, the main frames were economic prospects, public control, nature and globalization. In 2000, the frames of scientific progress, Pandora's box premonitions and fatalism became more important. The actors in the 1999 debate are local governments, producers and multinational corporations; by 2000, these are joined by scientists and the judiciary. The local scientific community tries to fend off 'ideology', and advocacy for GM crops declines.[2] The political polarization to which both newspapers contributed in the first place becomes thematic when the discussion shifts from 'ideology' to 'sound science'.

Political myth making

Local research also demonstrates the political mythology created around *transgenicos*. Menasche (2004) shows in detail how two particular events had become political myths by the election time of 2002. The burning of illegal local fields by the Federal Police on 22 April 1999, at the request of the federal Comissão Técnica Nacional de Biosegurança (National Biosafety Commission), provided a photo opportunity for Hoffman, the local Agricultural Secretary of the Partida dos Trabalhadores (PT). The PT was henceforth associated with burning crop fields, despite the fact that it was not directly involved in crop destructions. The field burning was further linked to the Catholic inquisition

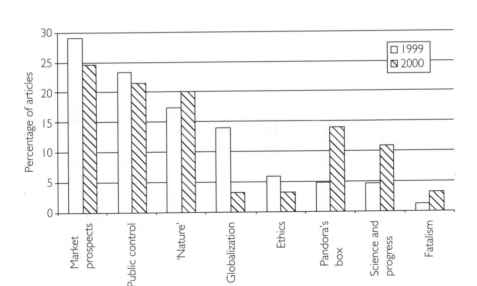

Figure 15.3 *Percentage of press articles in* Zero Hora *and* Correio do Povo *during March 1999 and March 2000 that frame the issues of GM crops in a particular manner (N = 151; p < 0.10)*

and to the book burning of the Nazis, two historical expressions of anti-scientific obscurantism and authoritarianism. Thus, the association of Hoffmann's image and crop burning came to signify an obscurantist and anti-scientific PT government.

The second event is José Bové's visit to the World Social Forum in Porto Alegre in January 2001. Bové, the French anti-globalization activist, visited a site where social movements had previously destroyed a GM crop field. The press and TV images turned Bové *ex post facto* into the main protagonist. Bové was applauded loudly at the World Social Forum but was then escorted to the airport by Federal Police to leave the country. This media event created a xenophobic discourse. For pro-GM protagonists the protest signified everything foreign to the true Gaucho: violence and disrespect for private property. The attribute 'foreign' was associated even with the MST, despite the fact that it originated as a social movement in Rio Grande do Sul (Fernandes, 2000). For the non-committed public, sceptical but disapproving of crop destruction, Bove also represented things foreign: violence, activism, *transgênicos* themselves and foreign interests. The effect of these two myths was that by the 2002 elections Gaucho politicians took positions as being either 'for research or for crop burning', for 'progress or obscurantism', leaving little space for differentiated arguments on either side. Polarization and mythology constrained the debate.

Public perceptions

We also observe agenda setting of the South in polls of awareness, consumer sentiment towards GM food, support for the moratorium and risk perceptions. After the surge of the national debate in mid-2000, the country as a whole moved towards the positions that were already prevalent in the southern regions of Brazil. A poll in Rio Grande do Sul showed 66 per cent awareness of GM issues as early as December 1999 (source: CEPA, 1999) and confirmed this level for the southern regions of Paraná and Santa Catarina, whereas Brazil as a whole had only 37 per cent issue awareness in 2002 (source: IBOPE 2001, 2002). The South of Brazil showed more issue awareness than many EU countries (see Gaskell et al, 2001). The question 'Given a choice, would you buy GM products?' was consistently answered 'no' by over 70 per cent of respondents in the South. Even the judicial moratorium on GM crops of 1998 carried growing support in the South: 58 per cent in 1999, 77 per cent by 2002. By 2002, two-thirds of all Brazilians supported the moratorium. Issue awareness did not affect support for the moratorium. The South and the rest of the country showed similar risk rankings: losing export opportunities due to transgenic production, health and environmental risks were the most salient.

In summary, our mass media analysis and the poll data showed media attention and issue awareness spreading from the South to the rest of the country. The controversy in Rio Grande do Sul raised awareness of GM crops and foods and by mobilizing civil society made this a national issue beyond the narrow circles of producers, scientists, governments and courts. For international corporations, environmental and consumer activists the South became a test arena, and political mythology crowded out many a good argument on either side.

The narrative of this controversy can be divided into four phases which show the paradoxical role of Rio Grande do Sul on this issue.

Phase 1: The judicial moratorium of October 1998

After initial failures, success in genomics research for Brazil came later in the 1990s (Azevedo et al, 2002). The Rio summit of 1992 had positioned Brazil as the centre of biodiversity and a leading voice on intellectual property rights. It was widely expected that Brazil would adopt the biotechnology revolution, as the US and Argentina had. Global companies including Monsanto, Dupont, Bayer and Novartis had developed a presence. By 2000, Monsanto controlled 75 per cent of crop field trials, or 90 per cent of the test area, and was pushing for commercialization. In January 1995, CTNBio had been created to regulate matters of GM crops.[3] By 2000, the commission had considered 1294 field test applications, of which 70 per cent were approved. Indeed, Brazil was turning into the testing ground for international corporations (Vigna, 2001). However, what happened in Brazil about that time must have taken many observers by surprise.

On 14 December 1997, Greenpeace activists blocked the port of São Francisco do Sul, in the state of Santa Catarina. US imports of GM soya authorized by CTNbio arrived for the production of oil. The activists' banners stated

'Frankensoja: don't swallow it'. In February 1998, federal police confiscated sacks of GM seeds in Rio Grande do Sul that had been imported illegally from Argentina. When CTNbio approved Roundup Ready soya in September 1998 with only a 13-vote majority against those of consumers and the foreign ministry, its decision carried no authority. Days earlier, the Federal Court supported a case brought by Greenpeace and IDEC claiming that the commercialization of GM crops should undergo an environmental impact assessment. The court drew on the precautionary principle in the constitution of 1988. This decision was challenged by industry and government. Nevertheless, in December 1998, crop *segregation* and labelling was required and the environmental assessment was confirmed as a judicial requirement even for open field trials. The Federal judge, Antonio Souza Prudente, stated:

> *I believe that the irresponsible speed of progress in genetic engineering would lead to damaging de-regulation of the global economy, that may at the beginning of the new millennium lead to a civilization bearing alien creatures. (translated by the author from Leite, 2000, p13f)*

These actions effectively established a *judicial moratorium*. Approved field trials, numbering 350 in 1999, collapsed in 2000 (Vigna, 2001). This moratorium continued until October 2003, when a presidential decree legalized GM crops on an annual cycle until the Law of Biosafety was ratified in April 2005.

Phase 2: Rio Grande do Sul to be a 'GM-free zone': September 1998–July 1999

Let us backtrack. In May 1998, a delegation of soya producers from Espumoso, Rio Grande do Sul, travelled to France on a sales mission. The expedition was unsuccessful, as the sample was 'contaminated' with *transgênicos*. Unperturbed, the region passed an aspirational law declaring itself 'zona livre dos transgêni-cos'. This sparked the 'batalha das prefeituras' (battle of the counties), where municipalities positioned themselves for or against GM crops. Other public bodies and organizations joined and formed networks, for and against. In October that year, *Zero Hora* published its first article in a series 'Seeds of Polemic'. Thus, the non-issue *transgênicos* had become an issue.

In the same month, the PT won elections in Rio Grande do Sul. In November, PT leaders and Greenpeace met to discuss GM crops. Thus, an election non-issue became policy. The new governor announced a 'zona livre dos transgênicos'. The outgoing agricultural secretary pointed to the facts: an estimated 15 per cent of the local soya crop is already GM. Notwithstanding, PT policy makers judge the issue compatible with the existing platform: environmental protection, public health and humans before profit.

In February 1999, the PT governor proposed to ban GM crops and to nor-malize the judicial moratorium in Rio Grande. This did not find a parliamentary majority, but small farmers and the landless movement MST started to enter and burn test fields. By March, the governor modified an existing decree, which now required notification of the planting of experimental and commercial GM crops and an environmental assessment. Thus, the law *enforcement* started. The closure of 50 experiments that did not have an impact assessment was followed by an injunction to prevent the harvesting of Monsanto's experimental crop. In April, federal agents burned experimental GM rice at a research station. Events cooled off, but the official policy, protests by social movements and the closure of test fields had become a threat to farmers whose interests were being voiced by the traditional FARSUL (Menasche, 2003). The Agricultural Secretary travelled to Europe to open markets for non-GM crops, a policy supported by other agriculture secretaries, who passed a motion to ban *transgênicos* in Brazil. He was convinced that PT was pursuing the right policy, consistent with its values, but also consistent with international markets. In July 1999, Greenpeace launched the campaign 'Rio Grande do Sul livre dos transgênicos'.

Phase 3: Escalation and stalemate: August–December 1999

The battle of the counties continued: networks of actors formed and declared their positions. In August 1999, the protests in France against 'mal-bouffe'[4] and GM crops were widely noticed. At the main agricultural fair, Agriculture Secretary Hoffmann emphasized that the policy of 'zona livre' would be enforced. A month later, the main seed producer declared 30 per cent of Rio Grande do Sul's soya to be transgenic. This estimate, which is cited internationally, is part of the controversy. Hoffmann accused the industry of constructing facts and called on the federal police to investigate. His own test kits ascertained only 4 per cent in November.

Throughout the harvest season, the conflict escalated, this time over the commercialization of GM crops. Some 700 silo tests were conducted and 3588 sacks of GM soya (1 sack = 60 kg) were confiscated in Cruz Alta, Palmerira das Missões, Passo Fundo, Erechim, Santa Rosa and Tupanciretã. A total of 24 producers were referred to the federal police. Traditional farming organizations, Clubes de Amigos da Terra, Sindicatos Rurais and FARSUL, mobilized civil disobedience, roadblocks and non-cooperation with officials. FARSUL, traditionally anti-PT, alleged an abuse of power and a threat to private property. Its political arm called for a debate in parliament to challenge the legality of law enforcement, claiming that GM crop regulation is a Federal, not a state, matter.

On 11 November 1999, the vice-governor, Rossetto, called a meeting of stakeholders (state ministers, the Federal Agriculture Minister, industry and producers). A compromise was reached: stop all enforcement for three weeks to allow farmers time to recover GM seeds and to replant the non-GM variety; costs to be covered by the state bank. The objective was to create a GM-free harvest for 2000/01 to position Rio Grande do Sul in the growing non-GM world market. While the processing industry supported the idea, FARSUL walked out and mobilized, and in *Zero Hora* (12 November 1999) the agreement was brandished as a 'pact against GM soya'. Rossetto's further attempts to mediate between the

Agriculture Secretary and soya regions failed. On 8 December, the parliament blocked all law enforcement on GM crops, on the grounds that it was not a state but a Federal matter. PT's policy of recovering the 'zona livre' through law enforcement was blocked.

A radio interview of 29 November with a Franciscan brother named Goergen, representing the landless movement in parliament, created a media event that became local memory. He insinuated that genetic modification introduces 'poison' into plants, and that some of the viral vectors used were HIV and hepatitis B. This triggered reactions by university scientists of all affiliations deploring the level of scientific information and arguing against the *anti-science moratorium* on plant genetic research. Goergen, asked to explain himself in parliament, admitted that his comments were intended to provoke debate. The radio interview was later published together with contributions from two plant scientists who translated soundbites into 'sound science' (Goergen, 2000). It was oil on the flames of polarization when the landless movement declared GM crops 'a criterion for invading land'.[5] MST in 2000 invaded two farms with GM crops in Santa Catarina, but not in Rio Grande. FARSUL retaliated by calling for the military to protect land and property.

On 13 December 1999, *Zero Hora* published a survey of the capital, Porto Alegre: opinions on the moratorium were split 50:50; but consumer sentiment was more sceptical and, given a choice, 70 per cent said they would not buy GM food (source: CEPA, 1999). This highlighted a contradiction in public opinion and what some observers recognized as a potential alternative strategy; while consumer sentiment is against GM food, criminalizing farmers carries no support. Instead of focusing on demand (for example, the markets already offered a 10 per cent bonus for non-transgenic soya, and high-level reconnaissance visits from European food retailers in search of non-GM soya were taking place), the Rio Grande government confirmed its commitment to law enforcement on production. In June 2000, there was a court ruling confirming the reliability of industry tests. Attempts to force crop separation in state silos failed. Not until November 2000 did the Rio Grande government regain the power to enforce the law.

In October 2002, PT lost the election in Rio Grande, but by this time *transgênicos* had become an election issue. The new centre-right government became a major driver towards the normalization of GM crops across Brazil, ironically supported by some Rio Grande PT deputies, thus revealing the split within the PT over this issue.

Phase 4: The nationalization of the debate: after 2000

After 2000, the focus of *transgênicos* moved north and to Brasilia. In November 1999, Greenpeace and IDEC launched the national campaign 'Por um Brasil livre dos transgênicos' across Brazil, and in May 2000 they won an injunction to block US BT-maize destined to feed poultry. Brazil, with an expanding poultry industry, is not self-sufficient in poultry feed. Poultry producers tried to avoid paying the premium on non-GM maize and to avoid labelling their chickens. In 2000, national information campaigns, websites, pamphlets and books on *transgênicos* were published (e.g. Goergen, 2000; Leite, 2000; Massarani, 2000). Increased corporate public relations activities tried to win the hearts and minds of the Brazilians. National opinion polls, sponsored by Greenpeace and IDEC, gauged public sentiment across Brazil (source: IBOPE 2001, 2002).

Figure 15.1 above showed that nationwide events peaked at the end of 2000. Henceforth Brasilia is the arena, as well as other regions of Brazil. The tussles between federal government, the two chambers of parliament and the courts continued. In December 2000, President Cardoso empowered CTNbio to make decisions on GM crops. Challenged by IDEC in January 2001, the court concluded that CTNbio had only 'virtual existence' because of an unresolved parliamentary veto of 1995. Earlier, in February 2000, a protocol had defined the environmental impact studies which the courts require. In June 2001, the President decreed labelling with a threshold of 4 per cent tolerance. This again was found to contravene existing consumer legislation and was therefore invalid. A 1 per cent threshold was implemented later, in 2004.

The widely anticipated liberalization of GM crops finally happened. The elections of 2002 brought a new government, the presidency of Ignazio Lula da Silva, but no majority in parliament. In the forging of a coalition government, *transgênicos* moved off the agenda. The Senate investigated illegal imports and planting of GMOs, and on 25 September 2003 the Vice-President signed a decree (MP 131) allowing planting of GM soya, regulating the handling of seeds and the monitoring of potential liabilities. The international press reported that GM crops had been finally accepted, overlooking that this decree allowed GM crops only for one year. In Paraná, the centre-right governor banned GM crops from the key harbour of Paranaguá and thus ensured segregated crops, while Santa Catarina opened its port São Francisco to GM soya. In March 2004, the Ministry of Justice required all products containing more than 1 per cent of GM crop to be labelled with a 'triangle', be they for human or animal consumption. Monitoring is coordinated by four research stations across the country. The rule allows for negative labelling, and applies equally to producers of poultry, pigs and milk, who must declare their feeding practice. In Rio Grande, this ruling is enforced by a team of 40 trained and equipped technicians. With liberalization in place, the focus of the debate shifts to consumer information – a Greenpeace campaign during April 2004 – and to the vexing issue of royalties for GM seeds. This ran into difficulties in Canada, the US and Argentina. Monsanto was accused of using royalty management to set incentives for GM crops (Azevedo, 2004).

The Federal parliament finally considered 17 proposals for the legislation of GM crops. Pressure increased to resolve the various contradictions: you cannot field-test GM crops without an environmental assessment, but for an assessment you need field tests; GM crops are illegal, yet GM seeds are used; labelling laws cannot be enacted because GM food ingredients are illegal and therefore do not exist; CTNbio, the body to decide these matters, does not legally exist; GM crop areas are illegal and thus there are no official GM crop statistics. International crop statistics do not include Brazil (James, 2002), yet international media have reported widely on GM crops in Brazil.

The policy of 'livre dos transgênicos', in stalemate in Rio Grande, moved successfully to other regions, although under different political colours. By 2001, restrictions on GM crops, foods or labelling had been introduced in Regio Norte, Paraíba, Bahia, Belo Horizonte, Minas Gerais, São Paulo and Espírito Santo. In July 2000, Greenpeace and IDEC published a list of products with GM ingredients, and Belo Horizonte confiscated GM foods in supermarkets. A total of 16 of the 26 states officially appealed to the President to protect Brazilian crops from GM varieties.

The main soya states, Paraná and Mato Grosso, both with centre-right governments, ruled against GM crops and campaigned to win farmers' support. Paraná destroyed illegally imported GM seeds before it admitted that part of its crop was GM. Mato Grosso do Sul introduced a campaign 'soja limpa' (clean soya) to persuade farmers to continue with conventional soya. These regions positioned themselves explicitly as GM-free, with law enforcement, segregation and public campaigns highlighting the market advantages in Europe, Japan and China. Greenpeace argued the market case in a well-documented report (Greenpeace, 2002). The president of the Agricultural Federation in Paraná declared:

> *70 per cent of the soya production of Paraná goes to Europe and Japan, with a value of US$1.6 billion. They restrict transgenic soya. We have already gained 50 per cent of this market, because we deliver what they require.*[6]

This position of producers in northern and central Brazil had a significant impact on the expansion of soya production and soya exports for Brazil.

We end this chronological account in April 2005. By now the situation had shifted. The Law on Bio-safety had been passed. The controversy over bio-technology had migrated from *transgênicos* to stem cell research and bio-medical progress. On 3 March 2005, a brief and emotive campaign, including the rolling of patients in wheelchairs into parliament, before television cameras, closed with a clear vote (352 'yes' votes to 60 'no'). Last-minute attempts by the Environment Minister, Greenpeace and others to lobby a presidential veto failed. The legislative package, covering both green GM crops and foods and red bio-medical genetics and stem cell research, ended the judicial moratorium of 1998. In the media reportage, one finds little memory of the *transgênico* debate. *VEJA*'s headline stated triumphantly: 'In Brazil, Galileo has not been burnt'.[7]

Resistance: Local failure – global success

The most startling outcome of the GM-free policy of Rio Grande do Sul between 1998 and 2002 was its complete failure. Rio Grande became the only state in Brazil where GM soya was the rule rather than the exception by 2004. Because it was an illegal crop, no official statistics on GM crops existed. Estimates ranged from 15 per cent in 1999, to 30 per cent in 2000, to 80 per cent by 2004. The uptake of illegal Argentinian seeds undermined the efforts of local seed banks. Soya farmers no longer use the seeds that are adapted to the local climate. The imported GM seeds are not suitable for a subtropical climate. In March 2004, during a southern drought, farmers experimented with traditional and GM crop and reported a 6 per cent yield lag for the GM variety (*Correio do Povo*, 19 April, 2004, p15; also Benbrook, 2004). The failure of the Rio Grande government to win the support of the farmers for its policy had immediate effects: Rio Grande lost its traditional export destination of Europe to other Brazilian regions.

With the controversy over *transgênicos* in Brazil, several things came to pass. First, Brazil massively expanded soya production and exports after 1998. With the European moratorium in place, Japan being sceptical and China demanding labelling of GM crops, it paid for farmers to reject GM technology and to satisfy demands for conventional soya. Brazil, de facto, sustains the European policy of GM-free crops, of labelling and offering a choice to consumers. Second, despite local policy failure, Brazil gained international attention as a place where globalization US-style is successfully challenged.

The Brazilian soya miracle of 1996 to 2004

Comparison of soya production in Brazil and the US points to the success of Brazil's precautionary approach. In 1996, US producers enthusiastically adopted Monsanto's Roundup Ready soya; by 2002, 66 per cent of the US crop was transgenic, with mixed results (James, 2002; Benbrook, 2004). By 2002, US production had increased by 40 per cent, but declined since 1998. In Brazil, where the adoption of GM crops was marginal and confined to Rio Grande, production increased by 160 per cent mainly after 1998, from 23 million tons in 1996 to 51 million tons in 2004. In 1991, it produced 19 per cent of the world's soya; the US produced 51 per cent. By 2003, Brazil accounted for 26 per cent, the US for 34 per cent. Argentina, which adopted GM crops even faster than the US, doubled its share to 19 per cent of the world production.

This expansion occurred mainly in the states of Paraná and Mato Grosso, accelerating the trend of relocation of soya production within Brazil (Bastiani and Bacha, 2002; Villarim, 2004). It is explained entirely by expansion of traditional non-GM crops for the export market. The producer optimism was exuberant. The Brazilian trade press reported the 'soya miracle' and the 'tiger of the agro-business' (see *VEJA Agronegócio*, April 2004).

GM crops in the South and GM-free crops in the other regions created a logistical problem. By 2002, export routes were segregated, resulting in non-transgenic crops being exported via the Amazon River through the northern route. Cargil International, a crop freighter company, has rapidly expanded its capacity in Santarém on the Amazon River. GM-free crops also reach the southern port of Paranaguá in thousands of truckloads, which due to lack of storage facilities serve as rolling silos lining the road. The governor of Paraná declared the port 'non-transgenic', and engaged in an image campaign defending the segregation policy against much opposition over such non-constitutional action. Only the two most southerly ports, São Francisco do Sul and Rio Grande, accept GM crops for shipping. Remarkably, of the states which sustained a GM-free crop, none had a PT government or majority. Where a PT government adopted such a policy, it failed utterly. The *transgênico* issue became aligned with ideology of being for or against PT and the economic argument was crowded out.

Brazil responded to European and Asian demand for GM-free soya, with a sizable premium: Japan pays 40 per cent more for the non-GM imports, Europe is willing to add between 4 and 10 per cent (Villarmim, 2004; *Nature Biotechnology*, October 2005, p1195; Brookes et al, 2005). By 2003, the cash crop soya con-tributed over US$8 billion, a quarter of the export value, to the country's trading balance, up by 100 per cent since 1994. Soya exports increased from 3.5 million tons in 1995 to 20 million tons in 2003, as shown in Figure 15.4. In 1992, 16 per cent of soya was exported; by 2003, this was 40 per cent, with a massive increase after 1998. Exports to Europe increased after 1998 and there has been a steady increase in soya exports to China and Japan since 2000.

Considering that the US, Brazil and Argentina produce 80 per cent of the world's soya and that Europe depends almost entirely on imports, it is noteworthy that Brazil alone has sustained the European moratorium on GM crops and foods since 1998. Indeed, GM future scenarios for GM food in Europe hinge entirely on the timing of the liberalization and adoption of GM crops in Brazil. After 1997, special missions of retailers like the French Carrefour and British Sainsbury's went to Brazil to secure supplies of GM-free soya to enable them to honour their consumer pledges.

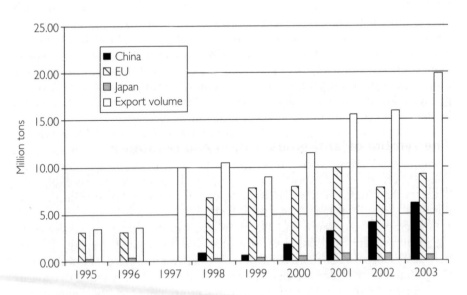

Source: MAPA; FEE Porto Alegre

Figure 15.4 *Brazilian soya exports for various destinations from 1995 to 2003 (no figures available for 1997)*

Delayed global diffusion of GM crops and the end of the 'life science' industry

Resistance to new technology delays the diffusion rate and geographically concentrates the process (Hagerstrand, 1967). The international monitoring of transgenic crops indicates that their diffusion suffered a setback with the European moratorium and the precautions in Brazil. The penetration rate of GM soya into the world production stagnated at around 63 per cent in 2001 and 2002 (James, 2002) and declined to 56 per cent by 2004 (James, 2004). Brazilian producer action reduced the world adoption rate. The world market split into GM soya supplied by the US and Argentina and non-GM soya supplied by Brazil. The soya case was instructive for wheat farmers. US and Canadian farmers deferred adoption of GM wheat in May 2004 to avoid a rerun of the US soya 'export disaster'.

The resistance, albeit temporary as history might show, to GM crops in Brazil adds to the global effects of resistance to biotechnology. International corporations such as Monsanto can no longer rely exclusively on lobbying policy makers and convincing farmers, their primary market, and have had to consider secondary markets. Farmers, in turn, respond to consumers, as policy makers might increasingly do. The Brazilian and European caution over the 'New Green Revolution' contributed to the demise of the life science industry vision in which pharmaceutical and agrochemical companies envisaged a joint future in the early 1990s. The marriage of Monsanto to Pharmacia ended in divorce in August 2002 after a short honeymoon. Equally short was Novartis's and Rhone-Poulenc's attempt to marry farm and pharmacy, divorcing Syngenta and Aventis in turn in 2000 and 2001. The global biotechnology movement is now clearly split into an agro-food sector (green) and a bio-medical sector (red). The European moratorium, the debate in Rio Grande do Sul and Brazilian farming practice are likely factors of this new global situation.

The symbol of 'anti-globalization and resistance'

Rio Grande do Sul became a symbol of anti-globalization resistance and democratic renewal (Sousa Santos, 2002; Herzberg, 2002). It positioned itself on the world map as a major soya producer adopting a GM-free policy. This was celebrated at the World Social Forum in Porto Alegre in 2000, 2001 and 2002 (Seoane and Taddei, 2001). The agricultural trade press and daily papers such as the *Guardian*, *Telegraph* or *Financial Times* in the UK, *Le Monde* in France, the *NZZ* in Switzerland, as well as *The New York Times* and *The Washington Post* in the US, regularly reported on the Brazilian crop policy. The region was keenly observed as the 'the last bastion to fall', the only basis upon which a European moratorium was viable. In May 2002, *The Washington Post* famously commented that Monsanto lost its way by ignoring the international GM controversy. Brazilian caution over Roundup Ready seeds had blocked its capability to raise money on the stock markets.

In summary, while the GM-free policy utterly failed in Rio Grande do Sul, farming across Brazil continued to be GM-free. As a result, soya production expanded massively between 1996 and 2004, exports increased sixfold and Brazil has ambitions to become the world's largest soya producer and exporter.

Conclusions: Explaining Brazilian paradoxes

Technological advances in food production such as the genetic modification of crops may reduce costs but, in the food chain as it is impossible for consumers to detect and make a choice. Market reputation is unlikely to be an effective regulator. Thus, the state can offer transparency with a food control programme and rules on labelling (Law, 2003).

Support for food regulation historically comes from established producers of 'quality food' as well as urban consumers concerned about public health. In Rio Grande do Sul, the policy of the PT government aimed at protecting small farmers, consumers and the environment (Almeida, 2003). This may explain what happened in Rio Grande, but does not explain what happened across Brazil, where industrial farmers observed the GM moratorium. Might one be able to model this resistance to a new technology as a rational economic choice contrary to innovation models?

Explaining the paradoxes of *transgênicos* in Brazil, the resistance to new technology by an otherwise high tech agri-food industry, is a far from easy task. The politics of innovation is conditioned by many factors at the regional, national and global levels, the unravelling of which would amount to an understanding of Brazilian politics, an impossible task for this space and my competence. I content myself with exploring some likely factors.

Geography

The location of Rio Grande do Sul with its 500 kilometre 'wild west' border with Argentina is a decisive factor in the failure of the GM-free policy. This extensive border is uncontrollable and has a long tradition of smuggling. Argentina readily adopted GM soya after 1995 (Sorman, 2001). No wonder, therefore, with demand for GM seeds (many farmers were naturally curious to experiment) it was easy to bring GM seeds from Argentina. Policing illegal imports of GM seeds from Argentina was impossible beyond occasional strikes. The incoming PT government of 1999 underestimated these circumstances when it adopted a policy that focused on law enforcement rather than on world market information and consumer awareness.

Political polarization

Political science distinguishes between polarization of the party system and polarization of the political culture. The political culture of Rio Grande is historically polarized, while many different parties compete for votes. This cultural polarization often translates into stalemate between the executive elected by majority, and the legislature elected proportionally. Rio Grande has a history of splitting in the middle, without a centre ground for compromise. The victory of the first PT local government in 1998, with a minority of 22 per cent in parliament, polarized all issues into pro- and anti-PT. This increasingly paralysed decision making, and not only on *transgênicos*, between 1998 and 2001. Decreasing numbers of laws originating from the government were debated in parliament, while increasing numbers of vetos by government and parliament can be observed in this period (Mello Grohmann, 2002).

GM crops were initially not a PT issue. The issue travelled from the centre-right to the left and aligned with established polarities only after the election of 1998: the governor and social movements working towards a GM-free region, while the parliamentary majority and traditional farming interests fought for the liberalization of GM crops. Symbolic politics blocked any compromise in Rio Grande do Sul. By mid-2000, many scientists and the press themselves deplored this polarization because it curtailed informed arguments, not least the economic one of a global market for non-GM crops. Ideological positions pro- and anti-PT divided opinions in 1999 more than any other variable.

This polarization is reflected in opinion polls. CEPA (1999) shows a 50:50 split for a GM-free region. Some 72 per cent of respondents would not buy GM products and 61 per cent would pay a premium for GM-free food products. But less than 40 per cent think the state should tell the farmers what to do, and only 35 per cent think that farmers planting GM crops should be prosecuted. The data shows the lack of support for an enforcement policy, but also the basis for a missed compromise: GM research 'yes', commercialization 'not yet'; 33 per cent are against a GM-free zone, against a moratorium and for research; around 40 per cent are for a GM-free zone, for a moratorium, but also for field trial research. A total of 43 per cent would not buy GM food, but would leave the decision over GM crops to the farmers, would pay more for GM-free foods or support the enforcement of the GM ban. The potential compromise would have had cross-party support: sceptical consumers supporting producer autonomy. Qualitative research reveals contradictory attitudes even among local producers: they liberally apply GM seeds and use chemicals for their industrial production, but for their own consumption they maintain an organic garden (Menasche, 2003).

Conflicts in government

Nationally, GM crops were not a party political issue. The Rio Grande policy to create a 'GM-free' state was not supported by the federal President, who was working towards liberalization by fighting off challenges in parliament and the courts. However, federal ministries were not pulling in the same direction. On the President's side were CTNbio, and the Ministries of Science and Technology and of Agriculture. On the other side, the Ministry of Justice supported labelling, and the Environment, Public Health, and at times the Foreign Ministry, supported the moratorium, or at least further public debate. Positions converged only with the passing of the Bio-safety Law and its ratification in 2005, which combined stem cell research and GM crop regulations.

Biased mass media

Many local observers see the failure of the Rio Grande *transgênico* policy in the light of a media conspiracy. Local researchers accuse RBS (the radio and television company of southern Brazil) and the newspapers of pernicious bias during the PT years in the South (see Guareschi et al, 2000; Menasche, 2003). This is demonstrated in issue framing and political mythology: the anti-scientific, obscurantist and authoritarian PT. However, the newspaper *Zero Hora* raised the issue before it was a party political one and thus set the agenda in the first place. However, they are an integral part of the political culture and they did not stem its polarization. The later anti-PT bias of the local mass media is likely to have contributed to the failure of the GM-free policy in Rio Grande, but by leading the debate nationally contributed to Brazil's national soya miracle.

The mentality of industrial agriculture

Brazilian soya production originated in Rio Grande do Sul in the 1970s as a modernization project of the military regime (Ruckert, 2003). With it came the mentality of industrial farming – cost consciousness and technology orientation – but it also brought the trauma of a credit crisis in the 1980s. In this context, GM crops entered with the equation of 'technological progress = higher productivity by decreasing costs' (Gehlen, 2001, pp73ff; Assouline et al, 2001). PT's misreading of this mentality of producers was recognized as a tactical error: farmers are experimenters; blocking experiments goes against the grain. Many farmers in Rio Grande planted part of their land with a GM variety, part with conventional seeds, testing for yield gains and drought resistance. Also, the gaucho is traditionally rebellious towards Federal governments, the historically secessionist spirit of Farroupilha. High-tech agro-industrial orientation and traditional rebelliousness contributed to the stalemate in the region. However, further to the north and in central Brazil the same agro-industrial mentality, resulting partly from gaucho emigration following the 1980s debt crisis, engendered cautious attitudes towards GM crops. Mentality is not a key factor. It is not mainly the traditional and small farmer who rejects GM technology in Brazil; on the contrary, it is the globally thinking entrepreneurial producer that is cautious. In the South, the small farmer is against GM crops, while the traditional cattle-based gauchos support GM crops, but mainly because they 'smell a rat' in relation to whatever is associated with the left PT.

External influences

International corporations such as Monsanto, Aventis, Syngenta and Bayer have major stakes in Brazilian agriculture, providing funding for research and development as well as seeds and agrochemicals. Monsanto was the major player in challenging court rulings against GM crops. It also stands accused of creating facts on the ground by encouraging 'illegal' soya planting. With liberalization after 2003, evidence emerges that Monsanto used royalty management to set incentives for farmers to switch to GM crops. Monsanto denied this in an advertising campaign in May 2003 (see Azevedo, 2004). And corporate public relations included the sponsoring of rural social events, intense image campaigning among farmers and lobbying with Chief Executive Officer (CEO) delegations in Brasilia. IDEC called for a public investigation on corporate lobbying over the GM issue.

On the other hand, there is also the presence of international environmentalism in the debate. Greenpeace found a local ally in the consumer organization IDEC. Together they staged stunts and successfully raised issue awareness. In 1999, 25 per cent of gauchos acknowledged that the local campaign for a 'GM-free Brazil' had influenced them (CEPA, 1999). Awareness of GM campaigns reached two-thirds of Brazilians by December 2002 (IBOPE, 2002). They successfully challenged the GM regulations in courts. Greenpeace input was key to the adoption of the GM-free policy by the incoming PT government in Rio Grande late in 1998 (see Menasche, 1998). Brazil became not only a testing ground for Monsanto's GM field trials but also an arena for the global debate. Whether these external influences were decisive for the failure of the policy and subsequent stalemate in Rio Grande do Sul is doubtful. What is clear is the existence of international backup on both sides of the argument.

In this chapter, we have explored the resistance to *transgênicos* in Brazil and its paradoxical motives and consequences. An ideological GM-free policy utterly failed in one region, while a cautious farming practice succeeded in northern and central Brazil. This led to massive expansion of soya production and exports between 1996 and 2005. Why did a high-tech agro-industry reject the 'New Green Revolution' in one region but not in the others? In the South, this is explained by the uncontrollable borders with Argentina, a culture of polarization and symbolic politics, and conflict within and between state and federal governments. Less clear is the impact of a partisan mass media, the mentality of industrial farming and external influences. The party political alignment of the GM issue in the South crowded out the economic prospect of a huge market for traditional soya in Europe and Asia. The entrepreneurial northern and central regions capitalized on this without the interference of party politics, and under governments from the other side of the political spectrum from those in the South.

The moral of my story: technological innovation does not always pay off, it might pay to wait; and resistance, not only from vested interests of old skills, but also from newer capital, might be a rational option. I end by wondering whether one could simulate this in an econometric model.

Acknowledgements

Research was undertaken with a CNPq Professorial Fellowship during a sabbatical in 2002; thanks to Professor Pedrinho Guareschi (PUC-RS); RBS and CEPA gave access to surveys and media data; interview partners and those who helped to arrange them (S. Jovchelovitch and R. Amaro in Porto Alegre, P. Noleto in Brazilia). Renata Menasche and Luisa Massarani offered me generous 'testing ground' for my hopeless attempts to understand 'Brazil' and gave me access to their own materials. I take the blame for all remaining errors and misunderstandings. A version of this chapter was presented in the Department of Sociology, UFRGS, on 16 April 2004.

Notes

1   Farroupilha refers to the secessionist civil war in Rio Grande do Sol in the mid-19th century.
2   This analysis was part of an exercise with Master's students in content analysis conducted by the author at PUC-Rio Grande do Sul, Department of Psychology. The categories used were from Durant et al (1998) (see also Verissimo and Felippe, 2000).
3   The regulation of biotechnology in Brazil is based on the constitution of 1988, which adopted the 'precautionary principle', and law 8974 of 1995. This law was vetoed by parliament but revised with presidential powers of 'provisional measures' (MPs). In 1996, this led to the creation of CTNbio and the 'Commission for the Administration of Biodiversity', in 2001 to the creation of an 'Inter-ministerial Committee', and in 2003 to the temporary legalization of crops on a yearly cycle. Regulation on the basis of presidential powers (MPs) creates legal uncertainty. Unless parliament approves an MP into law within 60 days, an MP needs to be continuously reconfirmed by the President. On these occasions it can be revised. No MP on biotechnology has ever been ratified by the parliament before the law on Bio-safety of 2005 (www.mapa. gov.br).
4   In Millau, southern France, protestors of José Bové's Confédération Paysanne attacked a McDonald's construction site as a symbol of the fight against globalization and 'mal-bouffe' (junk food).
5   The MST tactically occupy land to exert political pressure for land reform. They identify land that is unproductive using official agricultural statistics. By including GM crops, MST extended their usual set of criteria for occupation. Having spent time myself on a farm in the hinterland of Rio Grande, I have experienced an atmosphere of 'civil war'. Cattle farmers talk openly, albeit with exaggeration, of shooting invaders. Guns are clearly visible in these lands and sadly remain an option in land disputes, as is documented by an annual death toll among MST activists and supporters.
6   Paraphrasing an interview with Agide Maneguette on 12 July 2002 in *Diario de Maringa*.
7   This shift in public debate away from green biotechnology to red bio-medical issues, and the incoherent coalition that supported the new law, is beyond the scope of this chapter. At the time of final writing (June 2005), this law is again challenged in the Brazilian Supreme Court.

Sources

Interviews (November–December 2002)

Edelcio Vigna de Oliveira (INSEC, lobby and information group, Brasilia); Frei Sergio Goergen, OFM (Deputado Estadual since October 2002, for MPA); Marcia Mandagara (editor *RBS rural*, editor *ZH campo rural* until 2000); Miguel Rossetto (vice-governor, RS; January 2003 Federal Minister for Land Reform);

José Hermeto Hoffmann (Secretary for Agriculture, 1999–2002, Rio Grande do Sul); Renata Menasche (*doctorando* to UFRGS, Professora UERGS, was assessor to deputy Bohn-Gass in 1998; Greenpeace contact; discussion partner); Julia Guivant (food safety and consumer protection researcher, Florianopolis); Gerson Almeida (POA environmental secretary); Carlos Enrique Horn (Economist UFRGS, Director of the Regional Development Bank)

Surveys

CEPA (1999) is a quota sample (N = 418) conducted on 1–2 December 1999 in six boroughs of Greater Porto Alegre; face-to-face interviewing; 15 questions. The research was a commission by RBS and conducted by CEPA of UFRGS

IBOPE (2001) Pesquisa de opinião pública sobre transgênicos, opp081, Brazil, July (N = 2000, face-to-face interviews, national sample, commissioned by Greenpeace)

IBOPE (2002) Pesquisa de opinião pública sobre transgênicos, opp573, Brazil, December (N = 2000, face-to-face interviews, national sample; commissioned by Greenpeace)

References

Almeida Jalcione (2003) 'A agroecologia entre o movimento social e a domesticação pelo mercado', *Ensaios FEE, Porto Alegre*, vol 24, no 2, pp499–520

Assouline, G., Joly, P. B. and Lemarié, S. (2001) 'Biotecnologias vegetais e reestruturações do setor de provisos agrícolas: Um horizonte estratégico marcado por fortes incertezas', *Enasios FEE, Porto Alegre*, vol 22, no 2, pp30–52

Azevedo, N., Ferreira, L. O., Kropf S. P. and Hamilton, W. S. (2002) 'Pesquisa científica e inovaçao tecnologica: a via brasileira da biotecnologia', *DADOS*, vol 45, no 1, pp139–176

Azevedo Marques, V. de (2004) *Cobranca de royalties da soja transgénica – nota técnica*, Assessoria da Brancada PT/RS, POA, March

Bastiani dos Santos, A. and Bacha, C. J. C. (2002) 'Evolução diferenciada da lavoura de soja e de seu processamento industrial no Brasil – periodo de 1970 a 1999', *Economia Applicada*, vol 6, no 1, pp123–151

Bauer, M. (1995) 'Towards a functional analysis of resistance', in Bauer, M. (ed) *Resistance to New Technology: Nuclear Power, Information Technology, Biotechnology*, Cambridge University Press, Cambridge, pp393–418

Benbrook, C. M. (2004) *Genetically Engineered Crops and Pesticide Use in the US: The First Nine Years*, Benbrook Consulting Services & AgBiotech InfoNet, Iowa, Technical paper no 7

Brookes, G., Craddock, N. and Kniel, B. (2005) *The Global GM Market: Implications for the European Food Chain*, September (report commissioned by Agricultural Biotechnology Europe)

Durant, J., Bauer, M. W. and Gaskell, G. (1998) *Biotechnology in the Public Sphere: A European Sourcebook*, Science Museum, London

Fernandes, B. M. (2000) *A formação do MST no Brasil*, Vozes, Petropólis

Gaskell, G. and Bauer, M. W. (eds) (2001) *Biotechnology 1996–2000: The Years of Controversy*, Science Museum, London

Gaskell, G., Allum, N., Wagner, W., Nielsen, T. H., Jelsøe, E., Kohring, M. and Bauer, M. W. (2001) 'In the public eye: Representations of biotechnology in Europe', in Gaskell, G. and Bauer, M. W. (eds) *Biotechnology 1996-2000: The Years of Controversy*, London, Science Museum, pp53–79

Gehlen, I. (2001) 'Pesquisa, tecnologia e competitividade na agropecuária brasileira', *Sociologias*, vol 3, no 6, pp70–93

Goergen, Frei S. (2000) (ed) *Riscos dos transgênicos*, Vozes, Petrópolis

Greenpeace (2002) *As vantagens da soja e milho não transgênica para o mercado brasileira*, Amsterdam and São Paulo

Guareschi, P. et al (eds) (2000) *Os construtores da informação: Meios de comunição, ideologia e ética*, Vozes, Petrópolis

Guivant, J. (2001) 'Heterogeneous and conventional coalitions around global food risks: Integrating Brazil into the debates', Florianopolis SC (unpublished paper)

Hagerstrand, T. (1967) *Innovation Diffusion as a Spatial Process*, University of Chicago Press, Chicago

Herzberg, C. (2002) *Der Bürgerhaushalt von Porto Alegre. Wie partizipative Demokratie zu politischen-administrativen Verbesserungen führen kann (Region – Nation – Europa Bd 9)*, LiT Verlag, Münster

James, C. (2002) *Global Review of Commericialised Transgenic Crops: 2002*, ISAAA Briefs, Cornell University and Rockefeller Foundation, Ithaca, NY, no 29

James, C. (2004) *Global Status of Commercialised Biotech/GM Crops in 2004*, ISAAA Briefs, no 32, Cornell University and Rockefeller Foundation, Ithaca, NY

Lassen, J., Allansdottir, A., Liakopoulos, M., Mortensen, A. T. and Olofsson, A. (2002) 'Testing times – The reception of Roundup Ready soya in Europe', in Bauer, M. W. and Gaskell, G. (eds) (2002) *Biotechnology: The Making of a Global Controversy*, Cambridge University Press, Cambridge, pp279–312

Law, M. T. (2003) 'The origins of state pure food regulation', *Journal of Economic History*, vol 63, no 4, pp1103–1130

Leite, M. (2000) *Os alimentos transgênicos*, Publifolha, São Paulo

Massarani, L. (2000) 'A opinião pública sobre os transgênicos, História, Ciência, Saúde – Manguinhos', *Dossier 'transgênicos'*, vol 7, no 2, pp519–522

Massarani, L., Magalhaes, I. and de Castro Moreira, I. (2003) 'Quando a ciencia vira notícia: Um mapamento da genética no jornais diários' (Rio de Janeiro, manuscript)

Mello Grohmann, L. G. (2002) 'Relaçãoes executivo-legislativo sob polarização política: o caso do RS', paper presented to 3rd national meeting of the Brazilian Association of Political Science, Niteroi, 28–31 July

Menasche, R. (1998) *Transgênicos: o que esta em jogo? Subsidio para a discussão* (manuscrito gabinete deputado E. Bohn Gass PT/RS, November 1998)

Menasche, R. (2000) 'Uma cronologia a partir do recortes de jornais, História, Ciências, Saúde – Manguinhos', *Dossier 'transgênicos'*, vol 7, no 2, pp523–545

Menasche, R. (2003) 'Os grãos da discórdia eo risco à mesa: Um estudo antropológico das representaçãos sociais sobre os cultivos e alimentos transgênicos no Rio Grande do Sul', These de Doctorado, Departamento di Antropologia, UFRGS, Porto Alegre

Ruckert, A. A. (2003) *Metamorfoses do território. A agricultura de trigo/soja no planalto médio rio-grandense 1930–1990*, UFRGS Editora, POA

Seoane, J. and Taddei, E. (eds) (2001) *Resistências mundiais: De Seattle a Porto Alegre*, Vozes, Petrópolis

Sorman, G. (2001) *El progreso y sus enemigos. Verdades y prejuicios sobre los alimentos transgénicos, la clonación, el efecto invernadero y otras controversias*, Emecé Editores, Buenos Aires

Sousa Santos, B. de (2002) 'Orçamento participativo em Porto Alegre: para uma democracia redistributiva', in *Democratizar a democracia: Os caminhos da democracia participativa*, Civilização Brasileira, Rio de Janeiro, pp455–560

Verissimo Veronese, M. and Felippe, F. (2000) 'Os transgênicos na mídia: práticas sociais e ideologia', in Guareschi, P. et al (eds) *Os construtores da informação. Meios de comunicação, ideologia e etica*, Vozes, Petrópolis, pp297–316

VGM (2005) 'Brazil weighs cost of GM soy segregation', *Nature Biotechnology*, vol 23, no 10, p1195

Vigna, E. (2001) *A farra dos transgênicos*, Argumento 05, Insec, Brasilia

Villarim de Siqueira, T. (2004) 'O ciclo da soja: Desempenho do cultura da soja entre 1961 e 2003', *Rio de Janeiro, BNDES Sectorial*, no 20

Index

Page numbers in *italics* denote references to Figures, Tables and Boxes.